THE MASTER HANDBOOK OF
FINE
WOODWORKING
TECHNIQUES & PROJECTS

Other TAB books by the author:

No. 1247
$15.95

THE MASTER HANDBOOK OF
FINE
WOODWORKING
TECHNIQUES & PROJECTS

BY PERCY W. BLANDFORD

TAB **TAB BOOKS Inc.**
BLUE RIDGE SUMMIT, PA. 17214

FIRST EDITION

FIRST PRINTING

DECEMBER 1980

Copyright © 1980 by TAB BOOKS Inc.

Printed in the United States of America

Library of Congress Cataloging in Publication Data

Blandford, Percy W
    The master handbook of fine woodworking techniques
and projects.

    "TAB 1247."
    Includes index.
    1. Woodwork. I. Title.
TT180.B62   684.1'04   80-21246
ISBN 0-8306-9678-4
ISBN 0-8306-1247-5 (pbk.)

Cover photo courtesy of American Drew Inc.

Preface

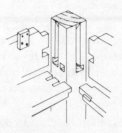

So much of modern furniture is, of necessity, mass-produced from manufactured boards and with designs adapted to the methods of construction. If we had to depend on the hand work of individual craftsmen, most of us could not afford to furnish our homes. This change has been a gradual process that has taken place during the last century. It was the development of power-driven machinery that could be adapted to production that heralded the change. Prior to that, all the processes in the making of a piece of furniture were done by hand. Gradually, power tools took over the laborious work and the need for an individual craftsman's skills lessened. Today, there are not many craftsmen who could call themselves skilled cabinetmakers in the original definition of the term.

It is unlikely that many cabinetmakers using traditional methods could now find enough customers able to pay fair prices for their work and provide them with a living. There are some craftsmen. But no matter how skilled they are, the markets for their products can never be very large. The continuation of the skills of fine cabinetmaking must depend on amateurs who pursue their craft for the love of it and do not have to relate man-hours to income.

Much woodwork done today by individual craftsmen, whether for profit or as a hobby, seems to be copying quantity-production methods. There is a feeling that a shop is only satisfactory if it has a machine for just about every process, then assemblies are tackled so that parts finish and are joined to suit the machines. Such results might be regarded as inferior copies of the products of factories equipped with better machinery.

Of course, there is satisfaction in any sort of woodworking, but there is more satisfaction to be obtained from making things that could not be produced by mass-production methods. There is no need to go back to using only hand methods. It is common sense to use machines where they can lessen labor. However, the best furniture is made with a greater regard for traditional methods, the use of joints that time has shown to be the best and where wood is fashioned in ways that do not lend themselves to repetitive production methods. Such a piece of work might be your original concept. It stands along as an example of fine cabinetwork. That is what this book is about. If you can master the skills outlined in this book, you will be keeping alive a tradition of the finest craftsmanship and will experience the satisfaction of looking at something that is yours from start to finish. A piece of fine cabinetwork is artistry as well as craftsmanship. To look at something good and say you made it gives a tremendous feeling of satisfaction.

Much can be learned by looking at examples of good furniture. Besides admiring it, try to analyze why you admire it. Consider the proportions and the detail work. Try to think through the steps in construction. There are books with pictures of good cabinetwork. They are the next best thing to the actual objects. Not many periodicals deal with fine cabinetwork, but help can be obtained by studying the bimonthly *Fine Woodworking* (Taunton Press, Newtown, CT 06470) and *The Woodworker* ((M & A Publications, Hemel Hempstead, 1HP 1EE, England). Greater details for some of the techniques involved in cabinetwork can be found in TAB book No. 860, *The Woodworker's Bible*, No. 1044, *The Woodturner's Bible*, No. 1004, *The Upholsterer's Bible* and No. 894, *The Do-It-Yourselfer's Guide to Furniture Repair and Refinishing*.

Throughout this book, all sizes are in inches unless marked otherwise. For near conversion to metric, treat 1 inch as 25mm, 1m as 39 inches and 12 inches as about 300mm. Scales are used as well as dimension so that other sizes can be measured. In the materials lists, widths and thicknesses are mostly finished sizes. Lengths are full to allow for cutting joints. Very small parts that can be cut from waste wood are not listed.

Percy W. Blandford

Contents

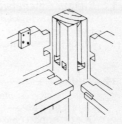

Chapter 1
What is Cabinetwork?

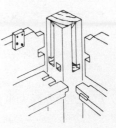

Very early man must have found ways of using wood. It was there to be picked up and broken off trees in most parts of the world. Besides using it for fires, he would have found uses for pieces of particular shapes and from that stage must have learned to fashion wood to suit his needs. He would have discovered that all wood was not the same. Different trees produced wood with different burning qualities and some was much harder than others. When he used wood as implements, the harder woods lasted longer than the softer ones, while the softer woods were easier to work to shape.

Throughout the Stone Age, the Bronze Age and the Iron Age it is certain that in the forested parts of the world, wood was always the most frequently used material. Early stone tools were used for killing animals for food, but they would also have been used to cut and scrape wood to make things of use in the primitive domestic life of our ancestors. When iron and bronze became available, better tools, weapons and implements became possible. With these improved tools, man made better things from wood. With the ability to fashion better and more useful things came a desire for more comfort. Men and women began to appreciate the comforts of home and wanted to furnish it with things that were inappropriate to the nomadic life.

With villages and towns, houses became more than basic shelters. Those workers that prospered wanted to make their homes better and equip them more lavishly. The one-room shelter developed into a multiroom house and the need for furniture of many kinds was felt. The majority of people still had to accept life with a few basic items, but those who had become wealthy wanted better furniture. Specialist woodworkers who could fill this need found scope for their skills.

Wood is not sufficiently durable for specimens of very early furniture to have survived. We have to rely on drawings and other indications to know how the earlier house dwellers furnished their homes. Furniture can last for hundreds of years and we can examine a few specimens from the Middle Ages. However, furniture making is a much older art and craft.

Civilizations in warmer climates seem to have managed with less elaborate and plentiful furniture. Warmer conditions did not require much of an enclosed life, so there was less inclination to equip homes with large quantities of furniture. The furniture they had was usually not bulky or heavy. Wall drawings showing early Egyptians portray stools, tables and other things of domestic use. Joints and details are indicated. Those early woodworkers obviously had begun to evolve practices that are followed today. Persian civilization followed very similar lines, but we have less pictorial help in visualizing details of their furniture.

Life in the Roman Empire, at about the time of Christ, had influence on furniture trends affecting us today. The Romans enjoyed comfort in their homes. Apart from furnishing, they had improved cooking and eating arrangements and even provided running water and central heating. This was not just as the exception for the very important people, but as something that those of only moderate wealth regarded as desirable and often possible.

The Romans spread all over most of Europe. The peoples they conquered were mostly living in a very primitive state. They moved into Britain and other countries and stayed for centuries. Many ruins are sufficiently intact today to show many of the details of their original form.

The Roman influence must have affected the work of native craftsmen and brought their ideas and methods much nearer to those Roman craftsmen. Surprisingly, there is not much evidence of this in the work of craftsmen after the Romans withdrew. The period known as the Dark Ages stagnated the Western countries for several centuries and furniture making in the Western countries did not produce anything of much note until what has been called the Middle Ages. From then on, furniture as sound examples of good craftsmanship has developed in a progression of examples up to the present day. Certain fashions that have blended into each other are known by the names of the reigning monarchs or the designer-craftsman concerned.

With the development of civilization came divisions. The wealthy man was able to commission the making of furniture of a quality that the ordinary man could not afford. There was domestic furniture in the ordinary household and those who had become moderately successful bought better items. But it was the feudal system, common in much of Europe, that brought power to the lord of the manor or the even more important earl or duke in his castle. At first, even those in positions of wealth and authority lived with comparatively crude furnishings, but gradually better furniture came into use.

Much of this was due to travel. Most people never went many miles from their home during their lifetime. But even a visit to a town might show a country craftsman examples that he might copy or adapt for local use. Others travelled more widely, often due to participation in wars, and they were able to see how people in other countries lived. If a leader saw furniture in the home of a foreign lord that appealed to him, it might have been plundered or bought and brought home. This would have been copied and the influence of the design was spread.

EARLY FURNITURE

Types of furniture varied according to available woods. In Britain and much of Western Europe, oak, elm and similar rather coarse hardwoods predominated. Some of these woods were very durable. This can be seen in surviving furniture that is many centuries old. However, this type of wood did not allow fine work or great detail, so furniture of these countries tends to be bold and substantial. Any carving or other decoration is sweeping and large. In countries nearer the Mediterranean, milder woods were available and more delicate work was done. Pines and firs were common in northern countries and a different style made use of these softwoods. Of course, as transportation systems improved, woods were imported and regional differences became less apparent. For example, mahogany became the most popular furniture wood in Britain even though no species of mahogany grows there.

The church also affected furniture development. Throughout long periods in the Middle Ages and earlier, almost all learning was related to the church. Schools and universities were linked to the church. About the only influence available to encourage learning, whether academic or in manual skills, was that of the church. Craftsmen of all kinds were employed in beautifying churches and other ecclesiastical buildings. Time was available to do the best work possible. In woodwork, this was shown in carving and other decorative work that must have taken months or years and could not have been done in even the comparatively simple and more leisurely commercial world of those days. All of this added to man's knowledge and appreciation of good woodworking and craftsmanship and affected the way household furniture was designed and made.

Another influence would have been the quality and availability of tools. When man had only a crude axe, wedges and simple hammers and spikes, the quality of woodwork he could undertake was obviously restricted. As iron and steel were developed, blacksmiths made better tools and the woodworker could do better work. With chisels he could fashion joints. With the chisel through a block of wood, he developed planes and produced smooth surfaces. Tools developed on similar lines in many parts of the world. The only major differences were in the way some of them were handled. Where most Westerners pushed planes and saws, Japanese and other Eastern craftsmen preferred to pull. Among Western craftsmen, the Germans still have planes designed to be pulled.

EFFECT OF POWER TOOLS

For most of history, woodworking tools have been for hand use. Turning has been done for a long time, but all lathes were hand- or foot-powered until comparatively recently. Water power has been put to use, particularly for sawing to convert logs to boards, but from that stage the boards were made into furniture by hand. Steam power, as it affected furniture production, did little more than take over from water power. The Industrial Revolution had a two-fold affect on furniture making. Better tools were produced in a larger range of types and sizes. Woodworkers everywhere were able to get tools of uniform quality produced in factories instead of the limited range of tools of varying standards from the local blacksmith. The engineering revolution also produced certain woodworking machines that lessened the labor needed to do certain woodworking tasks. At that time, the bulk of the work in producing furniture continued to be done with hand tools. Because these tools were better and more efficient, the standards of furniture design and making were raised.

The development of good woodworking power tools is comparatively recent. Most were designed during the present century and most came about due to the development of the electric motor. Power saws that would convert a log to boards were established first and planers and machines for molding, mortising, drilling and other operations were developed to acceptable standards later. If the work of a power tool had to be followed with hand tools, its value in production was mainly as a substitute for the sheer labor of doing it all by hand. Better machine tools were developed at the same time that good electric motors were developed.

Today we have the problem of the effect power woodworking tools have had on furniture design and production. Modern technology has brought us such things as *plywood* and *particleboard*. These have revolutionized the mass production of furniture. Nearly all of the processes in producing a piece of furniture can be done by machinery. This has meant that furniture of acceptable standard for general use can be made at a price within the reach of people who could not hope to buy individually made items.

Anyone prepared to accept the same sort of furniture as hundreds of other people will buy this factory produced uniform furniture. But, many of us would prefer to have at least some items which are individually produced by craftsmen capable of making furniture. It seems that those who are able to do the work cannot find enough customers at the prices they have to charge to give them a good living. This means that the tradition of good furniture making will have to be carried on by enthusiastic amateur craftsmen who do not have to equate the time needed to do the work properly with the rate per hour they are earning. It is mainly for those who would join this elite group of amateur craftsmen that this book has been written.

The reaction against mass production can be seen in the advertising of some furniture manufacturers with phrases such as "hand assembled joints" (where they would have to be, in any case) and "hand rubbed surfaces" (whatever that means).

Cabinet work or *cabinetry* means the making of furniture of all sorts. Maybe the pinnacle of skill was once shown in the making of cabinets, but tables, chairs and all kinds of furniture are collectively described as *cabinetwork*. This means that a worker in a furniture factory might describe himself as a "cabinetmaker", although he is a machine operator or an assembler of machine made parts. He could not begin to do the work of the traditional cabinetmaker who made a single item of furniture right through from rough wood to the finished product. To indicate the difference, the work of this latter craftsmen is better described as *fine cabinetwork* or *fine cabinetry*.

WOODWORKING DIVISIONS

In the days when woodworking was a young craft, all kinds of woodworking was done by one worker. That individual could repair agricultural implements, build a house, make furniture, repair a wagon or make a coffin. The standard might not have been as high as that of a later specialist, but it was acceptable in the local community. These conditions have prevailed in some places until quite recently. Early settlers in America were glad to have a general woodworker among them and would call on him to do any work in wood. In parts of Europe there are still such craftsmen. My uncle was a village carpenter, wheelwright and undertaker in Britain less than 50 years ago.

Woodworkers became specialists where there was sufficient demand for one sort of work—particularly in towns. The general name for a woodworking craftsman seems to have usually been *carpenter* and that is still an acceptable term. Where it is necessary to define different types of woodworking specialists, carpenter is the name for the man with the least skill or specialization who tackles simpler and rougher work.

A more skilled carpenter might call himself a *joiner*. A joiner makes windows and window frames, doors of various sorts and might even make and fit staircases. Much of a joiner's work is done in a shop prefabricating wooden assemblies that will be installed in a building as part of its fixtures rather than free standing furniture.

A *wheelwright* made more than wheels. He made all the parts of wagons, particularly those for agricultural use, and would also make barrows and the wooden parts of agricultural machines and implements. He cooperated with the blacksmith because many wagon parts had fitted wood and iron assemblies. A *coachbuilder* was a craftsman similar to a wheelwright. His finished work had to be of the high quality required in passenger carriages and coaches. These and other crafts involved making wood round on a lathe. Where there was sufficient demand a *wood turner* was a specialist. As a separate craft he made bowls, plates and similar things. A *wood carver* was also a specialist craftsman.

A traditional "cabinetmaker" regards himself as being at the top of the scale in relation to other woodworkers. The skills required in making the finest furniture are certainly greater than those required for other woodworking. This is particularly true when most of the work has to be done by hand. Most cabinetmakers could carve and turn, but perhaps not to as high a standard as the specialists. In general, a cabinetmaker produces individual items of furniture that are not secured in any way. However, he might make built-in furniture today where a cabinet or bookcase fits into a recess or into a wall. Most chairs and similar things are padded. This upholstery has always been the work of a specialist *upholsterer*. Most cabinetmakers could also do some of the work. An amateur cabinetmaker would find added interest in doing his own upholstery.

Some of the finest examples of traditional cabinetwork date from the days of the great cabinetmakers (mostly during the 18th century). Their work might not have been so well known if it had not also been a time of great development in printing. In 1754, the best known of these cabinetmakers, Thomas Chippendale, brought out his first edition of *The Gentleman and Cabinet-Maker's Directory*. The many pattern books produced by cabinetmaker/artists served as guides to a great many others. Therefore, much of the surviving furniture attributed to a famous name might actually have been made or designed by someone else.

Fashions in furniture change. We can admire the skill that went into some of this period furniture and we can admire the ornate decoration. Some of it might look nice in a museum or mansion of the same period, but it would not do for use in a modern house. However, there is much to learn from furniture of bygone years. In some cases, it is worthwhile reproducing or features can be taken and adapted to suit something more suited to modern needs. Fine cabinetmaking is not just the ability to reproduce the designs of older craftsmen. We have to make furniture that carries on the traditional skills, while making use of modern hand and power tools to evolve styles to suit today.

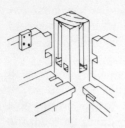

Chapter 2
Tools

Even the most enthusiastic cabinetmaker determined to carry traditional woodworking to its logical conclusion is unlikely to go into the forest, fell a tree, convert it to boards, season them naturally for many years and then make something from them. However, it would be an interesting exercise for any one with that much energy and time to spare. Anyone wanting to make furniture will have to decide how much of the work should be done by centuries-old methods and how much should be done using techniques that are only possible with modern equipment.

In a fully mechanized shop and using modern manufactured boards, it is possible to make furniture comparable with that turned out by factories. It might be custom built and it might have something that no other furniture has, but it is still following the modern trend of quick results and minimum effort. It can be described as cabinetmaking, but it would not justify the prefix "fine". Of course there are many reasons for making furniture in that way and the results can be quite satisfactory. But there is much more satisfaction to be obtained from making and owning a piece of furniture that is honest wood throughout and made with regard to traditional methods that are the mark of good woodworking craftsmanship.

To make furniture that displays all the attributes of good craftsmanship, the cabinetmaker has to decide how far to go with processes that are only possible with modern equipment. You must decide how much work to do with tools that have been available for centuries. Some of these tools have been updated and will function more efficiently than their earlier versions.

The finished furniture should show no signs of machine work. That does not mean that an item has to be made throughout with hand tools. It is better to use power tools to lessen labor. There is no virtue in slaving away at hand planing a board truly flat if it could be done with a power planer. What is wrong is leaving evidence of the power planing in the finished work. Power planing followed by power sanding would not be acceptable. The resulting surface would not have the correct character. To get the right finish, power sanding should be followed by hand planing sufficiently to get through the slight ridges from the power planing and remove the case-hardened surface due to the pounding of the power cutters. In many woods a good hand planed surface will need little or no sanding. If sanding is required it should be done by hand. The difference between this and a surface power planed and sanded is obvious to the discerning eye of a keen cabinetmaker or a connoisseur of furniture.

Most cabinetmakers have to leave the felling, conversion and seasoning of boards to someone else. Wood for cabinetmaking is bought already seasoned in boards and probably planed to thickness and probably to width. Wood might have to be bought in stock sizes, but it is unlikely that these will suit the things to be made. It is possible to get the lumber yard to cut wood to the sizes you need, but it is cheaper and more satisfactory to be able to do the cutting yourself. In any case, when making a piece of furniture you will want to cut wood to size to suit particular needs as the work progresses and you might not have been able to anticipate this at the time you bought the wood.

Having your own facilities for cutting wood down to size also allows you to use up oddments or to recycle wood obtained from discarded furniture. This means that you should have a table (circular) saw. It need not be very big, but it should be large enough and with a motor powerful enough to cut up to about 1½-inch hardwood. A combination rip and crosscut blade will do most cutting that is required. A wobble saw for cutting grooves and one or two other blades might be included, but for fine cabinetmaking the saw's main use will be in cutting wood into sections. Further work will be done with other tools.

A power surface planer can be used after the table saw to get a smooth surface on the wood. The surface quality it produces is not as important as its use in getting a surface flat without the hard work required to get to that stage by hand planing. The hand planing that follows only has to smooth a surface that is already very close to flat. Ideally, the planer will be large, but in the small shop there are limits of cost and space. A cutter width of 5 inches should be regarded as a minimum and anything over that is a bonus. A convenient arrangement has the planer and table saw in the same unit powered by a single motor.

One or more electric hand drills are useful. Chuck capacity of ⅜ inch or ½ inch might be desirable for one of them, but a lightweight drill with a capacity only up to ¼ inch will have many uses for screw holes and similar work. Power drilling in wood to larger sizes is possible with bits having reduced shanks to fit the drill chuck.

Traditional cabinetmaking did not include much *dowelling*. In normal construction, there were no dowelled joints of the type that are common in much modern furniture. That does not mean that dowelling is wrong in modern fine cabinetmaking, but its use should be limited and in many assemblies the joints that could have been dowels will be *mortise* and *tenons*. The oldtime cabinetmaker chopped out the mortises with a chisel. It is quicker and more accurate, as well as with less risk of cracking the wood, to drill out much of the waste. To do this properly means either using a drill press or mounting one of the electric drills in a stand.

Another useful power tool is a bandsaw. Whether it is needed or not depends on the type of work to be done. Its most obvious use is in cutting curves. Before the advent of electricity, cabinetmakers cut curves satisfactorily by hand, but some of this must have been hard work. A jigsaw, either hand powered or as an attachment for an electric drill, will cut many of the curves needed in cabinetry. However, there are other uses for a bandsaw. It will cut thicker wood than the table saw likely to be in the same shop. The cut might be slow, but even a small bandsaw will cut across a 4-inch thickness. It is also useful for general sawing. Cutting the waste material from the end of a strip will automatically be square. It might not be square from a hand cut with a backsaw.

One power tool that is considered desirable is a *lathe*. This really comes between a machine and a hand tool. Although the lathe rotates a piece of wood, the work on it is done by tools held by hand. Not every piece of fine cabinetwork includes turned wood and it is possible to make attractive and interesting furniture without the use of a lathe. However, the availability of a lathe extends the scope of the shop. Besides the turned spindles and legs found on much furniture, the lathe can be used for knobs and other small things such as tool handles and shop items that will improve your work. Most round work required in cabinetwork is turning between centers. But if the lathe can take large faceplate works, discs, trays and round table tops can be made. There are combination machines available, where the lathe is the basic part and saw and planer can be mounted on it, but make sure such a combination woodworker has a sufficient capacity for your needs.

The power tools so far described can be regarded as a back-up to hand tools and something which the traditional fine cabinetmaker did not have only a comparatively short time ago. They are there to take out some of the hard work and to provide mechanical accuracy. If your aim is to produce high quality craftsmanship, there should not be too much use of power tools. One of the marks of hand craftsmanship is the lack of absolute uniformity. If a set of dining chairs are made, they should be all the same, for practical purposes, yet there will be tiny variations among them. There will be deliberate differences in carving or parts that are not quite the same shape or size due to hand work.

BENCHES AND HOLDING DEVICES

It is almost impossible to do accurate work without a very strong surface to support the wood for marking it out, working on it and assembling parts. This means a firm bench and at least one vise and other holding devices.

There are some excellent complete benches available, mostly imported from Denmark and made of beech, with vises and *holding dogs* built in. However, if a craftsman claims to be a cabinetmaker, he should be able to make his own bench. The important part is a stout flat board to form the front working surface. A section of 2-inch by 10-inch will do if it is a close-grained hardwood and it can be further supported by a rather thinner apron (Fig. 2-1A). With the apron at right angles below the top, it serves as a guide for wood held in the vise.

If the bench is free-standing, there can be another top piece at the other side and a well made with a thinner piece of wood between (Fig. 2-1B). If that piece is removable, it becomes possible to use C clamps to hold work to the working top surface. If the bench is to go against a wall, it might be sufficient to have a narrow piece at the same height as the front and a wider well (Fig. 2-1C).

There should be substantial legs which are adequately braced. Boxing in below the bench for storage will also provide stiffness. How long to make the bench depends on available space, but length is often valuable when assembling large pieces or assembling at one end while leaving the other end free for further work.

Older vises were wood and they tended to not always grip with a parallel action. A steel vise that fits under the top and moves with a parallel action is better, but it should be mounted so that it can be given wooden jaws and no metal comes near the top (Fig. 2-1D). The inner wood is let into the top so its surface is flush with the apron.

Although a bench can go against a wall, it is useful to be able to move it so that it can be pulled out to allow for getting to both sides of a piece of work. However, it needs to be rigid and temporarily bracing to a wall is worthwhile. For a righthanded worker, the vise should be towards the lefthand end and it should be possible for work to overhang at the end. It helps if it can overhang at both ends. If space is restricted, ensure clearance to the left.

There should be a stop to plane against near the lefthand end of the bench. There are adjustable metal ones to let into the surface, but it is better to use wood. Wood will not damage the plane iron if it accidentally hits. A simple and satisfactory arrangement is a piece of hardwood through the top and resting against a leg (Fig. 2-1E). It can be hit up or down and it will stay in place by friction or there can be a bolt and butterfly nut through a slot (Fig. 2-1F).

Holes to take a peg can be made in the bench apron or leg to support long and wide boards held upright in the vise (Fig. 2-1G). If the ends of the well are closed with strips across, tools will be prevented from rolling out and there will be a place to put down a plane so that the cutting edge is kept clear of the surface (Fig. 2-1H).

The oldtime cabinetmaker always had a number of holdfasts of a simple type made by a blacksmith (Fig. 2-2A). To hold wood flat on the bench, the shaft was hammered into an oversize hole in the bench top. It went in diagonally and was gripped by friction. With many holes about the bench and several holdfasts, almost anything could be held. A modern version has a screw adjustment and the shaft goes through a metal collar let into the bench (Fig. 2-2B). Both shaft and collar are ribbed to prevent slipping as the shaft tilts.

One or two bench hooks can be used to push wood against when sawing or otherwise working on it. They can be narrow and cut from solid wood. They are always used in pairs (Fig. 2-2C). Wider bench hooks can be built up and used singly for many operations. So that there is no risk of tools touching metal, coun-

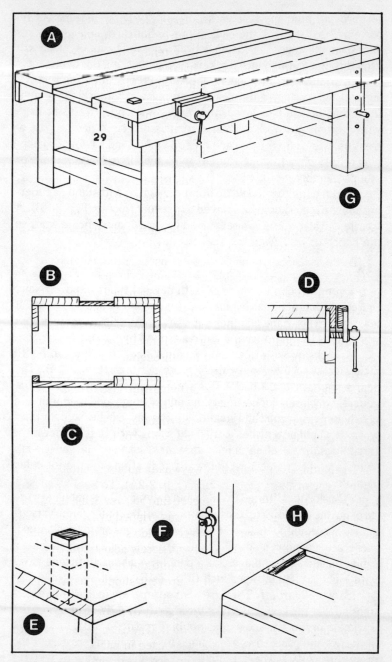

Fig. 2-1. A bench (A) can be plain and solid, with a well (B,C) for tools, a vise (D,G) and a stop (E,F) to plane (H) against.

terbore and plug any screws used (Fig. 2-2D) or assemble with dowels (Fig. 2-2E). If the ends of one or both cross pieces are set back from the edge (Fig. 2-2F), a backsaw used to cut off wood will drop through on the bench hook instead of marking the bench top.

In addition to the bench, there is often a need for a lower support for sawing or for assembling parts at a more convenient level than on the bench top. It is sometimes possible to manage with a stool or a broken chair, but it is better to have a pair of trestles (Fig. 2-3A). One can be used when hand sawing or chopping with a chisel, while the two will support a large cabinet or other assembly.

The trestle top should be stout enough to withstand hammering and the legs should be splayed to prevent tipping (Fig. 2-3B). A trestle will also serve as a seat when you are doing delicate work on the bench or just when you feel tired.

SAWS

Even if a shop is equipped with several types of power saw, there is still a need for hand saws. Many joints have to be cut (at least in part) by hand and there are several details in cabinetwork where it is better to have a cut controlled by hand.

A backsaw with fine teeth is most needed. This can be 10 inches or 12 inches long with 14 teeth per inch (Fig. 2-4A). The best saws have brass backs, but steel is satisfactory. This is the general bench saw for cutting joints and sawing wood to length on a bench hook. A second and smaller similar saw can be used for finer work. It would be 8 inches to 10 inches long with 16 teeth per inch. In catalogs, this is often called a *dovetail saw* and the larger one is a *tenon saw*. The names are not really indications for the intended uses.

A backsaw is limited to cuts where the saw does not have to go through the wood. For those cuts, a hand saw is given various names according to its size. The larger versions are only needed if there are no power saws. Even with a table saw available, a cabinetmaker will find uses for a panel saw about 18 inches along with eight or 10 teeth per inch (Fig. 2-4B).

Saw teeth are *set*. They are bent alternately in opposite directions so that the *kerf* they make through the wood is wider than the thickness of the saw and it does not bind in a deep cut. The teeth of backsaws and panel saws are shaped for severing fibers across the grain (Fig. 2-4C). These teeth will cut along the grain as well for short distances. Longer lengthwise cuts will usually be made with

22

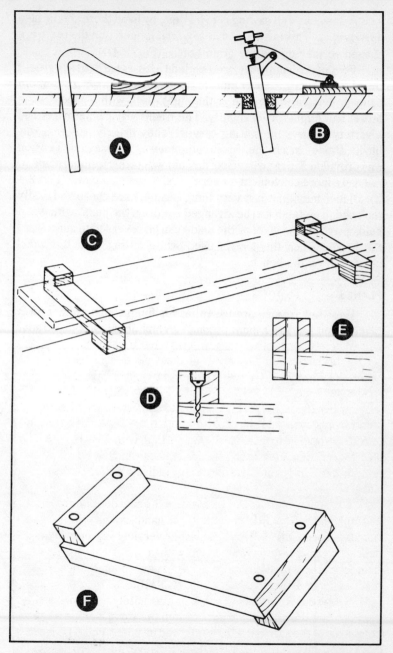

Fig. 2-2. Holdfasts grip work on the bench top. Bench hooks give support to press against while sawing: (A) holdfast; (B) collar; (C) hooks; (D) plugged screws; (E) dowels; (F) cross piece.

a table saw, but if all sawing is to be done by hand there should also be a *ripsaw*. This is like a panel saw, but longer, and the teeth are shaped so they divide the grain better (Fig. 2-4D).

Few other hand saws are needed. This is particularly true if there is a power jigsaw available. Hand sawing always gives more control. It is easier to stop at the right place with a hand saw. A power saw might run on slightly. The traditional cabinetmaker had a variety of saws for cutting curves. They usually had a narrow blade strained in a frame. Most common was the *bowsaw*. Tension was provided with a twisted cord. This was rather cumbersome to use and a more convenient modern version is a *coping saw* (Fig. 2-4 E). Blades might not last very long, but they are cheap and easily replaced. The teeth can be arranged to cut on the push, with wood held upright in the vise, or the blade can be reversed to cut toward the handle when the tool is used while sitting with the wood horizontal on the bench.

PLANES

Hand-held planes are essential for fine cabinetwork. Power planers and sanders cannot produce comparable results. A tradi-

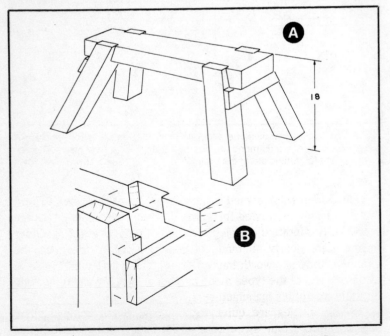

Fig. 2-3. A trestle (A) at knee height should be strong and rigid (B).

24

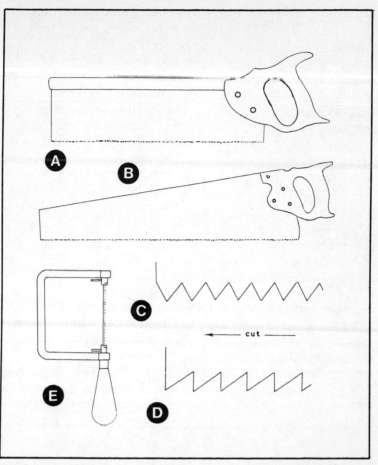

Fig. 2-4. A backsaw makes fine accurate cuts. A handsaw is for general purposes. Saw teeth are diamond shaped for cutting across the grain. They are more upright for cutting along the grain (A,B,C,D). A coping saw (E) will follow curves.

tional cabinetmaker owned a very large range of planes. There might not now be a need for quite as many, but anyone tackling moderately ambitious projects must still have several. Older planes were nearly all made of wood. If any of these can be obtained, they are worth having. Most planes today are made of iron and steel of the types made famous by Stanley and now made by them and other manufacturers.

Metal planes are quite satisfactory. Some traditionalists might claim a certain "sweetness" of use inherent in wooden planes and lacking in metal ones. A wooden plane has screw and lever adjustments that make adjusting simpler and precise. Other imported planes combine metal and wood and might have different adjustments. Whatever the construction, the important things are a flat sole and a blade at the correct angle rigidly held so that it cannot "judder."

There are three planes needed for dealing with flat and straight surfaces. If there is much wood to be taken off, as when sawn wood is planed, or a warped surface has to be trued, the plane to use is a *jack plane* (usually about 14 inches long). Its mouth is wide and the edge of the *iron* is curved (Fig. 2-5A) and set coarsely to take off thick shavings. To get a surface straight, the plane needs to be longer so that it bridges over a wavy edge or surface. This *shooting* (shutting) plane of *jointer* is 20 inches long and its mouth is closer with the cutting edge straight except for the corners being taken of (Fig. 2-5B). For taking off thin shavings to produce a finished surface, there is a shorter (10-inch) smoothing plane that is sharpened in the same way as the shooting plane.

In the Stanley method of construction, the operative parts are the same and differences are in the length of the sole (Fig. 2-5C). All these planes (Fig. 2-6) are used in both hands. For right-handed use, the right hand holds the handle (*tote*) behind the cutter, which is usually called an *iron* although it is made of steel, and provides push and pressure. The left hand provides pressure on the knob at the front of the plane. A useful small plane is the one-handed block plane that is about 7 inches long (Fig. 2-7). Its iron is at a low angle

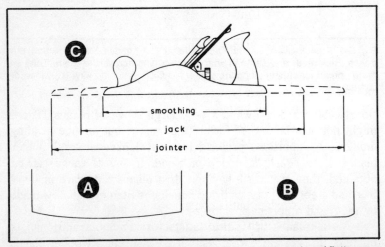

Fig. 2-5. Planes have rounded cutting edges (A) for rough work and flatter ones (B) for finishing. They are named according to their length (C).

26

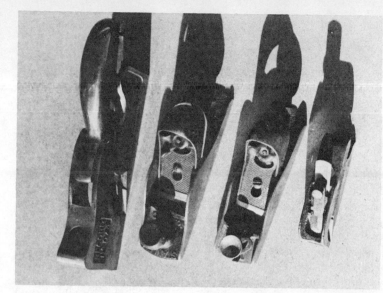

Fig. 2-6. A shoulder plane, two block planes and a bullnose rabbet plane.

for work across the grain, but it is also useful for taking off sharp edges and many light cuts.

Grooves (Fig. 2-8A) and rabbets have to made (Fig. 2-8B). A wobble saw in a table saw will cut grooves and some power planers will cut rabbets. If the work is to be done by hand, there are two special planes needed. Grooves are made with a plow plane. This can make different widths of grooves by changing cutters and the depths and distances from edges can be controlled with stops (Fig. 2-8C).

There are *rabbet planes* in which the cutting edge is the same width as the sole. One version has the iron at a low angle and is called a *shoulder plane*. Its particular use in planing across the grain of wide tenons. Another type has the mouth and cutter close to the front of the plane. This bullnose plane is made this way to get close into the angle of a stopped rabbet (Fig. 2-8D).

Rabbet planes can be used to follow the work of a power planer or saw, but if the plane is to cut the rabbet completely it needs stops and is then called a *fillister*. If the cut comes on the control edge (face edge) it is called a *side fillister* (Fig. 2-8E). If the cut comes at the far edge, but is controlled by a stop against the face edge, it is a *sash fillister*. (Fig. 2-8F).

Metal versions of these planes are more compact than the earlier wooden versions (Fig. 2-9). There are combination planes that will cut rabbets and grooves as well as a range of moldings. They are sold under names indicating the number of functions possible. Examples are the Stanley or Record Forty Five.

Moldings occur in most fine cabinetwork. The power tool for working them is a *spindle molder*. A spindle molder has a rotating cutter of the reverse profile that rotates at high speed while the wood is pushed against guides across it. This is satisfactory except that it suffers from the same fault as a power planer. It leaves the surface with minute marks and it pounds it. If molding for cabinetwork is made in this way, there should be a thorough sanding to disguise the fact that the work was done by machinery.

Traditionally, the moldings were cut by *molding planes*. The cabinetmaker would have had a large number of such planes. Unfortunately, they are no longer obtainable new, but used ones in working order might be worth buying. Each plane has its sole and iron shaped to the reverse of the molding to be cut. Additionally there were *hollows* and *rounds*. The names indicate the shapes they would cut. It is possible to form some moldings, with rabbets and convex curves, using rabbet planes, but for concave shapes a plane with a suitable sole is best. Or the waste can be removed with a plow plane and the shape can be finished by scraping or sanding.

Associated with planes are scrapers. The visual attraction of some wood is in its confused grain. Planing in any direction can cause this to tear up and leave a rough surface. The tool to use for

Fig. 2-7. Three wood planes: a hollow, a round and a molding.

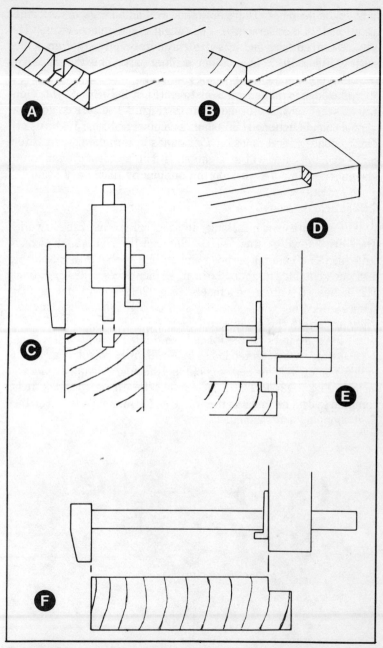

Fig. 2-8. A groove (A) is cut with a plow plane having stops to control depth and distance from the edge. A rabbet (B) is cut with a rabbet plane or fillister plane. Its stops (C) control the width from the near or far edge (D,E,F).

29

finishing is a *scraper*. There are modern handled scrapers, but the traditional cabinet scraper is a rectangular piece of tool steel. Its edge is burred over and it is this tiny turned edge that does the cutting (Fig. 2-10A). The scraper is tilted to an angle that makes it remove very thin shavings—not just dust.

The edge is rubbed on an oilstone (Figs. 2-10B and 2-11) then a hard steel tool is pressed along it (Fig. 2-10C). It could be a special round-sectioned burnisher or a chisel or gouge can be used. This is done several times on both angles to turn them over. After some use the burr will straighten. It can be turned over again several times before work on the oilstone is necessary again.

CHISELS

Chisels are used in making joints and much other cabinetwork. They are known by their widths and can be from about ⅛ inch upwards. The general purpose chisels are *firmer chisels* and the first ones obtained might be ¼-inch, ½-inch and a wider one about 1½ inches. Bevel-edged chisels (Fig. 2-12A) will do all that square-edged ones will and they will also get into acute angles. They are worth the slight extra cost.

There are uses for the longer and thinner *paring chisels* (Fig. 2-12B) which are not intended to be hit. Firmer chisels may be hit with a mallet, but for heavy chopping there are stronger *mortise chisels* (Fig. 2-12C). There is less use for these today as it is common to drill out most of the waste and firmer chisels can do the final chopping and shaping.

Fig. 2-9. A wooden plow or fillister (left) is a more bulky tool than the metal fillister (center) or plow (right).

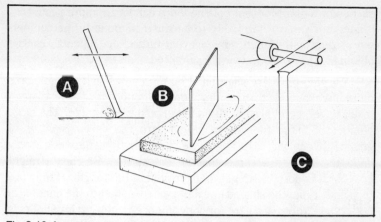

Fig. 2-10. A scraper cuts with its curved edge (A), make by first rubbing square on an oilstone (B) and then turning over with a hard steel tool (C).

Many modern chisels have plastic handles molded on. They are satisfactory, but wooden handles are attractive and give a different feel that seems to engender good work. If a chisel has to be hit, it is best to use a wooden mallet. Wide chisels will not roll off the bench. If the steel part is narrower than the handle, it is advisable to choose a handle with flats on it to prevent rolling (Fig. 2-12D).

In general work there is less use for gouges. A gouge ground on the outside (Fig. 2-12E) is used for hollowing. If it is *in canneled* it is used for paring concave cuts (Fig. 2-12F). One of these ½-inch wide might be the first purchase.

Wood turning on a lathe is done with special gouges and chisels which are longer than firmer chisels. Roughing to shape as well as some finishing is done with gouges. The cutting edge is usually rounded and it is sharpened on the outside (Fig. 2-12G). One that is ¾-inch wide will do most work, but another ¼-inch wide will also be needed. A turning chisel has its end angled and it is sharpened on both sides. (Fig. 2-12H). One that is ½-inch wide might be all that is needed. It is useful to have a parting tool for cutting directly into the work. The steel narrows behind the cutting edge (Fig. 2-12J) so that it does not bind in a deep cut.

Carving has more limited application. Until the beginning of this century, much cabinetwork was carved and some of this was quite extensive and elaborate. To do that sort of work involves a large number of gouges and chisels. During the peak of the carving era, tool catalogs listed hundreds of different cross sections and

31

shapes of tools. Modern tools now are in a much more restricted range. For the carving likely to be done in modern fine cabinetwork, they will suffice. However, if older carving tools can be obtained, they will be worth having.

Carving tools are sharpened on both sides, but gouges have more bevel outside than inside. Similarly, one side of a chisel has a major bevel, but there is a slight bevel on the other side. The large number of listed tools is mainly due to the varying *sweeps* of gouges. In any width, it is possible to get anything between a very deep U shape to a curve that is almost flat. Besides straight gouges, it is possible to get them curved in the length. If they are the spade type, the shaped end has a narrow shaft to the handle. In both cases, the shapes are for convenience in getting into hollows and awkward places.

Carving chisels have fewer uses. Besides straight ends, they have skew ends and can be curved or cranked in the length and might be spade shaped. A V tool is like a double chisel that will cut triangular grooves. What carving tools a cabinetmaker accumulates depends on what carving he expects to do, but about twelve tools will allow him to make a start (Fig. 2-13).

Fig. 2-11. An oilstone and a gouge slip, a thick mortise chisel, a thin bevel-edged paring chisel, a bevel-edged firmer chisel and an in cannelled gouge.

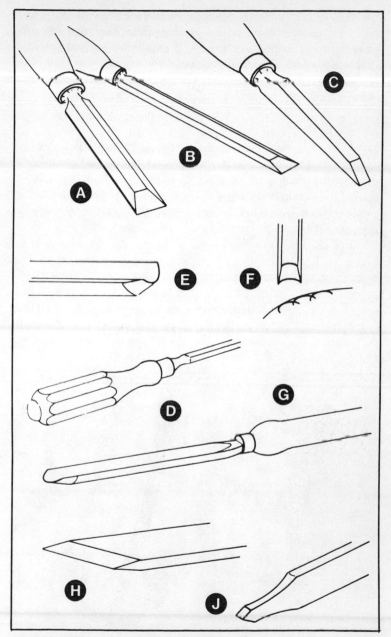

Fig. 2-12. Chisels can have bevelled edges (A) or be made extra thick (B,C). A gouge can be sharpened outside (E) or inside. Having flats (D) on a handle prevents rolling. Turning is done with long gouges, skew chisels and narrow parting tools (F,G,H,J).

Knives are needed for general woodwork and carving. There is a branch of carving, called *chip carving* in which there are uses for knives of many shapes. For most work, a knife with a sharp point is all that is needed. The traditional woodworking marking knife has a cutting edge sloping across the end, but today it is probably better to have a Stanley or similar knife with a replaceable blade.

SHARPENING

Edge tools must be kept sharp. This is particularly important with some of the hardwoods with difficult grains that are used in cabinetwork. Frequent touching up of edges before they have a chance to become very blunt is the best way of keeping tools in good condition. A cabinetmaker should have his oilstone ready for use and not begrudge time taken in sharpening.

For chisels and plane irons, a stone of the usual 2-inch by 8-inch by 1-inch size is suitable and it should be mounted in a wooden case. The manufactured stones, such as Carborundum and India, are quick-cutting, but coarse. It is best to also have a fine natural stone, such as Arkansas, for finishing. This might be all that is needed for touching up, but if much has to be taken off an edge is produced on the coarse stone. Sharpening repeatedly on the fine stone will remove the marks of the coarse stone.

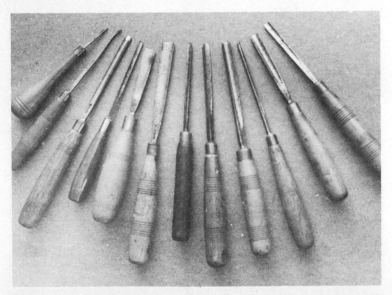

Fig. 2-13. Carving is done mostly with gouges of different curves and sizes, with chisels and with tools. Different handles help in identifying tools on the bench.

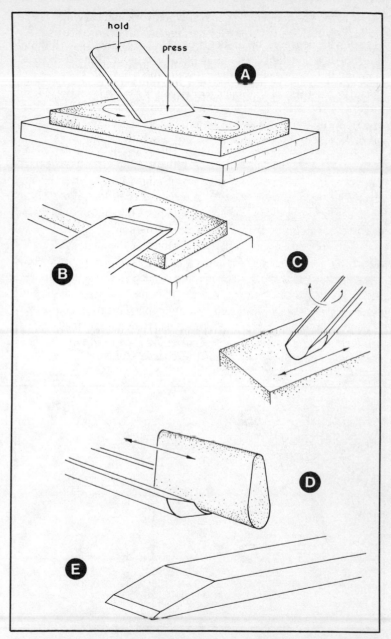

Fig. 2-14. Edge tools are sharpened by rubbing their bevels on an oilstone (A) and then the other side flat (B) to remove burr. A gouge is rolled as it is rubbed. Its inside is sharpened with a slip stone. Thicker tools have a grinding bevel and a sharpening bevel (C,D,E).

To sharpen a chisel or plane iron, note the existing bevel and hold the tool with that on the stone. In most cases this will be between 25 degrees and 35 degrees. There are jigs that will hold the tool at a constant angle as it is rubbed along the stone. With hand holding, there is a tendency to dip the hands at the far end of the stroke. However, with one hand holding the tool and the spread fingers of the other hand applying pressure (Fig. 2-14A), a little practice will allow you to maintain the angle. Use a thin lubricating oil or kerosene on the stone. Do not use a thick oil.

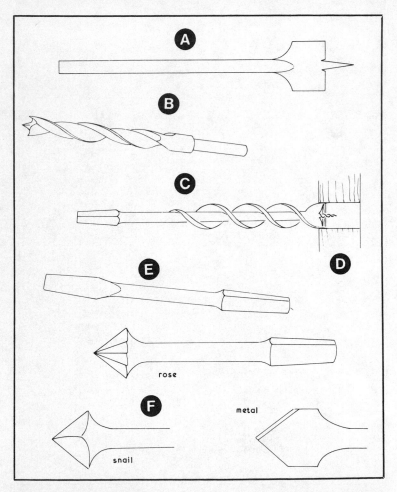

Fig. 2-15. Spade (A,B) and twist bits (C,D) are for power drills. Square-shanked bits are for hand use in a brace. Screwdriver (E) and countersink bits (F) are also used in a brace.

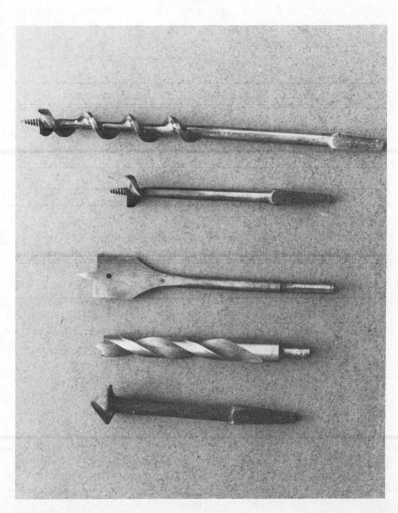

Fig. 2-16. A snail countersink bit, a power twist drill, a power spade drill, a screw center brace bit and an Irwin pattern brace bit.

Continue rubbing until a burr can be felt on the other side. This *wire edge* indicates that the bevel is meetiong the flat side and a little of the steel rubbed away is clinging to the edge. Put the tool flat on the stone and give it a few circular rubs (Fig. 2-14B). That should remove the wire edge. To make sure, slice the edge across a piece of scrap wood before putting the tool back into use.

To sharpen a gouge, you will need a *slip stone*. This is a small oilstone with a rounded edge. It need not fit the gouge, providing its cross section is curved smaller than the gouge. For a gouge bevelled outside, sharpening can be done on the ordinary oilstone by rolling the edge as it is rubbed (Fig. 2-14C). Follow by using the slip stone like a file flat against the inside to remove the wire edge (Fig. 2-11D). If the gouge is in-canneled all of the sharpening of the bevel will have to be done with the slip stone and the wire edge removed by rolling the outside flat on the ordinary stone.

Knives and other tools that are sharpened on both sides, should be rubbed a little at each side until the bevels meet and a wire edge can be felt. Then slice across scrap wood. A blunt edge can usually be seen. If the tool is held with its edge upward, light will be reflected from the blunt part. Examining in this way will show if any parts of an edge need further treatment.

Ordinary chisels and thicker plane irons have two bevels (Fig. 2-14E). Sharpening is done on the narrow edge bevel, but this will gradually get wider and sharpening will involve considerable pressure and rubbing. When that stage is reached the longer bevel should be reground. Care is needed to avoid overheating the tool to the stage where oxide colors appear and the temper is drawn. This would make the cutting edge soft. Woodworking tools were ground on a slot turning sandstone wheel lubricated with water. That would still be the best way, but in most cases grinding will have to be done on high-speed dry grinding wheel. Dip the tool into water frequently to keep the edge cool. Grind until only a narrow band of the oilstone bevel is left. With thinner tools, such as the irons of Stanley planes, sharpening need only be on the oilstone because there is a single bevel. It might be advisable, particularly if the edge becomes notched, to renew the entire bevel by grinding. Follow this with sharpening at the same angle on an oilstone.

Some planes have single irons which are fitted into the plane with the bevel upwards. Other planes have cap irons and are fitted with the bevel downwards. The cap iron provides some stiffness, but its main use is as a chip breaker. As the shavings come up

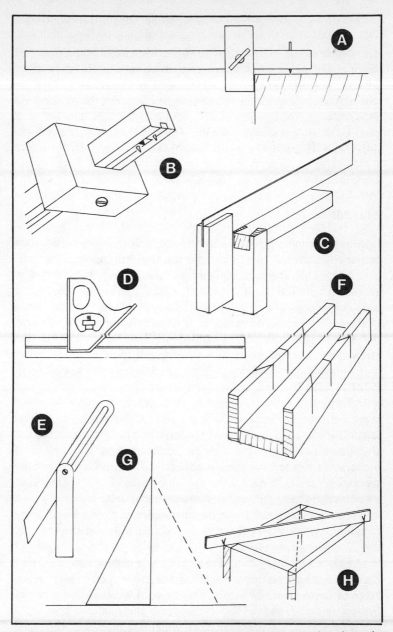

Fig. 2-17. A marking gauge (A) draws lines parallel with an edge. A mortise gauge (B) scratches two lines. A try square (C) for testing right angles can be rigid or have a sliding head (D). An adjustable bevel (E) tests other angles. Miters can be sawn in a box (F). Correctness of a square can be tested by turning it over (G). Squareness of an assembly can be tested by checking diagonal (H).

through the plane mouth, they are broken at frequent intervals and this reduces the risk of the surface grain of the wood breaking out.

The cap iron should fit closely to the cutting iron. Make sure that there are no particles of wood or anything else to prevent a close fit. For a coarsely set jack plane, the cap iron might be as much as one-sixteenth of an inch from the cutting edge. For the finer cuts of other planes, experiment with closer positions to get the best results. Also experiment with the width of the plane mouth if it is adjustable. Keeping the mouth narrow and the cap iron close on a finely set sharp iron is the way to get a surface with the finest texture when giving it its final planing.

DRILLING

At one time, all holes were drilled by hand using a bit brace and bits which were not very scientifically designed until a comparatively short time ago. Spoon bits, like gouges, were common and holes were often far from round or straight. Today, most holes can be made with an electric drill (except for the larger ones). However the common spade bits (Fig. 2-15A) for an electric drill do not make a perfect hole of much depth. For clean straight holes going well into the wood, use the type of bit that looks like a metalworking bit, but with a spur and woodcutting end (Fig. 2-15B).

For holes outside the capacity of the electric drill, use center bits with spur centers for shallow holes. Use twist bits, such as Irwin (Fig. 2-15C), for deeper holes (turning the bit with a brace). If the hole has to go right through, either drill against a piece of scrap wood or watch for the center to break through. Then turn the work over and drill back from the other side (Fig. 2-15D). This avoids raggedness due to the grain breaking out.

A ratchet brace is worth the extra cost. It allows a drill to be turned in a place where there is insufficient room for the brace to sweep a full circle.

Besides ordinary bits, it is worthwhile getting a screwdriver bit (Fig. 12-15E) so that the leverage of the brace can be used on large or stubborn screws. In addition, get at least one countersink bit (Figs. 2-15F and 2-16) for preparing the end of a hole for a flat-head screw. Countersinking at the slow speed of a brace gets better results than using a similar bit in an electric drill. Similarly, small holes for screws can be made better with a metal working bit in a hand-driven wheel brace than in an electric drill. A depth gauge for brace bits can be purchased, but be careful that it doesn't mark the wood surface.

MEASURING

For most of the history of woodworking, craftsmen have managed without the rules for the precision we regard as essential. The best way to measure a part is to try it against the position it has to fit. If that cannot be done, a *rod* can be used. This is a strip of wood with spacings penciled on the edge.

A 24-inch straight steel rule is a good tool to have on the bench for drawing straight lines and for measuring. A 10-foot expanding tape rule will take care of larger measuring. It might be worthwhile having a clearly marked 6-inch rule for setting gauges and other short measurements.

Distances from an edge often have to be marked and the tool traditionally used is a *marking gauge* (Fig. 2-17A). It is still the best tool for the purpose. A *mortise gauge* (Fig. 2-17B) is similar, but it has a second spur so both sides of a mortise or tenon can be marked at one time.

Right angles are checked with a try square (Figs. 2-17C and Fig. 2-18). The type with a wooden stock is traditional, but an

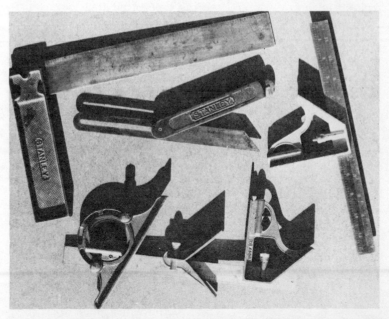

Fig. 2-18. A try square, an adjustable bevel and two combination squares; one has a center head as well as an adjustable bevel head.

all-metal type should be more accurate. A 12-inch blade will suit most purposes in cabinetmaking, but a 6-inch one is less cumbersome for squaring around smaller pieces of wood. A combination square, with a 12-inch rule sliding in a head that will test 45 degrees as well as 90 degrees, is a useful alternative (Fig. 2-17D).

For angles other than a right angle, there is an adjustable bevel (Fig. 2-17E). There are miters in many pieces of cabinetwork and it helps to have a miter box to guide the backsaw (Fig. 2-17F). Besides the plain wooden type, there are more acccurate ones with clamping devices included.

Many things will be made that are outside the reach of a 12-inch try square. It is possible to make larger wooden ones, but a set square, or triangle, made from thin plywood will be useful for checking. Test this during construction by turning it over on a straight line (Fig. 2-17G). Plane until you get the same result either way. Accuracy of many assemblies can also be checked by measuring diagonals. There is no need to use feet and inches. There is less risk of error if you keep a long straight batten for the purpose and pencil where the corners come on its edge (Fig. 2-17H).

CLAMPING

Much cabinetmaking consists of making parts which are then glued together and it is necessary to pull and hold the joints tight while the glue sets. You will usually find that you seem to never have enough clamps. It is worthwhile accumulating all the clamping devices you can. For the smaller grips, C clamps are probably the best choice. Although large ones can be closed to grip small things, they can then be rather clumsy. It is better to have some in smaller sizes. There are many places where two clamps have to be uses, so buy them in pairs if possible.

For larger assemblies you need bar clamps. They can be those with bars included or they can be heads to fit on a pipe or to the edge of a piece of wood. They should have a capacity of at least 3 feet and most jobs need two.

It is possible to improvise clamps with wedges to apply pressure. Two blocks of wood fastened to a base or a strip of wood provide the anchor points. The work is put between them and a pair of wedges driven across each other at one end to put on pressure (Fig. 2-19A). There is considerable power in a twisted cord, so a *Spanish windlass* can be made to pull frame parts together (Fig. 2-19B). Fortunately, with many modern glues, only enough pressure to hold the parts in contact will do. If it is possible to put the work under a weight, that might be enough clamping.

OTHER TOOLS

Not so many uses are found for a hammer because there are not many nails used in cabinetwork. A light (4-ounce) hammer is useful for panel pins. A larger hammer can be used over a block of wood to drive parts together, but this might be better done with a mallet.

Screws have to be driven and good quality plain screwdrivers in several sizes are probably more use than ratchet or pump-action screwdrivers. Short screwdrivers might be needed in restricted places, but it is easier to use long ones. File the ends to accurately fit the screw slots. In reproduction work, Phillipshead screws would be inappropriate because they are a recent invention.

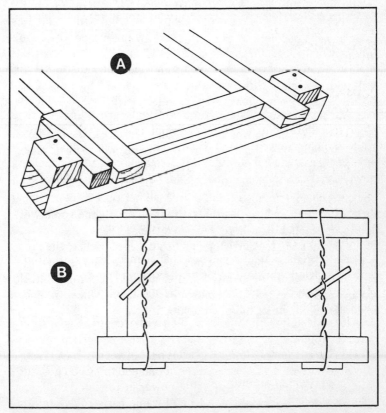

Fig. 2-19. Clamps can be improvised with wedges (A) or twisted cords (B).

Oldtime cabinetmakers used rasps, but the modern equivalent is a Surform tool. With flat and curved blades, these tools are useful for shaped work. They should be followed by sanding and with chisel or plane intermediately in some cases.

There are spokeshaves for curves. Modern metal ones are like small planes with a handle at each side. A flat sole is used on convex work, while a curved sole is used in concave work. These *spokeshaves* have a rather high cutting angle and are difficult to use to make a smooth surface. Surform tools are more effective. Older spokeshaves were made of wood with a cutter that sliced like a chisel and they generally gave better results.

A tool catalog will show a large variety of other tools and variations on those described. It is best to start with the basic tools of established pattern and add to the tool kit as the need is felt for more tools. To a certain extent, the type of work will dictate what tools are worth having. Standard tools have evolved over a long period and it is unlikely that new tools will make the popular ones obsolete. It is unwise to buy a prepared kit of tools unless you are certain that it contains what you need. Most kits include some tools you might never use and omit others that you will find essential. There is also the risk that in a kit there might be tools of inferior quality. If you select each tool individually, you know what you are getting.

Tools are a good investment and should be looked after. If you need to be mobile, they might have to be stored in a chest. Otherwise it is better to arrange racks in your shop. If there is a risk of dampness enclose the racks with doors and use a silica gel powder or paper to absorb moisture. Do not rush into arranging racks. Check their best positions after you have done some work and locate tools near where you need them.

Consider what would happen if you dropped tools to the floor. If the tool is wood, they might not suffer. If the floor is concrete, sharp edges would be blunted and cast iron parts might crack. Cover such a floor, at least in the vicinity of the bench, with rubber or linoleum or one of the plastic substitutes.

Chapter 3
Basic Techniques

For successful cabinetwork, there has to be attention to precision at all stages. In some general carpentry, there can be errors of flatness or straightness and often considerable tolerance in measurements. In something like a yard fence, posts and rails need not be straight or very exact to size. Even in the making of storage boxes and similar things, overall accuracy might hide discrepancies inside that do not matter. In the making of good quality furniture, there is little room for error. Parts have to be properly made or they will not do. Joints have to fit closely, surfaces have to match and most internal parts have to be as accurate as the outsides.

This means that a cabinetmaker has to approach the work with an attitude of restraint and care. Good cabinetmaking should not be rushed. Sometimes it is possible to use a piece of wood that is not quite the size originally intended or there might be a flaw in a piece that can be hidden where it does not matter. In general, wood selected has to be of good quality and suitable for finishing to the sizes required. Some wood might have to be discarded or put aside for use where it would be satisfactory reduced to a smaller size. What would be flaws in some woods becomes decoration in others. For load-bearing parts, such as legs, there must be reasonable straightness of grain. More information on woods is provided in Chapter 4.

FACE MARKS

The first requirement is the preparation of wood to the proper cross sections. They are usually slightly overlong to allow for cutting and fitting joints. Machine planing will bring wood to a reasonably accurate form, but there should be some wood left for truing by hand. This can be quite slight, but the power-planed surfaces have to be hand-planed. In doing this, the wood is brought to a true section and with flat straight surfaces.

Start on a wide surface with the wood against the bench stop. Check it by slighting under a straightedge, lengthwise and in the width (Fig. 3-1A). If this shows reasonable accuracy, use a smoothing plane to remove the machine plane marks and test again. If the surface is a long way from true, use a jack plane to remove the high spots. Follow with a shooting plane and finish with a smoothing plane after checking accuracy following the other two planes.

In moderate widths it is unlikely that there will be a twist. In wider pieces (6 inches or more), testing with a straightedge might show apparent accuracy. However, the surface could be *in winding*. This means that one end is twisted in relation to the other. This can be checked with *winding strips*. These are straight pieces longer than the width so that they exaggerate it when you are sighting (Fig. 3-1B).

Winding strips can be plain parallel pieces of wood. The traditional types have light or dark pieces let in the edges for sighting and dowels in one engage with holes in the other for storage together (Fig. 3-1C).

When one surface has been made true, an edge is planed equally true and at right angles to the first surface. Thin wood will have to be held in a vise, although benchtop support is better, because it prevents bending if the wood will stand against the stop. Use a shooting plane along an edge. Check along the length with a straightedge and use a try square the other way (Fig. 3-1D). Test at several places by looking towards a light.

These two surfaces are *face side* and *face edge* and are traditionally marked in pencil with a looped shape on the wider surface. They have a tail going towards a V meeting it on the edge (Fig. 3-1E). If it is a very long piece of wood or if it will be cut into several pieces later, use more than one set of marks.

In the assembly of a piece of furniture, all face surfaces are kept the same way (Fig. 3-1F). All measuring for joints and other things are made from face surfaces, so meeting parts will match. If there are any slight errors, they come at the other side.

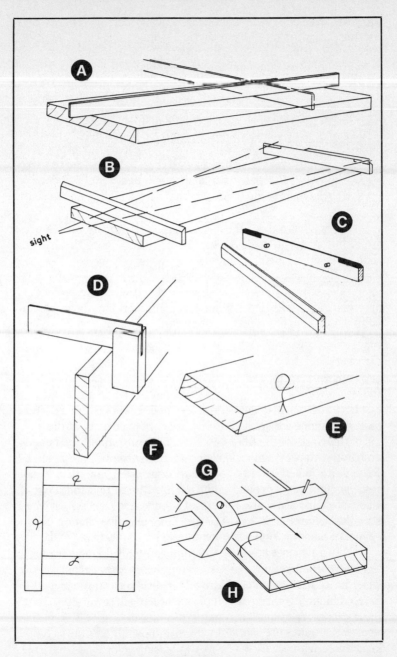

Fig. 3-1. A straightedge (A) tests flatness. Winding strips (B, C) test twist. Face marks are put on the first planed surfaces and these are used in further marking and testing (D, E, F, G, H).

47

With face side and edge of known accuracy, widths and thicknesses are marked from them. If there is much wood to be removed, putting the piece through a table saw with face surfaces towards the table and the guide fence will ensure accurate parallel cuts.

Mark the width with a marking gauge. Have its stock against the face edge (Fig. 3-1G). Do this on opposite surfaces so that you have a scratched line on both sides. Plane to these gauge lines, then gauge the thickness in the same way. If there is sufficient width to justify it, gauge across the ends as well (Fig. 3-1H). Plane to these lines. Also test flatness with a straightedge. You could have worked to the lines at the edges, but have left a high or uneven part elsewhere.

For most furniture, there will have to be many pieces prepared. It is advisable to do the same step to each piece that has the same dimensions before moving on. Whenever possible, avoid altering the marking gauge until all markings at one setting have been done. This way slight variations in resetting can be avoided. A busy craftsman will find having a second marking gauge worthwhile. Or one pin of a mortise gauge could be used for some single marking.

MARKING TO LENGTH

If a position has to be marked on wood, but not cut there later, it should be done with pencil. If a saw cut has to be made at the line, it is better to sever the fibers with a knife cut. Carpenters' pencils are made with rectangular leads so that they can be sharpened to chisel ends. When used edgewise to draw lines, they would not wear as quickly as a round point. If you cannot find this type of pencil at a hardware store, the end of a round lead can be sharpened to a chisel edge (Fig. 3-2A). A piece of fine abrasive paper glued to a piece of wood is kept for touching up the point (Fig. 3-2B).

If several pieces have to carry similar length or joint markings, deal with them together. In most assemblies, there are four legs or uprights that have to match. Mark all the distances on one piece and then put them together with all of the face edges toward the front. Use a try square to mark across all four pieces (Fig. 3-2C). In this case, the cut ends are marked with a knife and the limits of joints are marked with a pencil.

If parts have to be marked with matching dimensions, but they are of different sections or of different overall lengths so that they

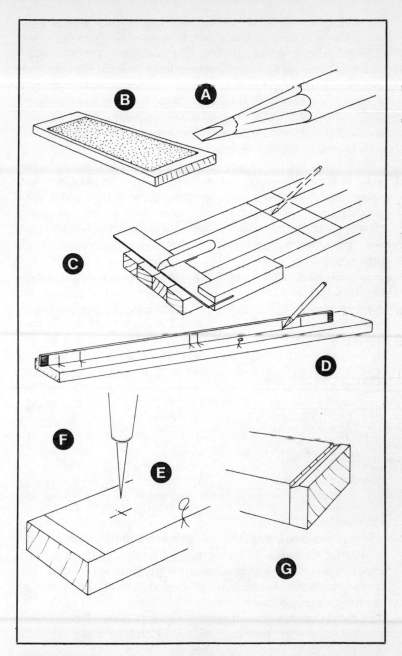

Fig. 3-2. A chisel-ended pencil can be sharpened (A) on abrasive paper (B).
Lines to be cut are marked with a knife. Distances can be marked with a rod.
Cross at hold positions (C,D,E,F). Recess at lines for accurate sawing (G).

cannot all be marked at the same time, it is convenient to make a *rod*. This is a strip of spare wood on which all the distances expected to be needed are marked. To mark one or a group of parts, the rod is put along the wood and the lines needed for that part are transferred. Other parts that have to match will have these and other marks transferred. It is best to locate each transferred position with a "peck." This is a freehand V with the point of a pencil (Fig. 3-2D). Then use the try square to put a mark through the point of the V where the line is to be marked.

Separate the pieces and "square around" the marks. At the ends, continue the knife cuts around all surfaces. At the other places, take the pencil lines on to surfaces where joints will come. In squaring around, it is best to put the stock of the try square against either the face side or face edge. However, it is unlikely that there will be an error if it is done the other way on wood already planed to size.

If holes have to be located, mark across them with a pencil on all pieces that have to match. Then use a marking gauge from the face edge to make a short line across them (Fig. 3-2E) so that all are at the same distances. Most pointed drills will locate without wandering. If you want to make sure of the drill entering properly, make a dent with a pointed awl (Fig. 3-2F). If it is a part with many lines marked and there could be confusion, put a penciled freehand ring around the crossing.

Cutting to length is often left until after joints have been cut. This is particularly true if there is a joint to be cut near an end and there could be a risk of the grain breaking out. If the saw cut at the end is to come against the knife cut line, it helps to use a chisel to pare a little from the waste side of the line (Fig. 3-2G). This guides the saw at the start and progress of it through the wood is easier to see.

CHISELLING

A chisel should usually be treated as a two-handed tool. This means that the wood being worked on must be held in a vise, gripped under a holdfast or clamped in place. It is rare that it is better to use a chisel in one hand. Striking the chisel with a mallet is an obvious exception.

Having two hands on the chisel is a safety factor. If both hands are behind the edge, they cannot be cut. Normally, one hand grips the handle tightly and provides thrust and control. The other hand is on the blade, pressing and ready to restrain if the cut has to be stopped.

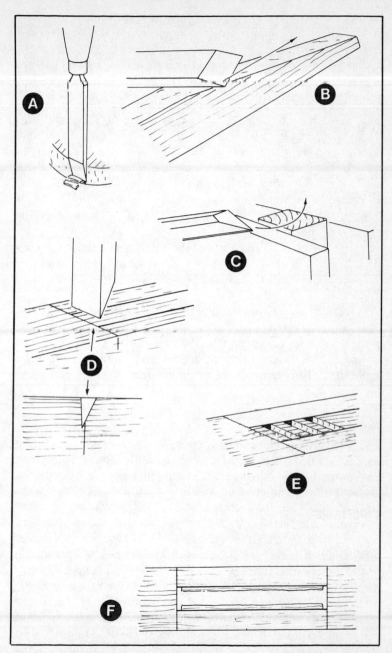

Fig. 3-3. Avoid breaking out by chiselling with the grain or slicing. Chop waste first away from a line before cutting to it: (A) paring; (B) tapering; (C) slicing; (D,E) chopping; (F) full cut.

Much cutting is directly across the fibers such as in vertical paring (Fig. 3-3A). This can be by hand for light cuts or with the help of a mallet when necessary. The edge is then making a direct shear and some fibers might bend instead of cut. This is particularly true if the chisel edge is becoming dull. The cutting edge will produce a smoother surface if it can be used with a slicing action. This might have to be done when tapering along the grain (Fig. 3-3B) or an end can be pared by slicing if it is held close to the vise jaws to prevent vibration (Fig. 3-3C).

A chisel enters wood with a wedge action. It pushes fibers aside on the flat side as well as on the bevelled surface. This must be remembered when you chop mortises or other slots, even if most of the waste has been removed by drilling. If the chisel is entered on the line at the end of the mortise, it will move slightly over the line as it is driven in and the mortise will finish too long (Fig. 3-3D). It is better to chop in a series of cuts to within a short distance of the line (Fig. 3-3E) and remove the waste. Then pare to the line by hand pressure only.

A chisel used across the grain will sever fibers with little risk of wood breaking out or a split developing. If driven in the direction of the grain, a split might spread further unless there is a cut across to stop it. This means that in cutting out an opening, cuts should be made the full width across the grain before working to size along the grain (Fig. 3-3F).

GRAIN DIRECTION

When using a chisel, plane, spokeshave or other edge-cutting tool, most wood will be found to work smoothly in one direction and tend to tear up the other way. If grain is regarded as a number of straws bound together, a diagonal cut that tends to stroke them straight should finish smoothly (Fig. 3-4A). Trying to cut the other way would catch in the straws, bending some and cutting the others raggedly (Fig. 3-4B). Grain appearance is not always as obvious as that, but grain markings sloping towards the surface will give a clue to the direction to cut (Fig. 3-4C). If the slope is slight or wavy there might have to be a trial cut to determine the best way. Some surfaces might have to be worked partly one way and partly the other. Some exotic woods with curling grain might not respond to any normal planing. Then it is sometimes possible to get a good surface by using a finely set smoothing plane at right angles to the general direction of grain. Finish would have to be with a scraper.

Grain direction has to be noted when working on a curve with a

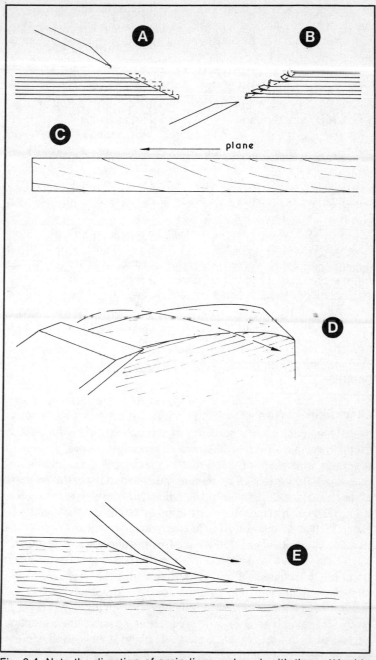

Fig. 3-4. Note the direction of grain lines and work with them: (A) with; (B) against; (C) plane direction; (D) slicing; (E) bevel.

chisel or spokeshave. It helps to have the tool cutting slightly on the skew to produce a slicing action (Fig. 3-4D). Internal curves might not be quite as obvious. A chisel can be used with its bevel downwards (Fig. 3-4E).

For cuts directly across the grain, care is needed to avoid breaking out at the far side. In some cases, a piece of scrap wood can be tightly clamped on to take the cut as it goes through (Fig. 3-5A). It is more common on a broad end to do the planing from both sides towards the middle and then get down to the line at each end and take the bump off the middle as the last step (Fig. 3-5B). In some cases, a small diagonal slice off the far edge stops breaking out (Fig. 3-5C). When chiselling across the grain, the work is easier and the result smoother if a broad chisel is used with a slicing action.

A plane with a low angle is easiest to use across the grain, but a finely set ordinary plane is satisfactory. In any case, avoid letting the wood have a long overhang from its support. It would vibrate and the plane would produce "chatter marks" as it jumped while cutting. Sides of metal planes are at right angles to their soles, so it is possible to shoot ends while the wood is held against a bench hook and the plane is used resting on its side on the bench (Fig. 3-5D).

SAWING

The natural grip would seem to be with all the fingers through the hole and around the saw handle. Actually, control is better if the first finger points along the side of the handle (Fig. 3-6A). It is useful to be able to use a backsaw in either hand to avoid the need to reverse a long piece of wood that has to be cut at both ends.

A cut can be started by pulling the saw back over the far edge of the wood. Guide the saw by the chisel cut against the knifed line (Fig. 3-6B) or by the thumb of the other hand. As you change to forward cutting, gradually lower the handle so that the cut comes down to the width of the wood (Fig. 3-6C). Once you are cutting the full width, the saw will be guided across and you can concentrate on watching its progress through the wood.

If it is important that a cut be accurate at both sides and you doubt if you can control the saw on one cut through, slope upwards on the near side (Fig. 3-6D). Then do the same from the other side (Fig. 3-6E). In both cases, go almost to the full depth. Then cut straight through (Fig. 3-6F) using the first cuts as guides for the saw.

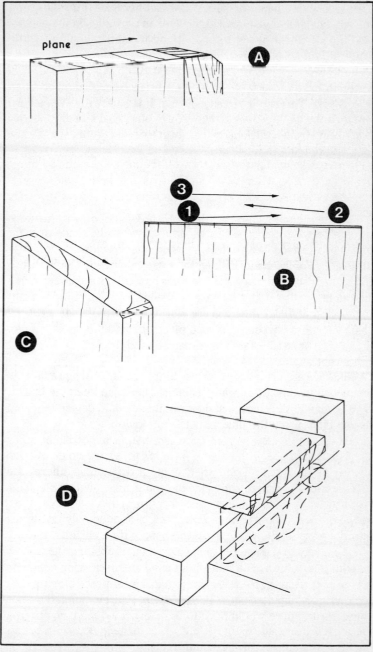

Fig. 3-5. Avoid breaking out when planing across grain (A,B,C). Small work can be planed with the tool on its side (D).

Cuts with a panel or larger saw can be made with the wood held vertically in a vise or with it level on a trestle. In the second case, kneel on the wood to hold it and to steady yourself while cutting. If the wood is fairly thick, there is less effort when cutting with the saw nearly upright (Fig. 3-6G). With thinner wood, it is better to have more teeth in contact by using a shallower slope (Fig. 3-6H). This applies to any sawing. It is better to have several teeth within the thickness of the wood by sawing at a shallow angle, than to cut straight through with only one or two teeth engaged at a time and tending to jump.

DRILLING

Some cabinetmakers say they *bore* holes, but *drill* is the more acceptable word today. Usually, holes have to be made at right angles to a surface. With a drill press or other machine, accuracy is automatic. For freehand drilling, the eye might need help. If a brace and bit are used, the operator can view how things are going in one direction. It also helps to have someone else sighting at right angles (Fig. 3-7A). When you are working alone with a brace or an electric drill, a try square can be placed beside the bit as a guide (Fig. 3-7B) or an adjustable bevel can be used if the hole has to be at a different angle.

If holes are drilled for dowels, there are several jigs available that act as guides to accurate spacing. They also keep the drill at right angles to the surface and one of these could be used for that reason even when the hole is not for a dowel.

If drilling is done to remove waste before a mortise or other slot is cut to shape with chisels, it helps to let the holes overlap slightly (Fig. 3-7C). Even when using a drill press, there is a tendency for the drill to slide sideways into an adjoining hole. This risk can be reduced if alternate holes are drilled and then those between them follow (Fig. 3-7D). Each hole need only just break into the next to allow trimming to shape with a chisel.

One way to supposedly judge a craftsman was to observe how he withdrew a bit from a hole. If he used an unscrewing action he was not a craftsman. He was a craftsman if he kept the bit going the same way as he pulled back. In the case of a screw-pointed bit in a "blind" hole, there would have to be a few reversed turns to free the point. After that, withdrawing while turning clockwise brings out the waste chips. Turning counterclockwise might leave some in the hole.

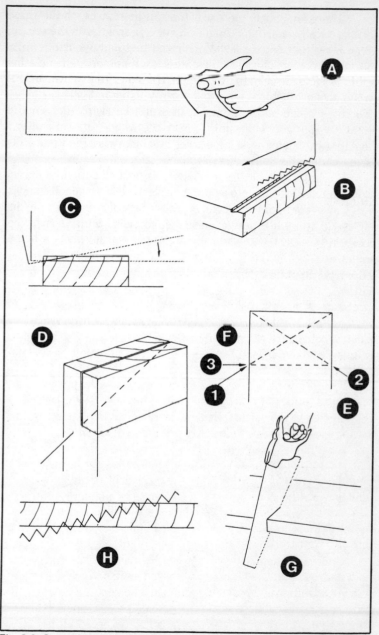

Fig. 3-6. Control a saw with a finger extended (A). Draw back to start a cut and lower the blade after it has started (B,C). Cut deep parts from opposite sides (D,E). Use a flat cut to employ more teeth on thin wood, but cut thicker wood more upright for less effort (F).

There is a limit to the size of the hole that can be made by hand drilling or power drilling. An expansive bit can adjust to 3 inches or even more, but getting it through hardwood to much depth might prove impossible. Larger holes are sometimes needed and other means have to be used to make them. If a lather is available and the wood is of a suitable size so that it can be mounted in the lathes, a hole of any size can be turned with hand tools while the wood is rotating. It might be possible to have the wood stationary while a tool rotates, but for most large holes in cabinetwork the wood is of a size outside the limits of an available lathe.

If a large hole has to be made, it is best to define its outline with a circle that cuts into wood. A circle made with pencil compasses leaves the fibers uncut and there is a risk of going over the line in later cutting. It is better to use steel dividers with a sharp point so that the circle is scratched into the wood. In many parts, it helps

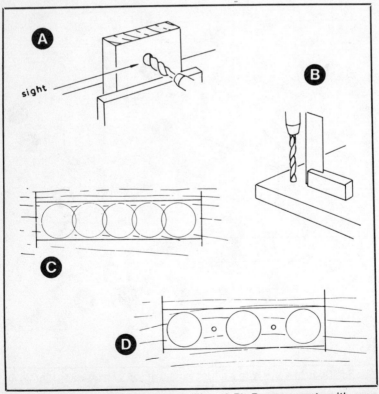

Fig. 3-7. Check squareness when drilling (A,B). Remove waste with overlapping holes (C,D).

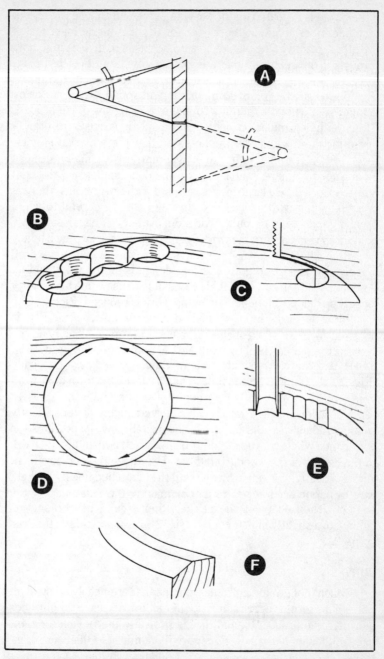

Fig. 3-8. Large holes can be drawn both sides (A) and then drilled around the edges to remove waster (B,C,D) before shaping with hand tools (E,F).

if the circle is repeated on the far side. This will reduce the risk of torn fibers breaking out there. Obviously, this circle must match the other exactly. One way of arranging this is to drill a small hole through at the center so that a leg of the dividers fits into it (Fig. 3-8A).

Waste can be removed by drilling all round the edges or by drilling at one point to admit a coping saw or jigsaw to cut around. Although holes might be drilled freehand, it is wiser to draw a circle for them and space the holes so that they overlap slightly (Fig. 3-8B). The size bit has to be a compromise. Small holes can be arranged so there is little work to be done in cleaning the final hole to size. While a large bit gets around with fewer holes, there is more finishing work to be done. In any case, be careful to avoid breaking out the grain on the far side. Either drill against tightly held scrap wood or turn the work over and drill back into each hole.

If the hole is sawn, move it slowly so fibers are severed closely. How close to go to the line depends on the wood and its tendency to break out. It should be possible to use a fine blade fairly closely so that the amount of finishing work is reduced (Fig. 3-8C).

How the large hole is finished depends on its size. If it is possible to get a spokeshave to bear on the edge, that is a convenient tool. Be careful to change direction to suit the grain (Fig. 3-8D). Alternatively use an in-canneled gouge and pare vertically (Fig. 3-8E). It might be possible to use a curved Surform tool. In all cases, finishing is usually best done by sanding with the abrasive paper around a block of wood with a curved edge to a very slightly smaller radius than the hole. Do not use abrasive paper loose in your hand. Whatever the methods used, watch both sides and work to the center of the wood from them. Use the scratched circles as guides. Ideally, you finish by dividing the scratched lines. The best way to obtain accuracy is to aim at making the side near to you correct. Then do the same at the other side, with the section sloping to a slightly higher center (Fig. 3-8F). Level this as the final step.

CURVES

Much modern furniture has shapes that are nearly all straight lines. This form is a characteristic of modern styles. Straight lines suit machine production and that is probably the reason for their use—although not all designers will admit it. Older furniture makes use of curves. Anyone reproducing antique furniture or designing modern furniture that differs from the general run of

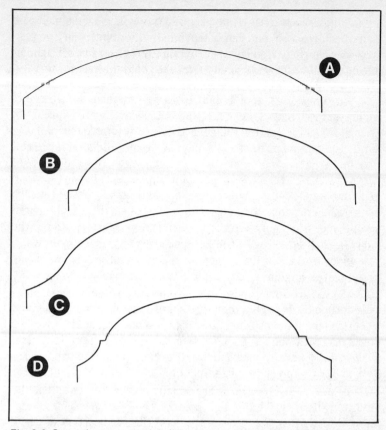

Fig. 3-9. Several curves are possible to decorate tops of furniture: (A) part of a circle; (B) ellipse; (C) reverse curve; (D) angular steps.

fashion needs to understand and use curves properly.

If some of the most attractive furniture with curves in it is examined, the curves will be found to be anything but simple. Some curves are free flowing and could only have been drawn freehand. The designer drew a curve he liked and that was it. If the shape had to be symmetrical, a half template was made and turned over on the centerlines.

There are places where the curve has to be part of a circle (Fig. 3-9A). However, making it part of an ellipse is usually more pleasing (Fig. 3-9B). For a backboard, it might include a reverse curve (Fig. 3-9C). But the ellipse rather than the circle is the base curve. Angular steps between the curves (Fig. 3-9D) are architectural devices that improve appearance in some places. They can also simplify the cutting of the outline accurately.

Where a curve has to be part of a circle, the radius might be considerably more than can be spanned with dividers or compasses. Use a strip of wood with an awl through it and a pencil against its end. If other curves have to be drawn, notch the side of the wood (Fig. 3-10A).

An ellipse, or part of it, can be drawn with the aid of a piece of string and two nails. There are ways of calculating the spacing of the nails, but for a partial ellipse it is probably simpler to mark the limits the curve has to pass through and experiment with the nail spacing to get a pleasing shape. Draw the long axis of the ellipse. Draw the short axis across it so that it comes centrally on the wood to be marked. Position nails on the long axis equally spaced at each side of the crossing. Loop string around to reach the intended limit at one end. Put a pencil in the loop and move it around. Keep the string taut (Fig. 3-10B). If the ellipse goes higher than you want, try wider spacing of the nails, For a curve that is too low, bring them closer together.

Curves are sometimes drawn around a strip of wood or a steel rule sprung to shape, but there are some possible errors that could occur. If one person springs the strip to shape and holds it while a helper draws around it, the curve should be satisfactory if the strip is not forced more by one hand than the other and it is not allowed to flex under the pressure of the pencil.

Known points on a curve are usually only at the center and the ends. If nails are driven at these positions and a strip is bent against them (Fig. 3-10C), the curve will be poor. It will be a tighter curve at the top than towards the sides. A better shape is obtained by using a longer strip so that it comes outside the three nails and is held down by others some way outside the limits of the wanted curve (Fig. 3-10D).

A good approximation of an ellipse can be made by first drawing a large sweep, which is part of a circle, then use something of circular form, such as a paint can, to draw around for the ends of the shape (Fig. 3-10E).

Errors of symmetry are usually more apparent in curved work than in that which is mostly straight lines. If the curves in opposite directions have to match, time spent in making a template is worthwhile. This applies where the shape is on one part as well as where there might be matching curved wings separated by another part. Paper is unsatisfactory because it will distort. Cardboard is little different and hardboard or plywood better. It need not be in one piece. Scrap pieces can be joined. Use measurements to

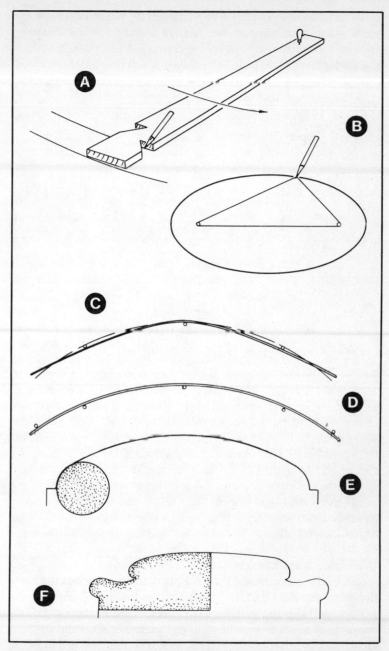

Fig. 3-10. Large curves (A) can be drawn with improvised compasses, while string (B) around nails can make an ellipse. Avoid kinks when drawing around a batten (C,D). Use templates to get opposite sides symmetrical (E).

provide a check, but have a true straightedge where the centerline comes and, usually, a base line at right angles to it (Fig. 3-10F).

CLAMPING

One problem in assembling a piece of furniture is getting it true to shape so that it looks right when it is viewed from any direction. There are often a great many parts to be joined and arranged properly and care is needed to avoid distorting one assembly when pulling another to shape. Sometimes there is no alternative to putting all parts together at the same time and using what skill you possess to get the assembly looking right. But many pieces of furniture are better put together in stages. Those that are framed from strips should certainly be dealt with in stages. If some parts are more solid and cannot distort, it might be possible to do more at one stage.

Many furniture assemblies can be related to a framed cube. A table or stool can be of this type. Any framed and panelled cabinet is basically similar. Assembly is then better done in stages. If there are longer sides, deal with them before the ends.

Assemble a side (Fig. 3-11A). Check it for squareness by measuring diagonally. Put it on a flat surface. Stand back and sight across it to see that opposite sides of it are not "in winding." Pull joints together by clamping. If the frame is slightly out of square, arranging a bar clamp a little out of true will move the frame as well as draw joints together (Fig. 3-11B). Assemble the opposite side over the first with the inner surfaces towards each other. Give that similar checks, but obviously the two parts should match and rest flat against each other. Leave them for the glue to set. If there is a risk of glue from the upper frame running on the lower frame and joining them together, put newspaper between them. If there are insufficient bar clamps to leave them on both parts and the joints are mortise and tenon, drive thin nails inside the joints of the first frame where they will be hidden to hold the tenons in when the clamps are removed for use on the other frame (Fig. 3-11C). Dowelled joints can be treated in a similar way.

With the glue set and the first two frames rigid, join the parts the other way (Fig. 3-11D). Check squareness on both of the newly assembled sides and pull out any distortion when clamping. Concentrate on squareness when viewed from the sides and get that right. But this is not the end of checking and truing. Have the assembly standing on a flat surface. Check diagonals at the top (Fig. 3-11E) and adjust the shape if necessary. It is also advisable

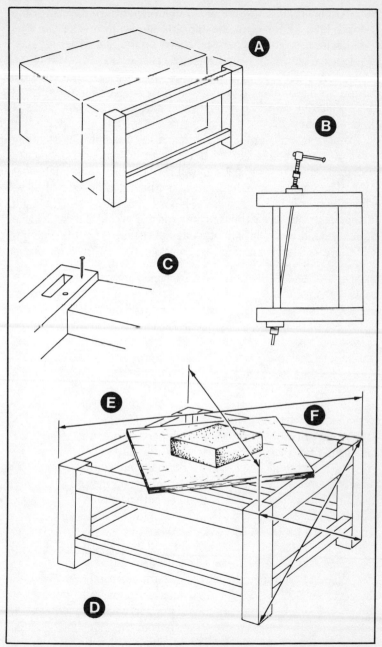

Fig. 3-11. Adopt a sequence (A) in assembly. Tilting a clamp will alter a shape (B). Nails (C) inside will hold a glued joint. Check all directions and leave under a weight while glue sets (D).

to check squareness lower down. Especially at the bottom or at the framing level. Even with the top and the bottom squared, it is possible for there to be a twist in the assembly. Stand back as far as possible and view your work from several directions. Sight through if it is open, otherwise sight outside and see that opposite edges are parallel with near ones. If you have to do any adjusting, go back and check squareness of the newly glued sides and see that none of them have moved.

If all parts are properly sized and the assembly is standing level, it should be possible to get it true. If accuracy only comes with the feet out of level, pack up where necessary and trim the feet later. The trued assembly might stand firm and be safe to leave while the glue sets. Otherwise, it helps to hold it if a weight is put on top, but make sure it presses down on all four sides (Fig. 3-11F). Step back and look all round it as a final check. Once the glue has set, there is usually nothing that can be done to correct errors of assembly.

Chapter 4
Materials

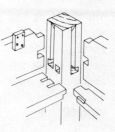

Wood is obviously the main material in furniture construction, but most wooden furniture has metal fittings and there might be fabric upholstery. Glues and finishes can be made from natural or synthetic materials. However, it is the choice of wood which is the main concern of cabinetmakers.

The varieties of trees in the world run into thousands. Not all are suitable for conversion to wood for making furniture and some have local uses. With modern methods of transport about the world, there are many fine woods coming into use in countries far from where they were produced. This means that it is almost impossible to keep pace with names and types of wood. Some furniture today might be made of wood that was uncommon even a few years ago. Even the generally accepted woods for furniture might appear in varieties that are very different from the traditional ones. Species grown in one part of the world can be very different from other species which are the same family in other parts of the world.

Some of the better woods are being used up. A tree can take 100 years to grow to a state suitable for felling and cutting into boards. Although new trees are planted, replacements cannot keep pace with demand. This means that furniture cannot always be made with the same woods that were favored by the famous cabinetmakers. Fortunately, world supplies of wood of all sorts are considerable and there might be other comparable woods that could be used. Many woods unknown to earlier cabinetmakers are very attractive.

Sizes of available woods depend on the size of the tree. Some trees never grow very large. Others grow to considerable sizes. A tree in a forest competes with others to reach up to the light and its trunk is long and straight. A tree that grows in the open, away from other trees, might be low and broad with a twisted trunk. Although the latter might produce wood with interesting grain markings, the available boards will be of limited size. It is the forest grown tree that produces long straight-grained planks. Some species of trees are naturally small. Some trees might not be worthwhile for converting into lumber. Others can only produce small pieces. However, some of these are used for attractive items within their range or for inlaying in other woods.

CONVERSION

A tree that is used for furniture wood grows by adding layers around the outside under the bark. Each year it produces an annual ring. A cross section of many woods shows these rings clearly. Counting them from the center outwards will indicate the age of the tree. Some trees grow to a considerable age and there can be hundreds of rings. In some woods, particularly some of the furniture woods, it is difficult or impossible to discern every ring.

The wood towards the center of the tree becomes compacted and hardened. This is the *heart wood*. The newer growth around the outside is the *sapwood*. In some trees this is a lighter color. It is not as strong and not as durable. In most woods, sapwood should be avoided for furniture making.

Sap is the lifeblood of a tree. It is most plentiful during the summer and least during the winter. However, in tropical climates there is little difference. Sap has to be dried out to an acceptable level. A tree felled in the winter has less moisture in it to be removed by seasoning. In natural seasoning, boards are stacked with spacers so that air can circulate with protection from rain and sun. Most woods then have to be left a long time. One year for each inch of thickness is usual. Quicker methods of seasoning are more common today. If properly done, they are quite satisfactory.

The cabinetmaker is usually introduced to his wood as boards or pieces cut to size and sometimes planed. If he knows something of the way wood is cut from the log, he can understand what has happened or might happen to the wood when he works it or after it has been built into a piece of furniture. It is always advisable to obtain wood some time before it is to be used. Wood for a particular project might be bought in just sufficient quantities, but it is worthwhile building up a stock of sizes expected to be used eventually in several projects. Keeping wood yourself continues seasoning it and it is likely to be in a more stable form when you finally use it.

A present-day problem is the effect of central heating. Normal seasoning reduces the moisture content of wood to something under 10 percent—depending on the type of wood. If the furniture made from it is to be kept in a centrally heated room, it can become dried out further. Consequently, there is a risk of shrinking or warping. It helps if the wood is kept in similar conditions for several weeks before it is made into furniture. That way it will dry to its final state before being worked to size.

The first conversion of the log to boards can be by "plain sawing" or "through and through" with a series of parallel cuts. There may be flat surfaces cut top and bottom for ease in controlling the log, but otherwise it is cut into a number of parallel slabs (Fig. 4-1A). The grain arrangement will be different according to how far a board is from the center. Boards further from the center might be expected to have more attractive grain marking, but they will have more tendency to warp.

More sap dries out after cutting into boards. This causes shrinkage, mainly in the direction of the grain lines, as viewed from the end. A board cut across the center of the log has the grain lines across and the effect of shrinkage will be to make the board a little thinner (Fig. 4-1B). Otherwise it should remain flat.

The effect further out is to make the end grain lines tend to shorten. This will cause the board to warp. If you can imagine the grain lines trying to straighten, that is the result (Fig. 4-1C). The tendency is greater the further the board is from the center. If the wood has been carefully seasoned, the risk of warping is slight. Of course, boards are not all used in the full width. If the outer cuts are for strips, shrinkage is less apparent. A look at the end of a strip will show what part of the log it came from and shrinkage along grain lines could pull an originally square piece out of shape (Fig. 4-1D).

A board cut right through will have "wany" edges that follow the uneven outline of the wood under the bark. This will have to be trimmed square, but it indicates the presence of sapwood. If it is a wood where it is inadvisable to use anything but heartwood, cuts must come further in and the amount of useful wood might be much less (Fig. 4-1E).

The most stable boards are cut radially from the log (Fig. 4-1F). This is wasteful, although smaller pieces can be cut from the intermediate parts. There are *medullary rays* that go approximately radially in all wood. They are very apparent in oak. A radially cut board shows them on the surface as *figuring* or *silver grain* (Fig. 4-1G).

One way of converting to get some boards with full figuring and adjoining boards with progressively less is to cut through a quarter section of a log diagonally (Fig. 4-1H). This does not waste as much wood, but only part of the boards are near radial and others have an increasing risk of warp as well as no figuring.

Cutting a quarter log parallel with one side produces some boards near radial (Fig. 4-1J). A variation on this has the cuts made in both directions (Fig. 4-1K) to get more boards nearer radial.

For structural stability, it does not matter much how the grain lines run if the part is to be securely jointed to other parts. If the board has to keep its shape without much external support, as in the flap of a table, it is better if it is cut radially so that any variation in moisture content will not tend to warp, twist or split the wood. However, appearance will also be a consideration and a piece of wood cut otherwise can be used. If it has been carefully seasoned, it will probably be satisfactory. The degree of risk varies between types of wood.

FLAWS

Part of the attraction of wood is that it is a natural material. Each piece of wood is different. A tree trunk is not a straight parallel cylinder. It might be far from round in section and it might be twisted and distorted in the length. Parallel cuts made along a log cross the grain lines and these give the final attractive appearance. In a large forest grown tree, each board will show the grain markings over a considerable length. Other trees have branches from the trunk at many places. A board cut past where there was a branch will have a *knot*.

Knots in a board are not necessarily a bad thing. They can be regarded as decorative in some woods. There are two types of knots. A *bound knot* is obviously part of the wood and is fully united with the grain around it. Providing it is not too large, it should not affect strength and it can be finished with the surrounding wood to provide a variation in appearance. A *dead knot* can usually be identified by a looseness and a dark line around it. Such a knot does not contribute anything to the wood. The wood might have a use where the flaw does not matter or the knot could be cut out and the wood used for smaller parts.

During its growth a tree might twist and bend in the wind so as to produce *shakes*. These are cracks along the trunk following the curve of the grain lines or cutting across them. Shakes are not found until after the tree is felled, but they are areas of weakness and normally boards should be cut around them.

Checks and *splits* are cracks along the grain. The end of a

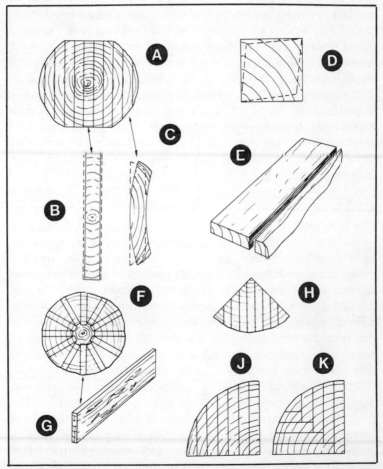

Fig. 4-1. Wood shrinks as it dries in different ways according to the position of the board in the tree section (A,B,C,D). In some woods, boards are cut radially (E) to show grain markings (F,G,H,J).

board might open in a split during seasoning. Even prepared wood might split slightly at an end. This is due to the end drying out more than the wood further along. Examine the end of any wood stored for a long time. Arrange for the final cut part to be a little way in from the original end so that any slight splitting will be cut off.

Some coniferous trees contain a lot of resin. A shake that develops might fill and become a *pitch pocket*. These small pockets will have to be accepted in structural work, but they should not be permitted on an important exposed surface.

Lumber yards preparing good quality wood for furniture do not have the time to allow for salvaging useful smaller pieces from boards of a stock size. Any pieces with flaws will be discarded and probably burned. A cabinetmaker who has his own power saw and planer can sometimes get these boards at a much cheaper rate and cut around the faulty part to yield useful material. He will also find that it is much more economical to buy boards that can be cut down than to go to the yard with a detailed material list for a large number of small pieces to be finished there to size. However, with a cooperative supplier who knows his stock, being armed with a fully detailed material list allows you both to select from stock wood that will serve your needs while not leaving the supplier with short ends that will not sell.

SPECIES

Identification of wood is only possible with any precision by scientific means. It is possible to recognize many of the commonly used woods, but as things are today, with varying supplies and changing uses, what were the common woods of a generation or so ago might be regarded as rarities by some woodworkers. There is the added complication of different names for the same wood in different places. Scientific names are the only safe choice, but it is the common names that will be mostly used. Long usage has made names acceptable. Craftsmen knew certain woods. When others with similar characteristics were introduced, they bracketed them together. There are many woods grouped as mahogany, but scientists would not agree that they are all truly mahoganies.

There are two broad classifications of wood: *softwoods* and *hardwoods*. These names are not as clear as they appear. They do not really define relative hardness or softness. Some hardwoods are actually among the softest woods. However, most hardwoods are harder than most softwoods. The names indicate the type of foliage on the tree. Coniferous trees with needles produce softwoods. Hardwoods come from broad-leafed trees. Most softwood trees are evergreens. Most hardwood trees lose their leaves during the winter (at least in temperate climates). The greater number of softwood trees grow in the cooler parts of the world, while most hardwood trees in quantities sufficient to be commercially worthwhile grow in the hotter parts. Trees are adaptable and many trees can be found in parts distant from where the majority of the type grow.

Much early furniture had to be made from trees that grew close to their point of origin because of transport problems. Hence the preponderence of oak in much medieval furniture from England and the nearby countries. Some of this has survived many centuries. More utilitarian furniture might have been made of local softwoods, but those woods are less durable and little has survived.

The great cabinetmakers of the last two centuries have worked almost exclusively in hardwoods. The commonly available softwoods were regarded as more suitable for rougher carpentry. Those cabinetmakers were probably influenced by the effects of improving worldwide transport. Woods not previously known arrived from distant places. Most of the countries being explored were tropical and they yielded hardwoods.

Cedar, with its aromatic oil that it exudes, was one softwood used sometimes to line clothes chests. Other softwoods had limited uses internally, but normally fine cabinetwork was entirely hardwood. *Knotty pine* furniture might be having a vogue, but it is a development of the kitchen furniture of the farmhouse rather than something that could be described as fine cabinetwork in its own right.

Softwoods

All of the trees that are called firs, pines, larches and spruce yield softwoods. Names are sometimes confused. What is a fir in one place is a pine in another. In Europe, woods from these trees were often called *deal*. *Red deal* is superior to *white deal* but these names are now discouraged. Such European softwoods were shipped from Baltic Russian ports and were also known by the name of the shipping port—to further confuse identification.

Besides cedar, cypress is an American softwood, but not normally a furniture wood. With the development of plywood, some American softwoods have found uses. Best known is Douglas fir. This is also known as Columbian pine, Douglas pine or Oregon pine (Pseudotsuga taxiflora). In Europe, most plywood is made from hardwoods.

Hardwoods

The furniture woods of the classic cabinetmakers came from a comparatively small range of hardwoods. All of the "new" woods being introduced are hardwoods and anything being offered today will have to be assessed in relation to the traditional woods.

The best known traditional furniture wood has been mahogany. Trees are large, so boards can be both wide and long. There are several varieties and some woods that are not true mahogany. Generally, the color is a rich brown. It is often treated or stained to a reddish hue. Much mahogany comes from tropical America. The type known to European cabinetmakers as Spanish or Cuban mahogany (Swietenia macrophyela) is found in Southern Florida, Mexico, Colombia and other parts of Central America. This is the true mahogany and probably the most popular furniture wood.

Early users confused mahogany with cedar. In Europe, it was probably used in boat building before being used for furniture making. It is still used in boats. Jamaica and Honduras are other places that give their name to species of mahogany. Philippine mahogany is coarser wood and it is not related to true mahogany.

African mahogany grows into very large trees on the West Coast of Africa. Its characteristics are very similar to the American mahoganies and might now be more plentiful and cheaper.

Much medieval furniture was made of oak (Quercus). The dark brown open-grained English oak was famous for its use in building ships as well as furniture. The need to build large numbers of sailing ships stripped many English forests. This is the oak that cuts radically to show the figuring or silver grain. It is also known in Britain as *wainscot oak* because of its use in panelling around a room. American white oak is very similar. Red oak has a coarser grain, but may also be used for furniture.

Walnut (Juglans nigra) was, and still is, a popular furniture wood. It predated mahogany in European cabinetmaking and gave way to it for some purposes. Color varies according to the part of Europe. It is a smooth wood that finishes well in anything from light to very dark brown. The American variety is called black walnut to distinguish it from the European walnut. Working characteristics are similar.

European chestnut (Castanea saliva) comes from the sweet

chestnut tree, not the horse chestnut, and it is so much like oak that it was used with it in furniture. It is distinguished by not having any obvious figuring when quarter sawn. American chestnut (Castanea dentata) is similar.

English elm (Ulmus procera) has a confused grain and resists splitting, but it is difficult to finish smoothly. Boards can be made wide. It was used extensively for seats and other parts of furniture, but Dutch elm disease has almost wiped out elms in Britain. Rock elm (Ulmus thomasi) and wych elm (Ulmus glabra) are straighter grained, hard, strong and suitable for bending.

Beech is plentiful in Europe and much used for chair frames, turnery and structural parts of furniture. It works cleanly and does not warp much. Its color is between white and reddish brown. It was much used for planes and other tools. There are several varieties of birch. Some of them have similar furniture uses to beech, as well as being made into veneers for plywood.

There are several varieties of maple. The wood is mostly light colored and some of it has a grain marking known as *bird's eye* which can be feathered in veneers. *Fiddleback* is another marking. It was given this name because of its use on the backs of violins.

Sycamore is a large tree. The wood is white/brown in color and suffers from a tendency to shrink considerably. It is clean for use with foods. It is the prepared wood for butcher blocks. Its furniture use is mainly as a veneer.

At one time, rosewood was comparable in popularity for furniture with walnut. Its sources are widely scattered. There are varieties from Brazil, Madagascar, India and Honduras. The latter variety is mostly used for cabinetwork. Color is from cream to light brown. Surfaces can be finished very smoothly.

Probably the main attraction of basswood or lime (Tilia americana) was in the great width of boards available. It could be used for backs and bottoms without joints. It is a nearly white wood from the tulip tree. It is also used for carving. As its place in furniture has been taken by plywood, little basswood is available for cabinetmaking. Popular or canary wood had similar uses.

Ash and hickory are the woods for bending. Some bentwood furniture is made of them and they are used in furniture with other woods. Hammer and other tool handles are made of them. Fruit woods, such as apple and pear, have been used in furniture. They are hard and have interesting grain. However, sizes are limited.

The foregoing brief descriptions are of examples of woods associated with furniture making. There are many others that are suitable. Some of them are traditional varieties and others are more recently introduced types that give scope for experimenting in cabinetmaking.

GLUES

In cabinetwork, joints are cut so that they fit together securely and then the meeting surfaces are coated with glue. In most places, there are no nails or screws to supplement the cut joints and glue. It is a characteristic of fine cabinetwork that the majority of assembled parts are jointed and glued.

Early glues would have been natural resins, but for many centuries the most successful woodworking glues have been based on animal, fish and vegetable products that usually had to be melted for use. Wood glues made from animal hooves and bones were in regular use until World War II. These glues were softened in a double pot, with the glue in an inner pot suspended in another of water, which was heated. The glued joint required tight clamping until it had set. Basically similar glues in a refined form are still available, for use cold or with slight heat, and these can be used to repair an antique or authentic reproduction work. Otherwise, it would be better to use a more modern glue.

Before the advent of the latest glues, the only plastic glue in use was *casein* (a milk product) which comes in the form of a powder to mix with water just before use. It produces a joint of good strength with a degree of waterproofness.

The modern plastic or synthetic glues are mostly known by trade names. Their strength and suitability for wood might not be immediately obvious. If an adhesive is described as being suitable for paper and other materials, its application to woodwork is probably useful for light construction and not furniture. If it remains flexible when set, it is not a powerful woodworking glue.

Most one-part glues depend on evaporation for setting. They have to be held in contact until the glue has set. Some are supplied in convenient container/applicators. Read the description and instructions. There are some good general woodworking glues of this type.

The strongest woodworking glues are also waterproof to varying degrees. While being particularly suitable for damp conditions, their strength makes them desirable in many furniture applications.

Urea-formaldehyde glues come in two parts. There is a resin, or a powder to mix with water to make a resin. This is the glue proper. With it comes a liquid hardener, which is a mild acid. They might have to be mixed before application or one put on each surface. Another make has a powder hardener mixed with the resin powder. When mixed with water a chemical, action starts and the glue begins to set. But there is ample time to fit and adjust joints. Any excess will harden in the pot.

Resorcinol glues are widely used in plywood construction. Some have a red color that might not be acceptable for some work. Application is similar to that just described, but the glue has greater waterproofness.

Both of these glues require joints to fit closely. They do not produce full strength if they have to fill gaps. This fault can be overcome in a joint known to be wide by mixing sawdust with the glue. Without the sawdust, the glue crazes as it sets and has little strength.

Epoxy glue (epoxide resin) is the strongest and most water-proof of this type of glues. Besides adhering wood to wood, it will join most other materials (including metals). The glue comes in two parts that are mixed just before use. Some of these glues have a setting time of as much as three days. Others are quicker, but with a slight loss of strength.

Animal-product glues had to be rubbed together and clamped tightly. The synthetic glues should not be clamped tightly. All that is required is to hold the surfaces in contact while the glue sets. Over tightening would "starve" the joint by squeezing glue out. Use glue only on bare wood surfaces. It has to penetrate the pores. If there is a polish or paint on the surface, penetration is prevented. There is a risk of staining if some of these glues are used in contact with metal on some woods. Avoid brushes with metal ferrules.

NAILS AND SCREWS

Not many nails are used in fine cabinetwork. In places where fitted joints cannot be made between parts, screws are more appropriate. It would be exceptional to use common or box nails in large sizes.

Small fine nails have uses in fastening fine moldings, fitting fillets that hold glass in frames and similar comparatively delicate work. If they have steeply countersunk heads (Fig. 4-2A), they are called *panel pins*. If they have brad heads (Fig. 4-2B) they are called *veneer pins*. The small heads can be punched below the surface so that the hole above is inconspicuous and easily filled with stopping. Very thin nails are called *pins*. All of these small nails may be made of steel and be untreated, but they may be bronzed or brassed to give some protection and make them less obvious if exposed. If they are made of brass, they will not then be so easy to drive straight.

Screws used in cabinetry are more correctly called *wood screws*, because a *screw* is also an engineering term for what most people would call a *bolt* (threaded almost to the head). Common wood screws are made of mild steel, but in cabinetwork it is better to use brass. Traditionally, brass was used because of its resistance to corrosion and because it was unlikely to stain the wood. Besides the stains that accompany rust, steel can cause oak and some other woods to discolor around each screw. Bronze and stainless steel screws should be satisfactory alternatives.

Screws are described by the length from the wood surface and

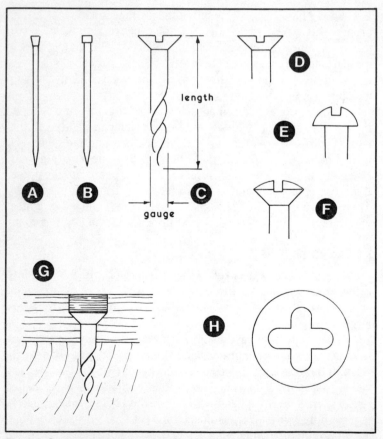

Fig. 4-2. Cabinetmaking nails have small heads (A,B). Screws can have several types of head (C,D,E,F,G,H).

by a gauge thickness (Fig. 4-2C). Flat heads are level with the surface and countersunk (Fig. 4-2D). A round head (Fig. 4-2E) is almost half a sphere and stands above the surface. Between the two is the oval head (Fig. 4-2F). It is countersunk with a curved raised top. Flat heads are normally used where they will not be seen or where they will be counterbored and either stopping or a wood plug put over them (Fig. 4-2G). If a screw head cannot be hidden, a round head looks better. An oval head may be chosen and it is appropriate to fastening metal fittings with countersunk holes. This will often look better than flat heads.

Slotted screw heads for standard screwdrivers have been usual until fairly recently when the star-shaped socket of the Phillips head (Fig. 4-2H) was introduced mainly to suit power screwdriving in quantity production. There are hand screwdrivers to suit, but in repairing antiques or making reproduction furniture the use of Phillips Screws would be inappropriate.

Screws are made from ¼ inch upwards. They are usually in ⅛ inch steps to 1 inch and then in ¼ inch steps and changing to ½-inch steps over 3 inches. Gauge thicknesses are numbered and a higher number indicates a thicker screw. In the small sizes, there are screws of odd and even gauge thickness, but in larger screws only the even numbered gauges are commonly available from the usual suppliers. There might be several gauge thicknesses available with each length. Some commonly available sizes are: gauges 2 and 3 only in lengths up to ½ of an inch; gauges 4 and 5 between ⅜ of an inch and ¾ of an inch long; gauges 6 and 7 from ½ of an inch to 1½ of an inch; and gauge 8 from ½ of an inch to 2 inches. Those are the sizes most likely to be used in cabinetwork. Gauges 10 and 12 are unlikely to be found in lengths under 1½ inches. Screws that are 3 inches and longer will be gauge 16 or more.

Wood screws have a parallel part for a short distance under the head. The screwed part has a parallel core which tapers to the point. The unscrewed part needs a clearance hole. If it is forced into an undersized hole, it might be impossible to drive or it might split the wood. Except for the smallest screws being driven into soft wood, there should be holes drilled for each screw. In the hardest wood there should be a hole of about the core diameter for the full depth the screw is to go and a hole to clear the parallel neck above it (Fig. 4-3A). In softer wood, the pilot hole need not go the full depth as the point will cut its own way in and its diameter could be slightly less than in the first case (Fig. 4-3B).

If the screw is holding a metal fitting to solid wood, the

clearance hole should not be any longer than the plain screw neck (Fig. 4-3C). If it is being used to pull two pieces of wood together and the plain neck is not as deep as the thickness of the top piece, make the clearance hole right through the top piece (Fig. 4-3D). Pressure on the joint is then put on between the head and the pull of the threaded part. If the pilot hole is partly in the top piece, the screw into that would resist pulling the two thicknesses of wood together.

For the smallest screws, a pilot hole can be made with a bradawl, but it is more accurate to use metalworking twist drills. Table 4-1 shows hole sizes for various screw gauges.

The countersunk part of a screw head may pull into some woods without any preparation of the hole. Use a countersink bit if necessary, but experiment on a scrap piece of similar wood to see how far to go. The screw might pull in level with only partial countersinking. If a panel that will have to be removed occasionally is held with screws, there are cup washers (Fig. 4-3E) that spread the pressure and avoid damage to the wood when used with flat or oval head screws.

OTHER MATERIALS

There are a great many metal parts, such as hinges, fasteners, catches and locks involved in making cabinets, tables and other furniture. Although plastics have made great advances and there are plastic alternatives to many traditional metal things, it is generally better policy to stick to metal for projects that are to be regarded as fine cabinetwork. This is particularly true when the item is either a reproduction or when it is based on earlier furniture. Exceptions might be the use of plastic drawer runners and other internal parts. Handles and other very obvious external parts should not be plastic. An exception might be a plastic insert in a mainly metal part. Suitable metal parts are described later in relation to projects where they are appropriate.

The materials used in upholstery have changed in recent years. Expanded plastic foam has taken over as the filling for most purposes. This replaces horse hair, flock, betting and a host of natural products. It has also reduced the use of springs and webbing. However, these are still needed in some seating. Covering materials might still follow traditional choices, but synthetic fabrics have advantages for some purposes. They can be difficult to distinguish from the natural materials (based on cotton and wool). Leather might be prohibitively expensive, but there are plastic

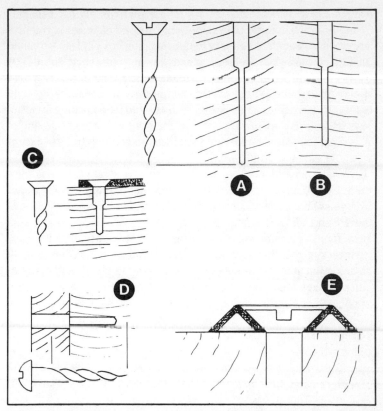

Fig. 4-3. Drill screw holes deeper in hard woods than soft woods and allow for the plain neck (A,B,C,D). A cup washer makes a neat finish where screws might have to be removed (E).

imitations that can be used. Changes have affected webbings and threads. These are now synthetic and stronger.

What materials are used for upholstering furniture will depend on the particular item. Even if external parts are of traditional types, there seems little point in using the older fillings. Foam is easier to use and should produce a better result unless your work is an attempt to make a very close reproduction of an old original. More information on upholstery materials and their uses is given in the description of furniture with upholstered parts.

Glass is used in doors and mirrors. For the comparatively small amount of glass needed by a cabinetmaker it is advisable to get it cut by a specialist working from measurement or a template. Bevel-edged mirrors and cut decoration on glass can be very expensive. It is advisable to have mirrors with simple rectangular frames and avoid decorated glass unless some stock patterns can be incorporated. Some old cabinets had leaded panes in the doors. This probably started as a way to use small pieces of glass when the making of good glass in larger sizes was not very successful. The effect is quite attractive. Making leaded glass assemblies requires specialist skills. It is unlikely that a craftsman will be found capable of doing the work, but there are kits available for attaching strips of lead or lead-like material to the surface of glass so that a pane of glass can be treated and it will look like the genuine thing—except on close examination.

Glass should not be used to provide strength. Whatever frames it has should take any load and be sufficiently rigid in itself. The glass should be a loose fit. If it fits tightly or has to be forced in there is a risk of it cracking later.

There are some clear rigid plastics that might serve as alternatives to glass. Surfaces would scratch in rough use, but in most places in a cabinet that sort of damage is unlikely. For the woodworker, they have the advantage of cutting with a saw and edges can be planed or filed. An exposed edge can be sanded smooth and polished with metal polish. The material can be sprung to a curve in a shaped door or it can be curved with moderate heat so that it keeps its shape.

If the making of a piece of furniture to an older design is being considered and there is any unusual glasswork or mirrors incorpo-

Table 4-1. Hole Sizes for Wood Screws.

Gauge	Shank diameter (inches)	Pilot hole diameter (inches)	
		Hardwoods	Softwoods
2	0.086	3/64	-
3	0.099	1/16	-
4	0.112	1/16	-
5	0.125 (1/8)	5/64	1/16
6	0.138	5/64	1/16
7	0.151	3/32	1/16
8	0.164	3/32	5/64
10	0.177	7/64	3/32
12	0.216	1/8	7/64
14	0.242	9/64	7/64
16	0.268	5/32	9/64
18	0.294	3/16	9/64
20	0.320	13/64	11/64
24	0.372	7/32	3/16

rated, the availability of these or suitable substitutes should be investigated before starting the wooden parts. Sometimes it is possible to modify sizes to suit available materials and avoid the cost of having glass parts specially made.

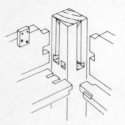

Chapter 5
Notched Joints

Of the large number of joints in fine cabinetwork, some of those commonly used involve notching one or both pieces. They are mostly simple to cut with hand or power tools. A beginner will find that the making of something involving notched joints only will provide practice in tool handling and joint cutting that will be of value in dealing with some of the more complicated joints in advanced construction.

If two pieces of wood have to cross at the same level, or nearly so, each piece is notched into the other. It might be called a *lapped joint* or *halved joint* or a *half lap* joint. The word *half* implies that half is cut from each piece, but that is not always so. The basic joint is seen where two rails of the same section cross (Fig. 5-1A) as they might in the framing between table legs. One piece stops at the other and this is a *T halved* or *middle lap* joint (Fig. 5-1B). If both pieces meet at a corner it is a *halved corner joint* (Fig. 5-1C). The parts do not have to be at right angles to each other. Some table rails cross at an acute angle. Pieces can cross edgewise ((Fig. 5-1D), but the joint construction is the same. When the parts are not the same depth, then the joint is stronger if somewhat less than half is cut from the thinner piece (Fig. 5-1E).

Halved joints are needed where parts cross and they can be used at the middle or corner of a frame assembly. If the frame is otherwise unsupported, it is better to use mortise and tenon joints or variations on them described later. Halved joints are adequate at any part of a frame that is being used to thicken or stiffen a piece of plywood or other thin wood (Fig. 5-1F).

The two parts of a halved joint should be marked out with both face sides or edges the same way (Fig. 5-2A). It is good practice in any jointing to scribble with pencil on the waste parts. You might not be confused with a simple lap joint, but making a habit of marking waste is good policy. Mark the width of the other piece on each piece. Where possible check the other piece against the markings. Do not just rely on measuring. Cut in these lines with a knife and square them down the edges using the knife (Fig. 5-2B).

Set a marking gauge to half the thickness and use this against the face side to mark both edges of both pieces. Even if the gauge has not been set to exactly halfway, gauging from both sides will keep the line at the same level. Saw cuts have to come so the kerf is

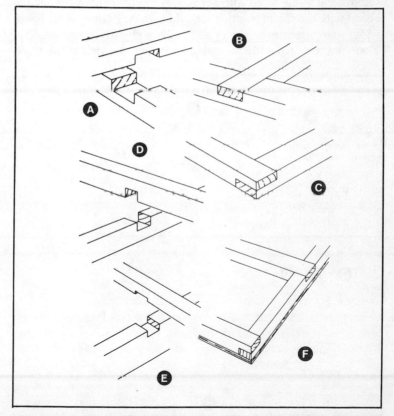

Fig. 5-1. Halved joints can have crossings (A, B, D, E) at the end of one pieces or at a corner (F).

on the waste side of the line (Fig. 5-2C). It will help in locting the saw if the waste is chisseled away inside of each line first (Fig. 5-2D). Accurate cutting is easier with a backsaw than a power saw. Aim to just leave the knife cuts at each position. Most joints can be cut with the wood in the vise or held against a bench hook. Then take the saw straight through. Be careful to just reach the gauged scratch. For large pieces, it might be wiser to cut with the saw sloping up until the cut has gone the full depth on the near side and then turn the wood around to cut the other side while watching the line there. If the amount to be removed is wide, it is simpler to cut away if one or more saw cuts are made in the waste part (Fig. 5-2E) almost to the full depth.

Have the wood held in the vise or held to the bench and start to remove the waste wood with a chisel. A narrow joint might have to be cut with the chisel pointing straight across. If there is sufficient width, use a narrower chisel and make a slightly diagonal slice. Slope upwards from the near side to reduce the risk of the wood

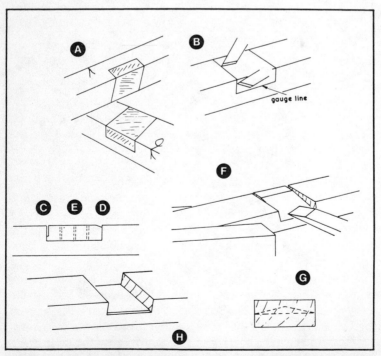

Fig. 5-2. Mark the meeting parts of a joint (A,B), saw (C,D,E) on the waste sides of the lines and remove the waste with a chisel (F,G,H).

breaking out with below the line on the far side (Fig. 5-2F). Turn the wood round and do the same from the outer side (Fig. 5-2G). Then level the center. Check across with a straightedge.

Trying a joint together might seem the obvious thing to do, but trials tend to wear edges. An experienced craftsman has enough confidence in his work to work to resist trial assemblies. His first assembly is his last. However, a beginner might feel that it is wiser to test assemble a joint. Make sure the bottoms of the parts are flat and there are no fibers that project between the bottoms and the sawn ends. If necessary, draw the saw back a few times over them. It might help you get a close fit if you make a slight bevel on the inner edges (Fig. 5-2H).

MIDDLE AND CORNER HALVED JOINTS

If one end of a piece is halved in a middle or corner joint (Fig. 5-3A), it can be cut with a saw. Gauge around the end as well as along both sides. At a corner, remember to keep the gauge against both face sides and scribble on the waste parts (Fig. 5-3B). Saw the shoulders in the same way as for a cross joint. Saw cuts the other way have to be just on the waste side of the line so that the finished edge just divides the gauge scratch.

In small sectioned wood and with sufficient skill and confidence, a cut can be made straight through. However, it is wiser to make the cut on each piece in three stages. Use a fine backsaw. Have the wood tilted in the vise and start cutting at the high corner, watch progress across the end and down the side (Fig. 5-3C). Go almost to the full depth. Turn the wood over and do the same the other way. Watch the marked line on the end and the side all the time (Fig. 5-3D). This leaves a high spot at the center. Put the wood upright and saw through to remove the waste part (Fig. 5-3E). If necessary, use a chisel to remove any lumps remaining. Be careful not to cut away too much. Check flatness across with a straightedge. With this type of joint, it is usually better to let the tongue be a little too long so that the end can be planed level after final assembly.

If a table saw is available, a fine circular saw blade can be used to make the lengthwise cut. The wood is advanced against the fence or guide (Fig. 5-3F). Be careful that the height adjustment is correct. If the saw cuts into the shoulder, it will show after assembly. The wood must also be kept at right angles to the table. With narrow wood, hold it against a temporary right-angled piece (Fig. 5-3G).

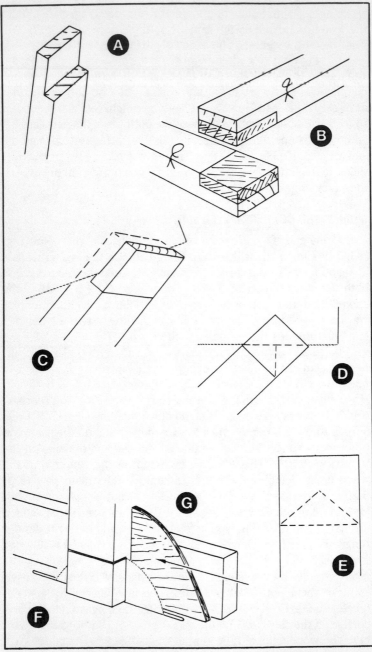

Fig. 5-3. At a corner, most of the waste can be removed by sawing (A,B,C,D) either by hand from opposite sides or with a circular saw (E,F,G).

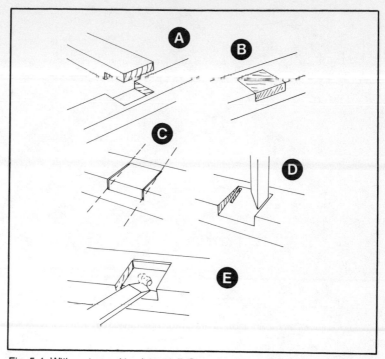

Fig. 5-4. With a stopped lap joint (A,B,C), more of the waste has to be cut with a chisel (D,E).

The many variations on this joint can be dealt with by applying similar methods. If a middle halving joint does not have to go right through, for the sake of appearance, the notched part has to be stopped (Fig. 5-4A). The other part is cut in the usual way. However, there cannot be any excess left on its end.

Mark the notched piece without taking the side knife lines right through and gauge the limit of the notch (Fig. 5-4B). Saw the sides with sloping cuts (Fig. 5-4C). Some of the waste can be removed by sloping the chisel, but there is no need to go as deeply as the saw cuts at this stage. Use a chisel to cut across the grain just inside the saw cuts. If you put the chisel into the saw cuts, it will make the notch too wide. Have the wood supported on the bench top while you drive the chisel in (Fig. 5-4D). After making the cuts across the grain, cut across near the gauge line (but not on it). Then chisel away more of the waste (Fig. 5-4E). Repeat cuts until you have gone to the full depth. Cut back to the lines across the grain and then along the gauge line. Make sure all waste is removed close into the internal angles.

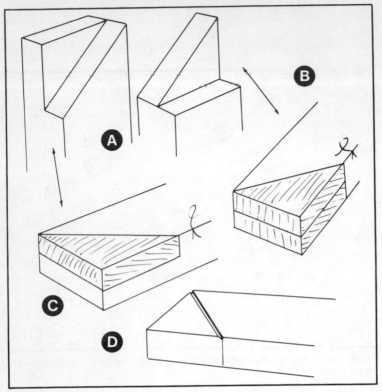

Fig. 5-5. A mitered lap joint (A,B) makes a neat corner at the front (D,E).

MITERED HALVED JOINTS

Sometimes for the sake of appearance, one face of a corner lapped joint should be mitered. If the wood is attached to a panel, it might be sufficient to cut a miter right through and let the panel provide strength. If there is strength required in the joint, half of it is mitered (Fig. 5-5A). Because the glued area is reduced, this is not very strong joint unless it is supported against something else. One piece is marked out in the same way as for a normal corner, then the miter is drawn with a knife (Fig. 5-5B). The other piece is marked in a similar way, except that the knife lines across the miter are avoided and there is no need to gauge down the outside (Fig. 5-5C).

The miter is the part that will show. Mark it with a knife on the face sides of both pieces and chisel away the waste against the lines (Fig. 5-5D). Saw the miters carefully. The internal one can be trimmed with a chisel, but the other can be planed if necessary.

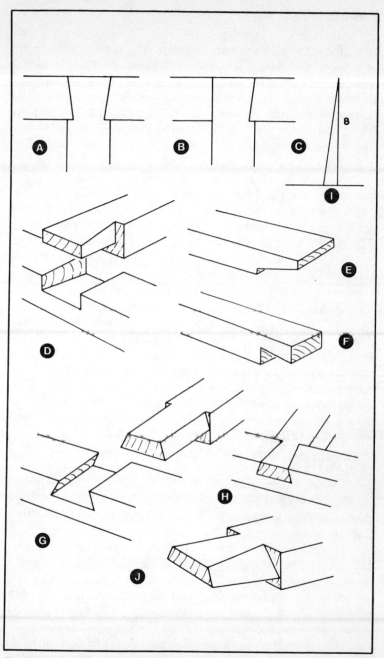

Fig. 5-6. Using a dovetail form with a lapped joint (A,B,C,D,E,F) gives strength and resistance (G,H,J) to pulling apart.

DOVETAIL HALVED JOINTS

If there is a load tending to pull on a T halved joint, it can be strengthened by giving it a dovetail form. This applies whether the parts meet at a right angle or not. Both sides of the tongue can be dovetailed (Fig. 5-6A) or it might be sufficient to do it at one side only (Fig. 5-6B). Too much slope could result in weakness of the short grain at the top of the tongue. A slope of 1 in 8 is about right (Fig. 5-6C). Set an adjustable bevel to this and use it instead of a try square on a right-angled joint. Alternatively, cut the dovetailed tongue first and place it over the other piece and mark its shape directly on the wood. However, be careful to allow for the thickness of the saw cut, by sawing on the inside of the lines.

In this joint, it is possible to compensate for the loss of wood in cutting the dovetail outline by sloping the underside of the tongue (Fig. 5-6D). It can be done in plain T halved joints and is a way of retaining maximum strength in the meeting piece if the part it joins is thicker (Fig. 5-6E).

Two other joints are sometimes called dovetail halved joints, but they do not have much use in modern construction. The tongue might be deeper at its end, so there is some resistance to a pull (Fig. 5-6F). The other type has the sides of the notched piece cut at a dovetail angle and the other piece tapered to match (Fig. 5-6G). A variation on this can be regarded as a trick. It does not really have much practical application, but it is a test of skill for a cabinetmaker if it is to appear to be impossible to disassemble. (Fig. 5-6H). The tongue slopes down to the full width and rises in the other part as it is pushed in (Fig. 5-6J).

DADO JOINTS

Dado or *housing* joints are related to halved or lapped joints, but the notched part takes the broad end of the other piece (as in a shelf attached to an upright). This is the basic "through dado joint" (Fig. 5-7A).

There is no special work on the shelf, except that it must be uniform in thickness and the end cut squarely. Work it completely to size. In some cabinetwork, it is best to leave final levelling of a surface with a smoothing plane until after construction work has been prepared. But in this joint, later planing would thin the wood slightly and loosen the joint.

The notched part is treated in a similar way to a halved joint, but the width of the notch should be marked carefully from the other piece. It is better to finish a little too narrow than too

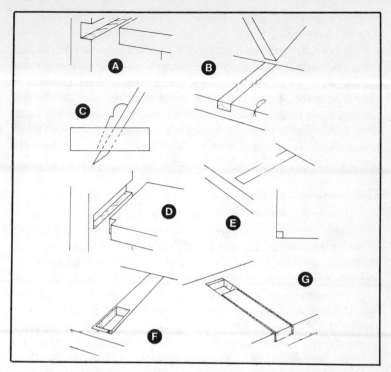

Fig. 5-7. A dado joint may go through (A,B,C) or be stopped (D,E). Care is needed to get the depth even, particularly in a stopped dado (F,G).

wide. The shelf can be thinned to suit, but a loose joint cannot be tightened. Mark with a knife and gauge (Fig. 5-7B). Pare with a chisel inside the lines. Usually the depth of the notch is kept less than halfway through the wood, but this has to be matched against the need for sufficient bearing for the shelf. Saw the sides of the notch and remove the waste in the same way as cutting a halved joint. Because of the greater distance across, be careful to get the bottom of the notch level. Check with a straightedge. If there is a hump anywhere in the body of the notch, the shelf will be held away and gaps will show at the sides. It is better to be very slightly hollow in the width so that the visible parts of the ends of the joint are close.

The bottom of the slot can be leveled with a hand router. If there are a large number of shelves to be fitted in a bookcase or similar item, it might be worthwhile to improvise a router if a manufactured tool is unavailable. This is made with a chisel through a sloping hole in a block of wood and held there with a wedge (Fig. 5-7C). It is adjusted to project enough to plane the bottom of the notch level.

The notches of dado joints can be cut with a powered router. For some purposes, it might be possible to rely on the careful setting of the router cutter and a guide to keep it on the right track across the wood. There might have to be more than one pass to get the notch to the right width and depth. It might be wiser to mark out the wood as if to cut the notches by hand. It can then be seen at all times if the cutter is working within limits and not about to produce a notch that will be too wide.

STOPPED DADO JOINTS

Having the form of the joint visible at the front will not be acceptable in most cabinetwork. However, it might not matter for some internal work. In a good quality bookcase or other block of shelves, it would be better to have the joint construction hidden. In a stopped dado joint, the back remains open and the front of the shelf is notched into a shortened supporting slot (Fig. 5-7D).

Use the same gauge setting to mark the limit of the notch and the part to be cut from the shelf (Fig. 5-7E). Cut around the shelf with a knife so that its end shapes cleanly and fits snugly against the upright. Be careful not to cut away too much. Ideally, the shelf closes tightly at the same time as the shelf touches the bottom of the slot. It is that front visible part that matters even if the shelf end does not quite tighten into the bottom of the slot.

To cut the slot, first chop out for a distance of about 1 inch inside the closed end. Cut across the grain first and lever out the waste between these cuts. Do not cut to the lines either way at first (Fig. 5-7F). With most of the waste removed, pare down to the knife cut lines. Leave about ⅛ of an inch of waste wood at the end of the slot. Now use a backsaw with short strokes into the cutout part to work the sides of the slot (Fig. 5-7G) and chisel out in the usual way. As a final step, trim the end of the slot to size with a chisel.

As with the through dado, a hand router can be used to level the bottom of the slot. A power router can be used to make the stopped dado almost completely. The closed end can be squared with a chisel or the end of the shelf can be rounded to fit. In a wide joint, the shelf can be cut back to clear the rounded slot without affecting strength.

How much to cut back the front of the shelf depends on the particular piece of furniture. There is no strength in the cutback part of the joint so it should be kept to a minimum. In most work ¼

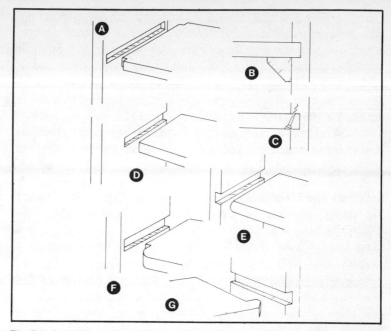

Fig. 5-8. A shelf can be narrower or wider than the upright and the joint altered accordingly (A,B). Strengthening can be by glued blocks or screwing from below (C,D,E).

of an inch to ⅜ of an inch is enough. If the back and front of a shelf will be visible, as in a room divider, there will have to be notches at both sides (Fig. 5-8A). The slot can still be cut with a power router, but for hand work it will have to be chopped out by an extension of the method described for dealing with a single stopped dado (Fig. 5-7F). Do the final trimming with a wide chisel to get a straight cut. This is particularly important for the top surface.

An individual dado joint is not very strong. Usually there are several and the whole assembly is part of a piece of furniture where other parts also provide support. If more strength is needed in a joint, a stiffening block of wood can be glued underneath (Fig. 5-8B). If the underside of a shelf will not normally be visible, there can be screws driven upwards diagonally through the joint (Fig. 5-8C). Under a wire shelf, there can be a glued block towards the back and one or more screws towards the front where the edge of the block might be considered unattractive.

Shelves and uprights are not always the same width. A narrow shelf can go into a stopped dado without its front edge being notched (Fig. 5-8D). If the shelf is wider, it can merely continue forward in a through dado (Fig. 5-8E). If it is not to overlap the front edge, it will have to be notched into a stopped dado (Fig. 5-8F). In another treatment, the front of the shelf overlaps a through dado and continues to the outer edge (Fig. 5-8G).

DOVETAIL DADO JOINTS

A way to draw a dado joint tight is to use the dovetail principle. There are several ways of doing this. The slot, whether through or stopped, can be cut with a dovetail section (Fig. 5-9A) top and bottom. However, it is easier and still will have enough strength to only have the dovetail angle on the underside (Fig. 5-9B). This can be further tightened by tapering the dovetail in the width of the board. Because it is entered from the back, it pulls tight as it is forced to the front (Fig. 5-9C) and can be done with a through or stopped dado joint.

Mark out this type of joint by first penciling the limits of the

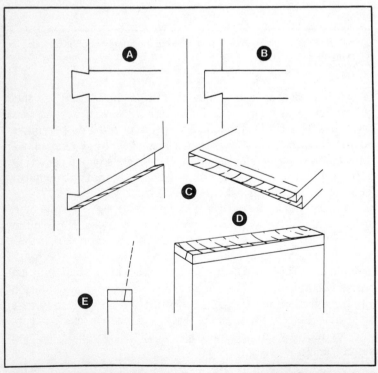

Fig. 5-9. A dovetailed dado (A,B) can taper across the boards (C) for the tightest fit (D,E).

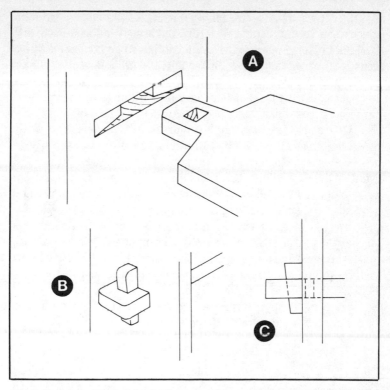

Fig. 5-10. A dado (A) combined with a tenon (B) can be locked with a wedge (C).

joint. If it is stopped, cut the notched corner of the shelf. On the shelf end, mark the amount of taper (Fig. 5-9D). How much to allow depends on the thickness of the wood, but taking too much away at the forward end will weaken the shelf. Cut in on this line with the saw tilted at the dovetail angle of about 1 on 8 (Fig. 5-9E). Having the wood in the vise and an adjustable bevel standing on the bench beside it should give sufficient guide to the angle.

Mark the mating shape on the upright. The surface size is at the root of the dovetail you have cut. Sever the fibers across the end with a knife. Use the adjustable bevel again as a guide when sawing the underneath of the slot. There will have to be some trial assemblies, but do not force the parts fully home. Check where any easing might have to be done with a chisel and make sure there are no obstructions to full assembly. Leave pushing the joint tight until it is assembled for the last time.

A joint associated with the dado joint has a tusk taken through and held with a wedge. This was used in much medieval furniture.

Possibly it was to allow for taking it apart. It was also a feature in much more recent German furniture and associated with parts that could not be disassembled. The tusk joint can be combined with a dado joint of normal shape. But where the horizontal part is narrower than the upright, it is tapered (Fig. 5-10A). This not a joint for light construction, but is used for such things as the rail between substantial slab ends of a large table (Fig 5-10B).

Only a slight taper is needed in the dado. The tusk is normally about one-third of the width of the rail it is cut on. Cut the wedge with a moderate taper and make it about one-third as thick as the width of the tusk. When the tusk is through the upright, the bottom of its slot must come below the surface by at least the amount the wedge is expected to tighten the joint (Fig. 5-10C).

It is advisable to leave some excess length on the tusk and on the wedge until after a trial assembly. Trim the wedge so that it has about the same amount projecting above and below the tusk when it is fully tightened. Do not cut too much off the end of the tusk because the wedge is tightening against the end grain and could break it away. In some furniture, the end of the tusk and both ends of the wedge are decorated by carving.

Chapter 6
Tenoned Joints

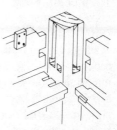

The framework of most pieces of good quality furniture contains mortise and tenon joints. The tenon is the projecting tongue which fits into the hollow mortise. Dowel joints can be regarded as variations on the mortise and tenon joint. The round dowel serves as a tenon into a round mortise.

Mortise and tenon joints have a long history. They were used in much early furniture and house construction. Because there were no glues of much strength, the joints were often assembled dry and tightened with wedges and by other means. Even so, there are examples that are still satisfactory after hundreds of years.

Nearly all mortise and tenon joints in cabinetwork are between parts at right angles to each other. When one part comes into the other obliquely, the same methods can be used. However, it is important that the grain lines on the tenoned part continue along the tenon. Keep the tenons in line with the part they are cut on and let any diagonal cuts be in the mortise. Never alter tenons to come at right angles to the mortised part. That would result in a weak short grain.

The basic "through mortise and tenon joint" comes between two pieces of the same thickness (Fig. 6-1A). In this case, it is best for the tenon to be about one-third the thickness of the wood (Fig. 6-1B). Because the mortise was traditionally chopped out with a chisel, there was an advantage in making the thickness of the tenon match the width of the chisel of the nearest suitable size. This is still a good idea, although we now remove most of the waste by drilling.

If the tenoned piece is narrower than the mortised part, as it is often when a rail is joined to a leg, the tenon can be thicker than one-third of the rail width. Therefore, there is less weakening of the rail. The thicker tenon can be made in the usual way (Fig. 6-1C) or it can be cut away at one side only to make a *bare-faced tenon* (Fig. 6-1D).

If rails meet in a leg, their length is limited.. To get the maximum glue area, they can be mitered where they meet (Fig. 6-1E). If the structure can be arranged so that the rails come into the legs at different levels, each joint is treated separately and the tenon can be longer and therefore stronger. When a mortise does not go right through it is called a "blind mortise and tenon joint with a stub tenon" (Fig. 6-1F).

In marking out and cutting a joint, the important considerations are the fit of the tenon in the mortise and the surfaces of the parts coming in the right relation to each other when the joint is tightened. Use the actual pieces of wood to get the sizes to mark on each part. For the through mortise and tenon joint in pieces of the same thickness, mark the depth of the part to be tenoned on the

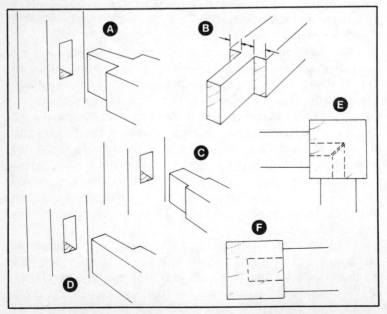

Fig. 6-1. A tenon is the projecting tongue (A,B,C). A mortise is the hole it fits (D). Sizes and form vary to suit the particular assembly (E,F).

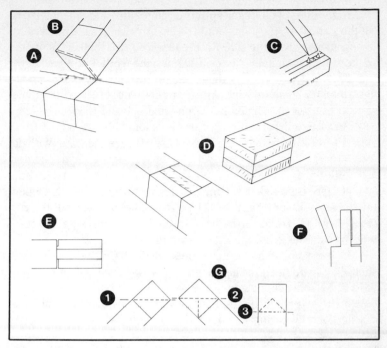

Fig. 6-2. Mark the parts of a joint from each other (A,B) and set the gauge to suit the chisel (C) to be used for the mortise (D, E). Saw tenons carefully on the waste sides of the lines (F,G).

other part (Fig. 6-2A). Use the thickness of that part to mark the length of the tenon. Allow for a little to spare for trimming later (Fig. 6-2B). Square around to the opposite side of the mortise with pencil. Square around the shoulder of the tenon with a knife.

If a mortise gauge is available, set the two pins to the correct distance apart. If it is the width of a chisel that is to be the size, use that as a guide (Fig. 6-2C). Set the stock to bear against the face surfaces. Gauge both sides of the mortise and gauge all round the tenon (Fig. 6-2D). Scribble on the waste parts. If a mortise gauge is unavailable, do the marking with two settings of a marking gauge. If there are many joints of similar size, do all the gauging at one setting so that there cannot be variations due to resetting.

Tenons can be cut in a similar way to that described for cutting the end pieces of halved joints in Chapter 5. Cut the shoulders carefully with the kerf on the waste side of the line (Fig. 6-2E). Stop exactly at the tenon. Letting the saw run into the tenon weakens the joint. It is better to cut slightly short and trim the angle later after cutting the sides of the tenons.

If the sides of the tenon split the gauge lines and the mortise is cut the same way, the joint should fit exactly. That is the perfection to be aimed at. Saw the sides of the tenon so that the kerf is on the waste side of each line (Fig. 6-2F). For hand work with a backsaw, tilt the wood and saw in three stages (Fig. 6-2G) in the way described for a halved joint. Alternatively, cut across with a table saw. Clean out the angles between shoulder and tenon cuts.

A mortise that goes right through should always be cut from both sides to ensure that both ends of the hole are accurate (with no torn fibers). To chop out entirely by chisel, start near the center and work towards the ends. Stop about ⅛ of an inch from each end so that there is no risk of cutting too far or damaging the edge when levering out waste (Fig. 6-3A). Use the chisel to lever out the cut chips of wood. Go about halfway through from one side and turn over to cut back from the other side in the same way.

If overlapping holes have been drilled (Fig. 6-3B), there should be little need for heavy hitting of the chisel. There might have to be some cuts made in the same way as when there are no holes. However, much of the shaping of the inside of the mortise can be done by paring without using a mallet.

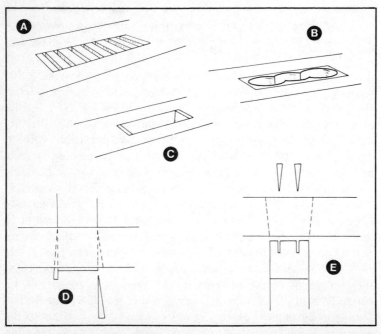

Fig. 6-3. Make a series of chisel cuts (A) or drill out waste wood (B, C) Wedges can compress or spread a tenon (D, E).

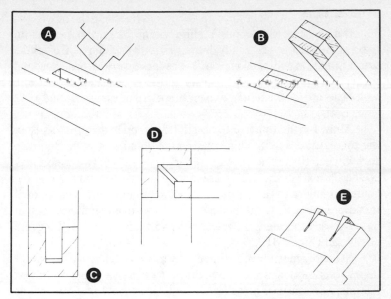

Fig. 6-4. A blind mortise (A) does not go right through. Make sure that there is clearance at the bottom (B, C). It can be spread with fox wedges (D, E).

In either case, concentrate on removing waste and getting the mortise to width for most of its length before paring back to the line at the ends (Fig. 6-3C). Do this in stages, so that the last cut at an end is only taking off a fine shaving and there is no risk of the cut being forced over the line. Work from both sides and see that the ends of the mortises finish straight through.

With modern glues in most cabinet construction, it will be sufficient to assemble a through mortise and tenon joint with no further treatment. For maximum strength or if a load on the joint will be in the direction to tend to pull it apart, it can be wedged. There are two ways of doing this. Wedges have to be driven so that the load they impose comes against the end grain in the mortise. Pressure the other way would put a splitting load on the wood. If the mortise is made slightly wide on the far side, wedges can be driven outside the tenon (Fig. 6-3D). Alternatively, the tenon can be expanded. Have the far side of the mortise widened. Put saw cuts in the end of the tenon (usually two) before assembly. Drive wedges into the saw cuts after the joint has been pulled together (Fig. 6-3E). Glue the wedges as well as the tenons. When the glue has set, cut off the surplus wood and plane the end of the tenon flush.

STUB TENONS

If a *stub tenon* goes into a *blind mortise* (Fig. 6-4A) steps in making the joint are basically similar to a through joint. However, there is nothing to be done on the reverse side of the mortised piece. Mark out on the surface only of the mortise and in the same way as before for the tenon, except there can be no extra length left (Fig. 6-4B).

Allow for the mortise to be slightly deeper than the depth of the tenon (Fig. 6-4C). This ensures the shoulders of the tenoned part will pull tight. The strength in a glued joint is between surfaces on the flat part of the grain. The end grain of the tenon would not contribute much to the strength of a glued joint in any case, even if it came tight against the bottom of the mortise. Similarly, if two mortises are to meet, cut the tenons so their miters will leave a slight gap (Fig. 6-4D).

Make the mortise in a similar way to a through mortise. Check depth frequently and get the main part of the slot to size before trimming the ends. If holes are drilled, a depth stop on the drill or on the drill press will help in getting the initial depth correct.

A stub tenon can be wedged with what are called *fox wedges*. The ends of the mortise are cut so that the bottom of the slot is slightly wider than the top (so the tenon can expand). Make saw cuts in the end of the tenon and make small wedges to fit in them and extend a short distance (Fig. 6-4E). You have to judge what size to make the wedges in relation to the size of the joint, but they must extend far enough to be forced into the cuts by the bottom of the mortise and expand the tenon.

HAUNCHED TENONS

If a mortise and tenon joint is to come at the corner of a frame, it needs special treatment because of the short grain at the end of the mortised part. One way is to let the mortise be an open part. This is more often called a *bridle joint* (Fig. 6-5A). Both parts are made with a little excess length to be planed level after assembly. The tenon can be cut in the usual way and the sides of the mortise can be sawn. This leaves only the bottom of the slot to be drilled and chopped out. Bridle joints can be used intermediately when they are a sort of reversed mortise and tenon (Fig. 6-5B). For most cabinetwork applications, it is preferable to use a mortise and tenon joint. If for the sake of appearance the end piece should run through, a bridle joint is better. An example is a table leg where the top rail is continuous (Fig. 6-5C).

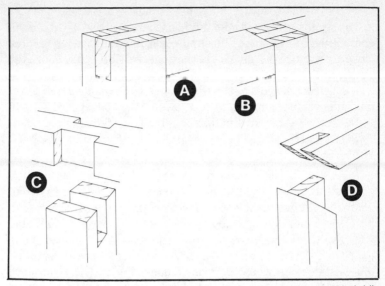

Fig. 6-5. An open mortise (A) and tenon joint (B) at a corner is also called a bridle joint. It can be used along one side or be mitered (C,D).

Another application of the open corner joint is where there is to be a miter on one or both surfaces. If the back does not have to be mitered, there is more glue area if that part goes right through. Otherwise, a neat miter is possible (Fig. 6-5D).

For strength at a corner, as in a framed door, the cabinetmaker haunches his tenons. This means cutting them back. It is usual to leave the mortised part with a little extra on the length as a guard against splitting. This is planed level when the door is fitted. If a door is made some time before it is needed, it is best to leave the extensions on to take any knocks that might otherwise have damaged the final corners.

In a simple haunched joint, the tenon is cut back to leave the small haunch to the end of the mortised piece (Fig. 6-6A). The sizes used will depend on the circumstances and will be a compromise between leaving as much tenon as possible and not weakening the end of the other piece. In close-grained wood, the mortise can finish nearer the end than in softer open-grained wood. The haunch keeps the parts in line.

Mark out and cut a full width tenon in the usual way. Then mark on it and cut the haunch (Fig. 6-6B). Use this to get the actual width for the mortise (Fig. 6-6C). Allow for the outer edge to come in the correct position.

Cut the mortise, which can be through or stub, and then saw and chisel the part that takes the haunch into it (Fig. 6-6D). If the end will be visible in the finished construction, make the stub a close fit without the gap at the bottom that there can be a stub tenon.

This sort of haunch might be acceptable in many assemblies. But if the visible haunch is to be avoided, it can be tapered so as to come to the surface on the finished line (Fig. 6-6E).

WIDE TENONS

If something like a deep rail has to go into the top of a table leg, a full-depth tenon would require a considerable amount to be cut out in the mortise and this would weaken the leg. At a corner, with a rail the other way, the top of the leg would lose considerable strength. In this case, two or more tenons are used instead of one long one. If it is at the end of the mortised piece, there is a stub and this continues between the main tenons (Fig. 6-7A). The piece between the tenons might not always be necessary, but it helps in lining up the parts and provides extra glue area.

If parts are very thick, a single tenon in the usual proportions would be quite large and not provide an adequate glue area for heavy work. In that case, there can be twin tenons (Fig. 6-7B). If

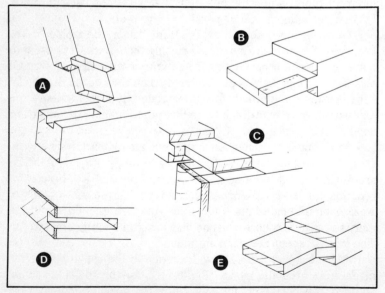

Fig. 6-6. A mortise and tenon joint (A,B,C) has to be set back at the corner of a frame (D,E).

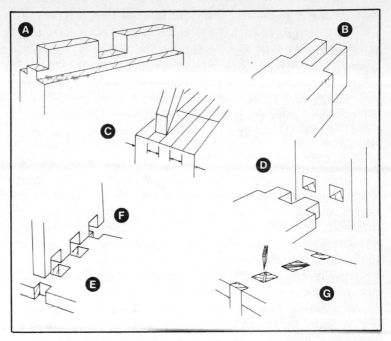

Fig. 6-7. Wide mortise and tenon joints (A,B,C), are stronger if divided (D,E).

the mortised piece is the same thickness, dividing the dimension by five should give suitable proportions with an allowance for matching the tenon thicknesses with a chisel (Fig. 6-7C). If the mortised part is wider, the shoulders outside the tenons can be less and the tenons a little thicker. The tenons can be through or stub and there can be haunches if the joint comes at a corner.

This type of joint can be used even when the tenoned part is not very thick the other way (Fig. 6-7D). Although it might be considered a place for a dado joint, twin tenons going through are stronger. Appearance might be improved by cutting a shallow dado for use in conjunction with the twin tenons.

This type of tenoning can be extended to wide boards with multiple tenons (Fig. 6-7E), as in divisions inside a cabinet, where wide boards secured together will have a mutual resistance to warping. The tenons should be about square and the spaces between them about the same as their width. If the assembly looks better with the tenoned piece going through at the edge, there can be narrower tenons outside (Fig. 6-7F). If the tenons are to be wedged, it is best to do this diagonally. Use saw cuts made before the joint is assembled (Fig. 6-7G).

RABBETED AND GROOVED TENON JOINTS

Many of the assemblies that require mortise and tenon joints in cabinetwork are frames that hold glass or panels and the parts are not of simple rectangular section. A rabbeted frame holds glass or a mirror. But as the tenoned part meets the mortised part at two different levels, it needs special treatment. It is usually possible to arrange the mortise inside the wider part. If it is a simple square-edged front, the tenoned part can be given long and short shoulders (Fig. 6-8A). If it is the corner of a door, there can be the usual haunch.

Mark out the tenon, working from the bottom of the rabbet first. Square this around and measure from it where the cut for the shorter shoulder will come (Fig. 6-8B). Gauge around so that one line comes on the line of the rabbet. Cut to this and mark the haunch on the tenon (Fig. 6-8C). Cut this to shape. The mortised part might have been marked at the same time, but for a first joint it helps to have the tenoned part complete to see what has to be marked and cut on the other part (Fig. 6-8D).

If a wider part is molded or bevelled, the joint would not be satisfactory if it is merely cut back. It would be better then to miter the front (Fig. 6-8E). The arrangement of the joint is best visualized if the front edge is regarded as a separate molding put on to an otherwise rectangular sectioned piece. Start by cutting back both pieces to the same level as the inside of the rabbet as far as the joint will be. Then cut the projecting pieces to 45 degrees. From this stage, marking out is the same as for a haunched mortise and tenon joint between plain pieces of wood (Fig. 6-8F). If this sort of joint is needed elsewhere than at a corner, as with an intermediate rail into the stiles of a frame, cut back and miter the front both sides (Fig. 6-8G).

Grooved frames are used to enclose panels. If the plowed groove is about one-third of the thickness of the wood, the tenon can be the same width. Usually, the groove is narrower.

If the grooved wood has square edges, the mortise and tenon joint needed is little different from a plain one. Make the tenon of a suitable thickness and cut this back to the bottom of the groove. If it is a corner joint, make a haunch that will come to at least the full depth of the groove in the other piece (Fig. 6-9A). Mark and cut the mortise in the other piece. Doing this will remove the groove and leave the parts ready to assemble in the usual way (Fig. 6-9B).

If one or both edges are molded or bevelled, they will have to be mitered in a similar way to the corner of a rabbeted frame. If

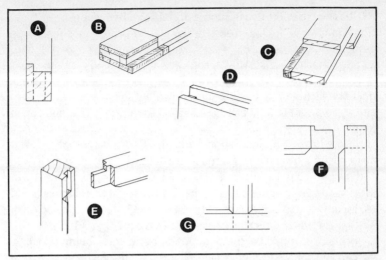

Fig. 6-8. If the parts are rabbeted (A), tenon shoulders (B) have to be at different levels (C) or the extending parts can be mitered (D,E,F,G).

both edges are to be treated, cut them back on both pieces and miter them. Then make simple joints at the new levels. If only the front edge has to be shaped and the back still has a square edge, it will still be better to cut them both down to the level of the bottoms of the grooves and miter the meeting parts. However, it is possible to only miter the front and let the back of the tenoned part lap on to the edge with a shorter shoulder (Fig. 6-9C).

In joining to a molded edge, a joiner assembling a house window makes a "scribed mortise and tenon joint." Instead of cutting back and mitering, he shapes one shoulder to fit over the edge (Fig. 6-9D) and this could be on grooved or rabbeted wood. The method is not often used in cabinetwork, but it has occasional applications.

DOWEL JOINTS

Dowels are not new in furniture construction. Pegs of varying degrees of accuracy were often used in older furniture. One use that has almost gone is in securing other joints when there was no satisfactory glue. Mortise and tenon joints were drilled through and a dowel driven in. With the glues available now, there is no need to do this except sometimes for the sake of appearance in reproduction work. Dowels were also used in places where we would now use nails or screws. This was because of the scarcity or cost of these metal fastenings.

Dowels are often used today for assemblies where they function something like inserted tenons. Dowels were once fashioned as needed and were not always very accurate in shape or size. Modern machine-made dowel rods are accurate and convenient. If holes can be drilled so that they are guided accurately with a drilling machine or by using jigs, dowelled joints are satisfactory and in some situations can be used in place of mortise and tenon joints.

The dowel and hole should match. This means that a dowel coated with glue and then forced into a hole will compress air inside and possibly burst the wood. A groove sawn along the dowel will let air and surplus glue out (Fig. 6-10A). A slight bevel at each end of the dowel also helps assembly. Make the holes a little too deep so that the meeting surfaces can come tight (Fig. 6-10B).

Satisfactory dowel joints depend on the holes being properly spaced and square to the surface. There are jigs available to clamp on to adjoining parts so that they can be drilled to match. However, these have limited application and in many places it will be the care with which you mark out and drill that will affect the result.

As an example of marking out, an edge-to-edge joint can be reinforced with dowels. Have the two boards in the vise with their face sides outwards and high enough for a marking gauge to be

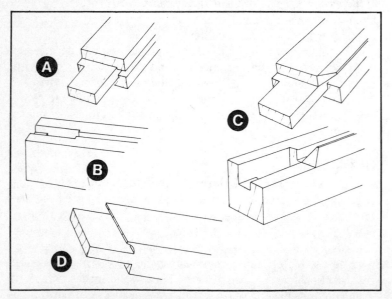

Fig. 6-9. Tenons are cut back in grooved parts (A,B,C), where one piece could be mitered or shaped over a molded edge (D).

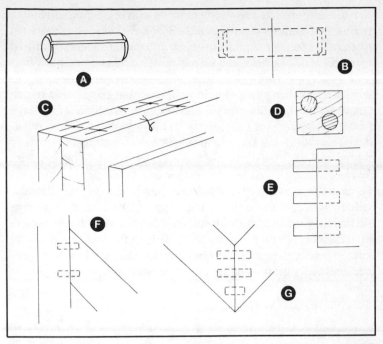

Fig. 6-10. Dowels should be grooved (A,B) to prevent bursting. Marking out (C,D) and drilling (E) must be carefully done if parts are to match (G).

used. Use a square to mark across where the holes are to come. Set a marking gauge to half the thickness and gauge each piece from its face side (Fig. 6-10C). The holes have to come where the lines cross. To prevent the point of the bit from wandering, push a spike in to make a dent at each crossing.

If dowels are to be used in place of tenons at the end of a rail, always use at least two. A single one would allow twisting. If there is not much space, use thin dowels diagonally spaced (Fig. 6-10D). For deeper rails, use two or more (Fig. 6-10E). How many and what size to use depends on several things, but dowel should project at least as far as a tenon would and expose about the same area for glue if the joint is to be satisfactory.

One situation where dowels are superior to tenons is where the joint comes diagonal to the grain and a tenon would have to be cut across grain lines. One part meeting another at an acute angle is an example (Fig. 6-10F). They can also provide strength across a miter (Fig. 6-10G).

It is not always easy to make adjoining parts together. It might be possible to make a template from which to mark the meeting surfaces or there could be a strip of wood with projecting nail points to mark hole centers in both pieces. Some markers are available in the form of shouldered plugs to press into the holes already drilled in one piece. They have projecting central points so that the first piece can be pressed against the other to mark its holes.

Any dowelled joints should be assembled completely in one operation. It is unsatisfactory to fit dowels into one piece and leave it to fit to another part later. Have all the dowels cut and grooved. Make sure there are no ragged edges or other things to prevent easy assembly. If the mouths of any holes are rough or ragged, trim around them with a chisel or knife or use a countersink bit. This treatment might help to pull a dowel into place. Tap the dowels, with their glue, into one piece. Then apply glue to the other surface and carefully insert the dowel ends into their holes before hammering or squeezing the parts together. It is difficult to avoid having surplus glue come out and spread around. Use newspaper to protect finished surfaces and be ready to wipe away excess glue.

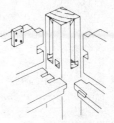

Chapter 7
Dovetail Joints

Probably more than any other joints, dovetails are the cabinet-maker's joints. The dovetail form gives a joint that is secure in one direction without dependence on glue. A series of dovetails will lock two broad boards together so that they expand and contract together to prevent warping. Dovetails can be made so that they are not visible in one or both directions and it is possible to examine a piece of furniture without knowing there are dovetails between parts. Exposed dovetails are regarded as design features in some furniture. There is nothing to equal dovetails for joining drawer sides to the front. Some connoisseurs pull out a drawer to see its side joints as an important point in assessing the quality of a piece of furniture.

The name comes from the parts in one direction. They are usually called *tails* because they are like the tail of a dove. The projections on the other part that go between the tails are *pins*. The construction is seen in a single, through dovetail (Fig. 7-1A). In general carcase work, several dovetails are arranged across the joint (Fig. 7-1B). There are no recognized rules about the spacing of the parts of the joint or the number of parts to be used or their relative width. Individual cabinetmakers have their own ideas and a beginner can discover customary arrangements by examining good furniture. The tails and pins have to be spaced across the wood and arithmetical considerations will settle exact sizes. In general, very wide tails should be avoided. Making them a little wider than the thickness of the wood is often satisfactory.

There was a time at the height of the handmade furniture period when cabinetmakers took a pride in making the pins very narrow (Fig. 7-1C). This might have shown their skill in cutting joints and the joints appear to have held together well, but there is more strength in wider pins. In reproduction work, it may be necessary to make joints with the narrowest possible pins. Otherwise, it is stronger and easier to give them a moderate width (Fig. 7-1D).

There are many places, like a drawer front, where the dovetail has to be hidden one way. This is a *half blind*, a *stopped* or a *lap* dovetail joint (Fig. 7-1E). Details are the same as for a through joint. A part covers the ends of the dovetails. Most dovetail joints have to be made by hand. However, there is a way to make this type of joint by machine. Machined joints can be identified by checking widths. The tails and pins will be found to be the same (Fig. 7-1F). Inside the joint the parts are rounded (Fig. 7-1G). It is possible to make such a joint with a template that clamps to the wood and acts as a guide to a cutter mounted in an electric drill. The result is quite satisfactory, but it would not really be classed as fine cabinetwork. In good quality work, it is better to make the joints by hand and arrange the pin widths to be narrower than the tails.

The slope of the side of a dovetail has to be enough to prevent it from pulling back, yet not so much that its tip cuts across short

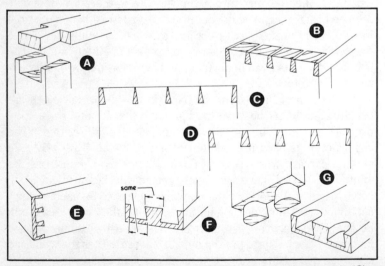

Fig. 7-1. Dovetails can be single (A) or multiple (B) and with pins wide (C) or narrow (D). A stopped dovetail (E) is hidden in one direction. Machine-made dovetails have tails and pins of the same width (F,G).

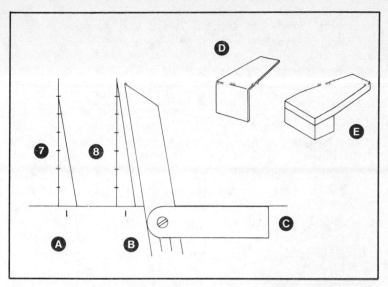

Fig. 7-2. Dovetail angles are slightly wider in softwoods than hardwoods (A,B,C). Simple gauges can take the place of an adjustable bevel. Wood or metal templates (D,E) can be used.

lines of grain that might break off. In soft woods, a slightly wider angle is needed than would be satisfactory in harder woods. However, the difference is slight. The angle should be between 1 in 6 and 1 in 9. For soft woods, a slope of 1 in 7 can be used (Fig. 7-2A). For hardwoods 1 in 8 is better (Fig. 7-2B). Uniformity of slope is essential for the sake of appearance. An adjustable bevel can be set to the slope after laying out the angle on the edge of a board (Fig. 7-2C). A piece of sheet metal can be bent and used as a template (Fig. 7-2D) or a similar thing can be made from wood (Fig. 7-2E). A more elaborate tool, if much dovetailing is to be done, has a blade with softwood and hardwood angles on opposite sides (Fig. 7-3).

When laying out dovetails, allow for having to remove the waste between them with a bevel-edged chisel. Make sure that the gaps are somewhat wider at their bottoms than the chisel you intend to use. It is common for there to be pins at the edges of the joint (Fig. 7-4A), but in some situations it is better to have half dovetails outside (Fig. 7-4B). This is satisfactory, but if there is no particular need for it, choose the other arrangement. Dovetails do not have to be all the same widths and some craftsmen mark them out by eye. In any position that will show, they should be uniformly arranged. Some traditional cabinetmakers used one narrower tail near an unsupported edge (Fig. 7-4C) where it might be considered to provide a little extra strength. This also allows him to make up for taking less trouble in spacing the main tails.

MAKING THROUGH DOVETAIL JOINTS

Dovetail joints can be marked out and cut with the tails first or the pins first. For an ordinary through dovetail joint, it does not matter which way is chosen. The ends of the pieces of wood should be planed square to the face sides and edges, but they can be just slightly too long. If much excess length is left, the gaps between tail ends will get closer and removing the waste becomes difficult.

If the tails are to be cut first, mark the width of the other piece back from the end. Leave just a little excess for planing after assembly. Do this with pencil and square it around all four faces. Space the tails and mark them with pencil (Fig. 7-5A). If two parts, such as the opposite sides of a box have to match, mark the tails on one piece. Then square across the two while they are clamped or held in a vise (Fig. 7-5B). Saw down the sides of the tails with a fine backsaw. Keep the kerfs on the waste side of the line and watch the cut at the far side as well as at the front to see that it does not go below the line. Two or even four pieces can be sawn at one time.

Turn the wood on edge and cut each side. For the cleanest

Fig. 7-3. If much dovetailing is to be done, an adjustable gauge can be made to suit the usual angles.

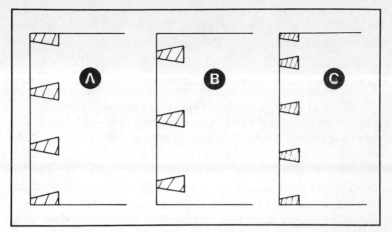

Fig. 7-4. Pins (A) or dovetails (B) can come outside and sometimes a smaller tail is used at the top of an open box (C).

ends, go over the pencil line at each place with a knife to sever the fibers before sawing. Have each piece supported on a flat piece of scrap wood on the bench top while chopping out the waste between the tails. Cut about halfway from each side to avoid breaking out. Be careful that the chisel is not levered against the ends of the pins where it would either damage them or break them off. Clear the waste by chopping from each side to within a short distance of the line. Then pare by hand back to the line (Fig. 7-5C). Check in each space to be sure that the cut goes right through straight and just touches the lines at each side. A lump in the middle or fibers still clinging in an angle will prevent close assembly. A very slight hollow is preferable to a lump.

Although matching parts can be sawn together, it is unlikely that they will finish so uniform as to be interchangeable. From this stage, mark each mating tail and pin part with numbers inside or some other means so that corners do not become mixed.

Have the thickness of the dovetail part, plus a little extra for planing, marked all round the part that will have the pins. Support the tail part over it (Fig. 7-5D). Use a fine steel point or a finely sharpened pencil to mark the outline of each tail (Fig. 7-5E). Use a try square to draw down to the line at each mark. The marked lines indicate the actual sizes of the tails. To get a close fit, the kerfs must be kept on the waste side of the lines (Fig. 7-5F). For a first attempt it is advisable to scribble with pencil on the waste parts as a guard against sawing on the wrong side of a line.

The waste can be chopped out, but it is possible to remove

117

some of it by sawing diagonally (Fig. 7-5G). Work back to the lines by chopping from each side. Remember to taper in the width when chopping from the wider side. Tilt the chisel to avoid damaging the far side of a pin. Then carefully pare back to the line on each side with a wider chisel than was used for chopping out.

If the pins are to be made first, space the tail outlines across the end and square down to the thickness line (Fig. 7-5H). Cut away the sockets between the pins in the way just described. Stand the pin part in position on the piece for the dovetails and mark the shapes (Fig. 7-5J). One advantage of this method is that there is more room for using a spike or pencil. Square across the ends of the wood and cut the tails on the waste side of the lines.

Another way of marking the pins from the dovetailed part is to saw the sides of the tails. Do not chop out the waste. Put the wood in position on the other piece and draw the end of the saw back in each kerf a few times to mark the end grain (Fig. 7-5K). Remove the top piece and finish it by cutting between the tails. The mark made by the saw does not allow for the thickness of the cut. Do not continue to saw in the positions marked. Instead, relocate the saw for each cut on the waste side of that initial shallow kerf. Otherwise the joint will finish loose by the thickness of the saw cut at each place.

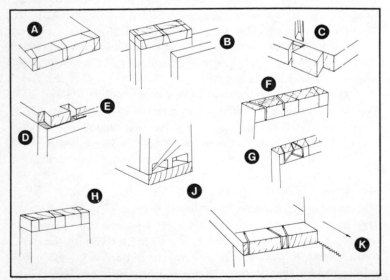

Fig. 7-5. Tails can be cut first and used to mark the pins (A,B,C). Alternatively, mark the tails from the pins (E,F,G). Another way is to mark through saw cuts (H,J,K).

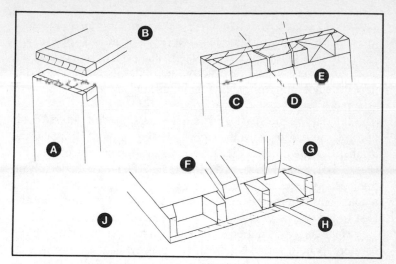

Fig. 7-6. A stopped dovetail (A,B,C,D,E) involves more work with chisels (F,G,H,J).

A skilled craftsman depends on his ability to work accurately and does not make a trial assembly of a dovetail joint. As with the mortise and tenon and other joints, a trial assembly might cause wear at the edges of a joint and there will be a better fit if the first assembly is the last. If you want to try a joint together, enter the tails only partly into their sockets so that you can see if they are correct. Do not push the parts tightly together yet.

In the final glued assembly of a wide joint, be careful to avoid local pressure that might cause cracking or difficulty elsewhere. Make sure that all tails are entered in their sockets. Then spread pressure with a strip of wood across and clamp over that at both ends or use a mallet or hammer over it. Most of these joints have to finish at right angles, so check squareness before allowing the glue to set. If it is a four-sided assembly with dovetail joints at the corners, check squareness by measuring diagonals.

MAKING LAP DOVETAIL JOINTS

The half-blind or lap dovetail joint is particularly associated with joining drawer sides to the front, but there are many other uses for it. In effect, it is the same as a through dovetail joint with a piece behind the pins covering the ends of the tails. Usually that part is thicker than the other to allow for it. The overlapping piece should not be too thin, although it looks neater if kept to a minimum.   The sockets for the tails have to be chopped towards it and a very thin part might crack or allow the chisel to break through. For the usual cabinet drawer, allow about 3/16 of an inch.

The dovetailed part is similar to that of a through dovetail joint. However, it must be exactly the proper length because this joint does not allow for planing the ends later. Mark on each piece how much the other will overlap (Fig. 7-6A).

If the dovetailed part is to be made first, mark it out and cut it in the same way as for a through dovetail joint. Put it in position against the line on the other part and mark the shapes of the tails (Fig. 7-6B). Square down to the line (Fig. 7-6C). Saw diagonally on the waste side of the line at each position (Fig. 7-6D). A small amount of waste can be removed with the saw (Fig. 7-6E), but the rest of the waste will have to be cut out with a chisel.

Have the wood flat on a piece of scrap wood on the bench top (preferably held with a holdfast). Chop away diagonally first (Fig. 7-6F). Make other cuts first across the fibers (Fig. 7-6G), then pare towards these cuts (Fig. 7-6H). Do this a little at a time, with the cross grain cut always ahead of the paring along the grain, until the socket is to shape (Fig. 7-6J) and there are fibers left in the angles. It might be possible to remove some of the waste by drilling or a router cutter could be used. Great care is needed to avoid going too far. When chopping or paring, be very careful not to break through the thin covering part.

The pins could be marked and cut first if you prefer to work that way. Carefully position the wood on the part for the tails at the exact limit when you are marking on the end grain.

For a drawer, the bottom will fit into a groove at the front and into each side. The lap dovetail joint has to be arranged to enclose this so that the groove is not visible outside. The groove could be in the bottom tail in a normal arrangement, but to get it lower it is better to use a half tail at the bottom (Fig. 7-7A) with the groove through it meeting that across the front.

At the back of a drawer, it is common for the bottom to go through with the back above it, usually held to the sides with through dovetails (Fig. 7-7B). If the drawer slides on runners there will be a piece to increase the bearing surface on each side (Fig. 7-7C).

HIDDEN DOVETAILS

The next step after the lap dovetail joint is one where the details of the joint are hidden in both directions. This is a *stopped lap* or *blind lap* dovetail joint. The pins and tails meet normally, but

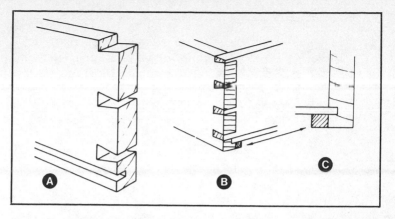

Fig. 7-7. In a drawer, the groove for the bottom can be hidden in the front bottom tail (A) and taken under the back (B,C).

both parts have extra thickness outside to cover them (Fig. 7-8A). When the joint is closed, only one overlap is visible (Fig. 7-8B).

Mark both pieces with the amount they overlap and cut back one piece by the covering part (Fig. 7-8C). Mark one part and cut it out. A small amount of sawing can be done on the part without the overhang, but most cutting of both parts will have to be with chisels. Mark the second part from the first. If the actual joint is visualized as a through dovetail joint and the outer parts are considered as additions, the steps in cutting the joint will be understood.

That joint assembles with a narrow piece of end visible in one direction, but it can be eliminated by altering it to a "housed and mitered dovetail joint." Both pieces are given extensions which meet in a mitered corner (Fig. 7-8D). The extensions have to be pared carefully so that they will meet throughout their length when the joint is pulled tight. A safe way to do this accurately is to clamp a thick piece of wood that is planed to 45 degrees below the dovetail and use this as a guide for a wide chisel (Fig. 7-8E).

When that joint is closed, the outer corner will be a tight miter. At the edges, part of the form of the joint can be seen (Fig. 7-8F). For many purposes, this does not matter. If the edge is also to appear as a miter, it is necessary to make the joint into a *secret dovetail* or *blind dovetail* joint.

The secret version is best visualized as the *housed and mitered* joint with extra thickness top and bottom. It is mitered (Fig. 7-9A) so in marking out there has to be the parts that will make the joint dealt with as for a through dovetail joint. Then extra thickness goes

121

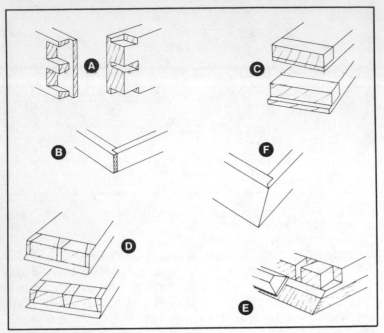

Fig. 7-8. A dovetail (A,B) can be hidden by parts cut (C) outside, either squarely or mitered (D,E,F).

outside each part for the corner miter and more is needed to continue this miter at the edges (Fig. 7-9B).

After cutting back for the corner mitered parts, it might be best to cut the edge miters so that what is left can be marked out for the tails and pins. Leave cutting the main part of the long miter until the sockets have been cut. You will almost certainly cut into the extension pieces at some stage, but this will not matter if there is

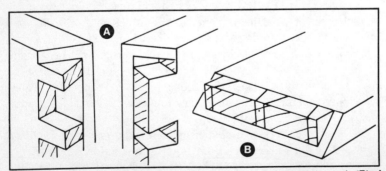

Fig. 7-9. In a fully hidden mitered dovetail (A), there are miters at the ends (B) of the joint.

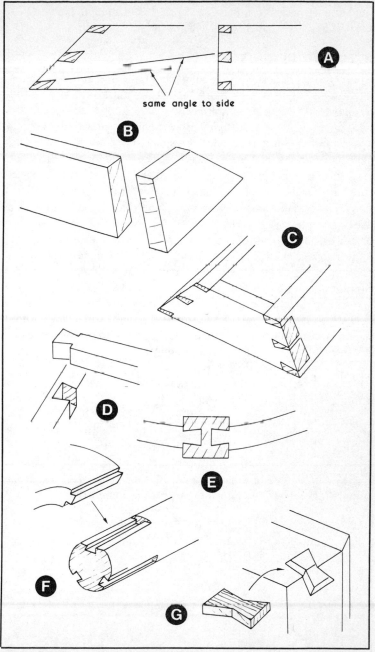

same angle to side

Fig. 7-10. Dovetail construction (A,B,C,D) can be adapted to angled and round forms (E,F,G).

123

still some surplus wood there. Very little of the joint can be sawn and it is mostly careful work with chisels

OTHER DOVETAIL JOINTS

Most constructions involving dovetails are at right angles both ways. When one or more angles are different, any of the dovetail joints can be used. Care is needed to keep the angles at the sides of the tails correct. Do not alter them to conform to a sloping surface, but angles in relation to the side of the wood should be the same as when the joint is a square one (Fig. 7-10A). Work to what would be 1 in 7 or 1 in 8 to a right-angled end, but set the adjustable bevel to this in relation to a straight edge of the wood.

If the corner slopes both ways, plane the ends to the correct relevant angles (Fig. 7-10B). Where you would normally square across with a try square, use an adjustable bevel set to the corner angle and have another adjustable bevel set to the dovetail slopes in relation to the edge of the wood. There are no right angles in the joint details (Fig. 7-10C).

Single dovetails can be used anywhere that there might be an extending strain on a rail. An example is a rail holding sides at the correct distance under a cabinet top (Fig. 7-10D). Curved rails under a table top could be dovetailed into the legs (Fig. 7-10E).

The three feet at the bottom of a central spindle under a round table will be strongest if they are dovetailed in what might also be called a *dovetail dado joint* (Fig. 7-10F).

Dovetail keys are used on the undersides of bannisters and other places that have to be pulled together. The method of connecting will not show. They can be used on the undersides of mitered corners of plinths under cabinets or other mitered frames. The key is a piece of thin wood cut at both sides with the usual dovetail angles and let into the parts to be joined (Fig. 7-10G).

Chapter 8
Other Joints

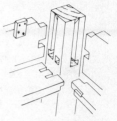

If a cabinetmaker thoroughly masters the joints described in the previous three chapters he will be able to cope with nearly all the assembly problems in making good furniture. Many other joints are adaptions of the standard ones. When faced with the need to devise a method of joining two parts, a craftsman will find that he can often modify joints he already knows. However, there are a few special techniques not already covered.

Modern strong glues have made some of the earlier complicated joints unnecessary. In many situations, a flat surface-to-surface glued joint can be trusted where it could not have been relied on with the glues available only a few years ago. Then the cabinetmaker would have had to use a joint that provided some interlocking to supplement the rather poor grip of the glue. Plywood and other manufactured boards have also reduced the need to join boards to make up large areas. In fine cabinetwork, where the emphasis is on solid wood dealt with in a traditional way, the craftsman needs to understand ways of increasing widths.

EDGE JOINTS

An edge or butt joint is used to glue two boards together along their edges a piece of greater width. Edges have to be planed straight and square. If edges are machine planed they should then be hand planed to remove the case-hardening effect of the rotating cutters. Otherwise the glue might not penetrate the pores adequately.

There are several points to watch. Check which way each board planes best on its surfaces and get the boards the same way. That way cleaning up the combined piece will be simpler. Marks across the joint will remind you which way to assemble it.

Check flatness (Fig. 8-1A) with a straightedge. The boards might have to be assembled with the end grain the same was for the sake of surface appearance. However, they usually can be arranged so that heart sides alternate. Any tendency to warp later will be partially cancelled (Fig. 8-1B) instead of being exaggerated if all boards went to warp the same way.

If the two meeting edges are absolutely flat and straight you can expect the joint to be perfect. It usually is, but there is sometimes a tendency for the ends to open. This can be avoided by planing the edges very slightly hollow in the length (as shown exaggerated in Fig. 8-1C). When the joint is clamped, this puts more pressure on the ends than the center and all should be well.

Joiner's dogs are useful tools for clamping joints (Fig. 8-1D).

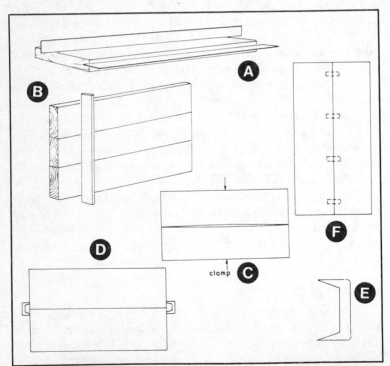

Fig. 8-1. In making up widths, boards should be planed true. (A). Alternating the grain reduces warping (B) Planing slightly hollow helps in tight clamping (C). Pinch dogs will hold joints (D). Dowels across provide strength (E).

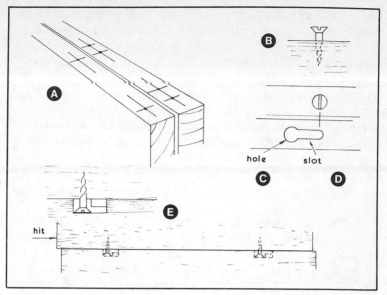

Fig. 8-2. Secret slot screwing clamps and strengthens a joint: (A) mark; (B,C,D) Drill; (E) drive.

The outside of each leg is upright and the inside slope so that driving them in draws a joint together (Fig. 8-1E).

If greater strength is required across a joint there can be dowels (Fig. 8-1F). They need not be thicker than one-third the thickness of the boards and their spacing depends on circumstances. However, six times the thickness of the wood is a reasonable distance. If a jig is not used, mark out carefully from the face (upper) sides and make sure that holes are at right angles to the edge (as described in Chapter 6).

There is an ingenious use of screws called *secret slot screwing*. This provides strength across a joint, but also serves to pull the joint together without clamps. Mark out as if for dowels, but not as closely. Nine-inch spacing should do. At each position on one board, make another mark a short distance away (Fig. 8-2A). One-half inch will do for most woods, although it could be a little more for softwoods.

Use flat-headed steel screws. For ¾-inch boards, they could be 1 inch by 8 gauge. On the edge with single marks, drill for screws and drive them until the threaded part is buried and not more than ¼ inch projects (Fig. 8-2B). On the other board, drill holes at the second marks that are just large enough to clear the screw heads (Fig. 8-2C). At the first marks, drill holes that will clear the necks of the screws. Remove the waste between the holes, possibly by drilling another small hole and chiselling out (Fig. 8-2D).

Bring the boards together so that the screw heads go into the opposite holes. Then drive one board along the other until the screw heads have cut their way along the bottoms of the slots to the other ends (Fig. 8-2E). If that assembly of the joint is satisfactory, drive the boards back again so the screws will lift out. Give each screw a quarter turn. Apply glue to the edges and drive the boards together again. This method can be used in other assemblies, where the fastener has to be hidden, but it can only be used where the slot can be arranged for the screw head to cut in the direction of the grain.

If many boards have to be used to make up a width, there has to be some allowance for expansion and contraction due to changes in the moisture content of the wood. If a table top is solid wood, its width might vary by perhaps ¼ of an inch. This would be enough to cause breaking or damage if it was held down rigidly all round to its framework underneath. Changes in the length would be so slight as to be ignored. Instead of being fastened tightly, the top is held by buttoning. The rails have grooves in them that are either cut where each button is to come or plowed in their full length. Buttons are glued and screwed under the table top. At each position, the tongue goes into the groove. Some clearance is allowed for movement (Fig. 8-3A).

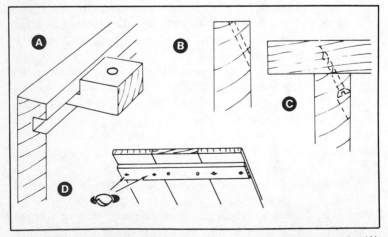

Fig. 8-3. A wide table top can be attached with buttons to allow for expansion (A). Screws can be driven diagonally (B) upward through framing (C). A screwed batten should have a slot screw holes to permit movement (D).

128

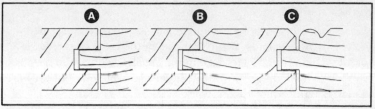

Fig. 8-4. Tonque and grooved joints (A,B) allow boards to make a width. Decoration at the front disguises expansion and contraction (C).

To keep the top symmetrical over the framing, there can be rigid attachments near the centers of the ends using one or two *pocket* screws. Drill diagonally down through a rail to suit a screw (Fig. 8-3B). Use a gouge and chisel to cut away enough to clear the screw head when it is driven upwards into the top (Fig. 8-3C).

If several boards glued together have to remain flat without being held on framing, there might have to be battens across their undersides. However, gluing and screwing them rigidly in place would lead to trouble if there was any expansion or contraction. To allow for this, the battens are slot screwed. Screws near the center can be through round holes, but near the ends of the battens the holes should be made into slots so that the screws can move with any alterations in the boards (Fig. 8-3D).

Before the days of plywood, hardboard and similar things had to be made up with solid boards and changes in width had to be allowed for. Backs of hutches, blocks of shelves, glass-fronted cabinets and similar things had many boards arranged upright. They were not joined to each other rigidly, but joints were used that were decorative and disguised any movement.

Basically, there is a tongue in one piece and a groove for it in the other (Fig. 8-4A). The groove and tongue are wide enough for shrinkage to not open the joint wide. Usually, the tongue is slightly less than one-third the thickness of the wood. At one time, there were special combination planes that would make the groove on one piece and a matching tongue on the other. The groove could be made with a plow plane or a wobble saw and the tongue formed by working two rabbets.

To draw attention from any movement, the front edges can be bevelled to form a V (Fig. 8-4B). A more traditional treatment is a bead worked on the tongued piece with a bevel alongside it and on the opposite edge (Fig. 8-4C). The ends of the boards are held in grooves or screwed only near their centers. Therefore, slight expansion and contraction does not cause splits at the fastenings.

HINGES

There are ways of making one part swing on another without the use of metal hinges. Some of these methods are described later for furniture designs which use them. Usually a door or lid has to be fitted with metal hinges. Plastic hinges are available, but they are inappropriate to fine cabinetwork.

In a hinge, the point on which the door pivots is the center of the knuckle. In most situations, this has to be located outside the front line of the wood (Fig. 8-5A). It throws the door clear and in a flat-fronted piece of furniture it can swing back flat through 180 degrees. If the knuckle is allowed to come within the thickness of the wood, the door will begin to bind against its frame once it passes 90 degrees. That can be intentional, as in a box lid which can be stopped by bevelling edges (Fig. 8-5B). If the door and its surround are not in the same plane, the knuckle might have to be some way from the surface of the door to make it swing clear (Fig. 8-5C).

All doors have two or more hinges and it is important that their knuckles are all exactly in line. Otherwise the door will not swing smoothly and screws might be pulled due to the distortion.

The simplest hinges to fit are those on the surface (Fig. 8-5D). They do not require any preparation of the wood and the knuckle

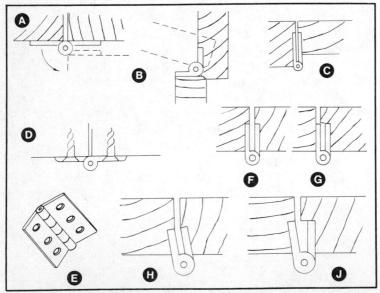

Fig. 8-5. Hinges may go on the surface (A,B,C,D,E) or be let in in various ways (F,G,H,J).

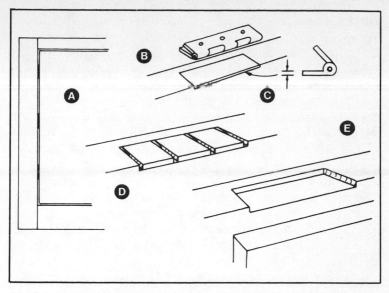

Fig. 8-6. Let hinges (A,B,C) into shallow recesses (D,E).

comes in the right position automatically. In some furniture, there are decorative hinges on the surface and these usually match handles and other metal parts to serve as features in the overall design. Plain hinges on the surface might be appropriate in some general carpentry, but not in cabinetwork.

Butt hinges can be made from sheet metal wrapped around the pin or they can be cast metal (Fig. 8-5E). Small hinges might have the knuckle divided into three parts, but five parts are more common. The hinge closes with a small gap between the flaps. Holes are drilled and countersunk for a particular gauge of flat-headed screw. There is not much clearance when the hinge is closed, so projecting screw heads would foul the other side. If necessary, countersink further.

In the standard construction, each flap is let in level (Fig. 8-5F) with the whole diameter of the knuckle above the surface. Sometimes the hinge is only let into the door and the flap on the post goes on the surface (Fig. 8-5G) to throw the door slightly further clear as it swings open. However, the surface attachment does not look satisfactory when the door is open. Some cabinet-makers let one or both flaps in at an angle (Fig. 8-5H). This increases clearance between the flaps and would be a way of dealing with a flap that would otherwise remain on the surface (Fig. 8-5J).

131

There is no exact rule about where to put hinges on the side of a door. Because optically a gap at the bottom seems less than at the top when it is exactly the same, it is best to arrange a lower hinge further from the bottom than the upper hinge is from the top (Fig. 8-6A). For the same optical reason if there is a third hinge, have it slightly above halfway between the others.

Use the actual hinge to get the length of the recess on the wood. Use a marking gauge set to the distance the flap is to go into the wood. This is usually the width of the flap up to the knuckle (Fig. 8-6B). In most doors, the gap between the flaps when the hinge is closed can be assumed to be the same as the clearance between the door and its post. Therefore, set the gauge to the thickness of the flap (Fig. 8-6C). Mark all hinge recesses at the same time. Use a knife to mark the ends across the grain. A common fault is to cut recesses too deep. If this happens, there has to be a shaving or paper packing under the hinge. This is undesirable so remove waste cautiously.

Saw the ends of the recess and in all but the smallest recesses make a few more cuts intermediately (Fig. 8-6D). Chisel the end cuts squarely and lightly cut in along the grain at the back of the recess. Have the wood projecting slightly above the vise and pare out the waste (Fig. 8-6E) with your hand over the blade ready to restrain as necessary to prevent the far side from breaking out. Try the hinge in position and check that its surface does not go below the level of the wood.

Slight alterations in the hinge position can affect the way the door shuts. Hinges can be screwed to the door with all screws, but another way is to try one screw only in each hinge. Then move the door. If it does not close properly, try moving a hinge in or out slightly in its recess with another temporary screw in another hole. When you are satisfied, drive all the screws.

There are a great many different hinges, but most are fitted in a generally similar way to butt hinges. If the fact that they pivot on the center of the knuckle is understood, the movement of whatever they control can be arranged as required. One special hinge that looks like a wide butt hinge is a backflap (Fig. 8-7A). An ordinary hinge will not open much further than with the flaps in line. A backflap goes further to more than 90 degrees the other way (Fig. 8-7B). This is appropriate to any position where greater movement is needed, but the hinge is particularly intended for a rule joint in the flap of a table.

The name comes from the similarity in section to the sort of joint once used in most carpenters' rules, and it is arranged to give

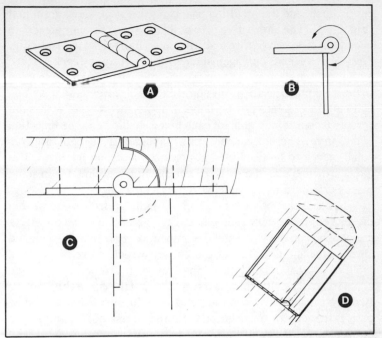

Fig. 8-7. A backflap hinge (A,B) swings far enough to allow a rule joint to be used on a table flap (C,D).

a better edge when the table flap is lowered than would be possible with the edges cut squarely. The edge of the table has a rounded lip on it and the edge of the flap is shaped to go over it. The whole thing pivots on the backflap hinge knuckles (Fig. 8-7C). For accurate, neat working the curves of the edges have to be with their radii matched to the knuckle position (based on a fullsize section drawing). Besides the flaps letting into the wood, there has to be clearance for the knuckle as well (Fig. 8-7D).

LAMINATING

In older cabinetmaking, there were interlocking joints or metal fastenings to reinforce the glue and to maintain the hold even if there was a partial failure of the glue line. Light gluing, such as the attaching of veneers, was satisfactory with older glues. However, glue alone could not be trusted in load-bearing situations. It is now possible to use glue in situations where nothing else assists it. Constructions are available to us that could not be used by cabinetmakers of less than a generation ago.

If a shaped part is made from solid wood, quite a lot of wood is cut to waste and the resulting part can have weak short grain in it (Fig. 8-8A). The alternative is to build it up from thinner pieces. In one method, the layers are made in pieces like bricks in a wall (Fig. 8-8B). Let the ends butt against each other tightly and each part can be approximately shaped so that there will be less finishing shaping to the assembled parts. Allow some excess at the ends so trimming and cutting of joints can be done in the same way as with solid wood. Of course, the grain of each piece should be in the direction of the curve. Therefore, short grain is avoided. This method allows small pieces to be used up and produces a strong member. The joints are visible on the surface, but this might not matter in some places or where it will be covered by veneering.

In another method, the shape is built up from several thin pieces bent to the curve and glued (Fig. 8-8C). How thin the strips are depends on the wood and the amount of curve, but they should spring to shape dry. To get the curve correct, there has to be a mold or pattern to bend the strips around. It can be built up from scrap wood. The vital thing is the accuracy of the curve (Fig. 8-8D). Arrange for the strips and the mold to be longer than the finished part. If the length stops abruptly, there is a risk of straightness or unevenness at the end. It is better for there to be some to cut off.

Newspaper placed around the mold will prevent excess glue from causing the part to stick to it. It helps to spread pressure if you

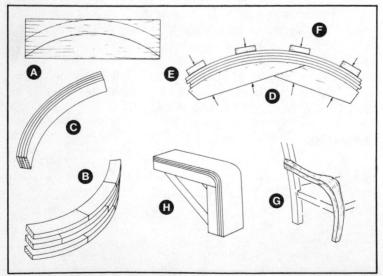

Fig. 8-8. A curved part cut from solid wood may have part with weak short grain (A) but laminating allows the grain to follow curves (B,C,D,E,F,G).

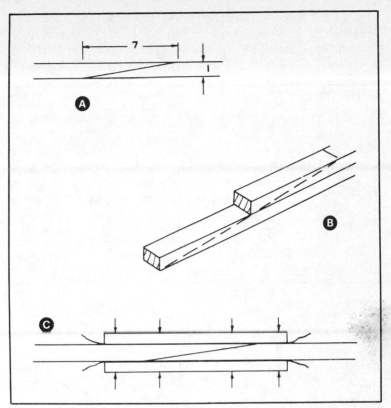

Fig. 8-9. Glued lengthwise joints (A,B) should be angled acutely (C).

make some pads to put under the clamps (Fig. 8-8E). Glue all the parts at one time and put on enough pressure to hold them close without being so tight as to force too much glue from the joints (Fig. 8-8F).

With laminating, it is possible to make parts that would have been impossible with earlier methods. Therefore, some good quality modern cabinetmaking might develop into a style of its own. For instance, a chair arm and leg could be in one finished part (Fig. 8-8G) with several laminations over a former and the shape the other way cut before thoroughly rounding the parts (Fig. 8-8H).

A glued splice is associated with laminating. No glue holds very well on end grain. Its grip is at its maximum on side grain. If meeting parts are cut diagonally, the grain comes sufficiently near being sideways to be satisfactory. In practice, this means that the angle should be at least as acute as 1 in 7 (Fig. 8-9A). If parts have to be joined to make up a length or to add a larger part to a smaller one, a glued splice at that angle should be satisfactory. If the parts are the same thickness, they can be planed together with very little marking out (Fig. 8-9B). Clamp between boards that extend past the joint. Use paper to prevent sticking (Fig. 8-9C).

KEYED JOINTS

If grooves are plowed in two meeting surfaces and a strip of wood is put in, the effect is like a tongued and grooved joint. If the strip has its grain across, the joint should be stronger than if a tongue had been cut on one piece (Fig. 8-10A). In the past, this joint was often used with the spline cut diagonally to get a greater length from a given width of wood. Today it would be satisfactory to use plywood with the grain of the outer layers across the joint (Fig. 8-10B). If necessary, several pieces can be used to make up the length of a joint.

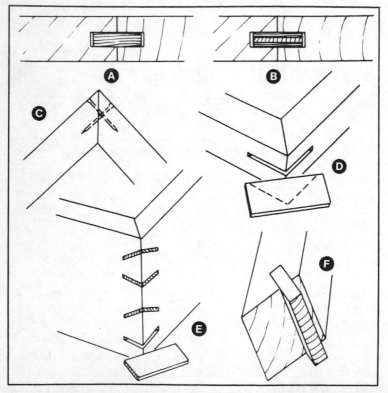

Fig. 8-10. Joints can be strengthened (A,B) with cross-grained pieces let in (C,D,E,F).

Miters are simple to cut, but the plain diagonal surfaces are too much across the grain for satisfactory gluing alone to hold. In a picture frame, there could be thin nails or pins in each direction (Fig. 8-10C), but they provide little strength. One way of making this joint stronger, either for a picture or in cabinet construction, is to cut across the corner and glue in a strip of wood with its grain across the joint (Fig. 8-10D). For light construction, this could be a piece of veneer in a saw cut. Otherwise cut a wider groove for thicker wood.

In a deeper mitered corner, there could be several pieces of veneer in saw cuts and they might come at alternate angles to give something of a dovetail effect (Fig. 8-10E). Of course, the edges of the veneers would show on the surface. If this is to be avoided, a spline could be fitted the other way (Fig. 8-10F). Keep the grooves towards the inside of the joint to avoid the risk of breaking out the thinner edge. In this and in other splined joints, let the spline be slightly shallower than the combined depths of the grooves so that it does not prevent the main surfaces meeting when the joint is pulled together.

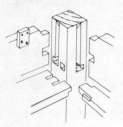

Chapter 9
Basic Steps
For Turning,
Carving and Veneering

In production work, any turning would be done by a specialist wood turner and any carving would be done by a specialist wood carver. Both would follow the cabinetmaker's instructions, but they would employ their specialized skills to produce work of a quality that would usually be of higher standard than he could produce. Similarly, any veneering would be done by a specialist. However, this was a craft that many cabinetmakers included in their own work.

If wood turning and carving are to be carried to an advanced stage, instructions for each would require separate books. Only sufficient information is included here to show the cabinetmaker the basic steps so that he can include turning and carving in his work without the need to go to a specialist for the simpler processes. That is all that are needed in many cases. Further information can be found in TAB book No. 1044, *The Woodturner's Bible*.

TURNING

Round articles are produced with hand-held tools on a lathe (which rotates the wood). It is a hand process more than a mechanical one and there is plenty of scope for a craftsman to show his skill. A lathe need not be very complicated and for most purposes it is better for being simple.

The important part is the headstock (Fig. 9-1A) where a shaft takes its drive from a motor. Its bearings should be as free of

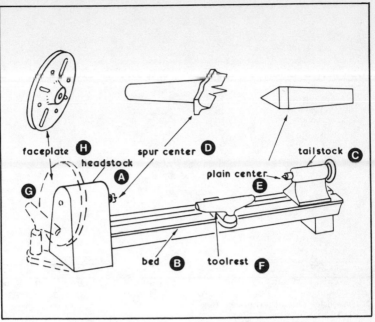

Fig. 9-1. A wood turning lathe is of simple, but rigid, construction.

vibrations as possible. At one or both ends, the shaft is threaded to take fittings that drive the wood.

The headstock is mounted on the bed (Fig. 9-1B). This can be a parallel flat or round piece or a single large round rod or tube. The bed should be straight and stiff. Also on it is the tailstock (Fig. 9-1C). It has a center at the same height as the headstock spindle. It can slide and be locked at any position on the bed. A bed long enough to give a capacity of over 30 inches allows table legs to be turned.

Drive at the headstock is made with some form of spur center. It locates the wood and has teeth to dig in (Fig. 9-1D). At the tailstock, there is a plain center (Fig. 9-1E) or a live center that revolves with the wood. Tools are used on a T-rest (Fig. 9-1F). It can be moved about the bed and locked in place with the actual rest adjustable in height and angle.

For bowls and similar large diameter things, the limit of size is determined by the height of the centers above the bed. This can be described by the largest diameter or radius that can be cleared. Some beds have a gap near the headstock to give a greater clearance, but a better arrangement is to allow for bowls to be turned at the outboard end of the headstock (Fig. 9-1G) with another mount-

139

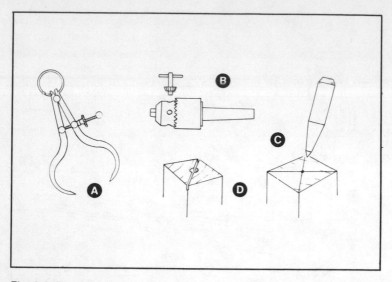

Fig. 9-2. Round work is checked with calipers (A). A tailstock drill chuck (B) makes central holes. Square stock is carefully centered (C) and prepared for the lathe centers (D).

ing for the tool rest there. There are several devices for holding shallow large diameter work, but the standard one is a faceplate with many holes for screws (Fig. 9-1H).

Wood turning tools are gouges and chisels. They are longer in both blades and handles than ordinary bench tools. Gouges are the roughing tools. They are also needed for some finishing processes. Chisels are mostly used for smoothing after working to shape with gouges.

Wood turning gouges are in many widths. A ½-inch one will do most general turning, but a ¼-inch one will be needed for small hollows. The end of the tool is ground outside and given a rounded end (Fig. 2-9G). Chisels are also made in many widths, but a ½-inch one will suit most purposes. The end is skew and bevelled both sides (Fig. 2-9H). Sharpening on the oilstone should be at the ground angle so that there are no second bevels. A parting tool (Fig. 2-9J) cuts directly into the revolving wood for deep grooves as well as for cutting off.

Calipers (Fig. 9-2A) are needed for checking diameters. A drill chuck to mount in the tailstock (Fig. 9-2B) allows holes to be drilled centrally in turned work. It is possible to use the lathe as a drilling machine for other work as well. This is particularly true if the drill chuck can be mounted on the headstock spindle.

Most of the woods used for cabinetmaking can be turned. The close-grained ones are better than the open-grained ones and beech turns more easily than oak. Harder woods are better for fine detail. Some softwoods need care or they will break out.

Wood for turning between centers should be square. Most woods can be turned from square. If there seems much risk of splintering, the corners can be planed off to make it roughly octagonal. Mark the center at each end and make a dot with a center punch (Fig. 9-2C). For a two-prong driving center, there could be a shallow saw cut across the center (Fig. 9-2D). Put the wood in the lathe with the tailstock adjusted to bring its center tightly into the wood. If it is a plain center, put a spot of grease on it. There might be wear at the center during turning, so tighten it occasionally.

Set the tool rest to clear the wood and just below center height. Hold the gouge with one hand on it at the tool rest and the other on the handle. It might be sufficient to have your thumb over the tool rest or you might have to put your hand on top for a heavy cut. Start the lathe and advance the tool to take off the high spots of the wood. Move it along as well as in and aim to reduce the wood to a cylinder. At first you could scrape by pointing the tool towards the center (Fig. 9-3A), but you get a better cut if the tool points

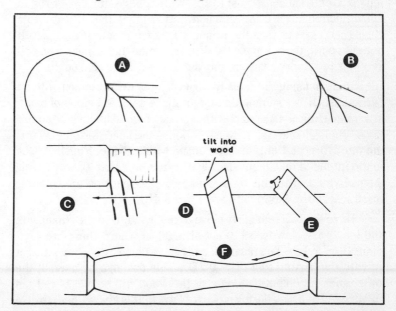

Fig. 9-3. Using a tool near horizontal scrapes (A, B), sloping it up pares, while a sideways movement slices as well. In shaped work cut toward the thinner parts (C, D, E, F).

141

more around the curve (Fig. 9-3B). You will also get a better surface if the gouge is tilted towards the direction of cut along the wood so that its side is working with more of a slicing action (Fig. 9-3C).

On the practice piece, the chisel action can be learned on the cylinder. For shaped work, the chisel is not needed until after shaping with gouges. More care is needed in handling a chisel to avoid digging in and to keep the cut smooth. Slope the chisel in the direction you want to cut and keep the shorter edge toward you (Fig. 9-3D). It can be turned over and used either way along the wood.

Approach the wood with the bevel of the chisel rubbing on the surface and the center of the cutting edge over the highest part of the circumference. Rock the chisel on the rest so that the cutting edge enters the wood and then begin to slice along (Fig. 9-3E). Use both hands to control the movement and the angle of the tool. It might not matter if the lower corner of the edge enters the wood, but if the top corner does it will dig in and spoil the surface. Aim to always keep the long corner out of the wood. Practice slicing in this way in both directions. Change hands the other way.

There are many decorative spindles with hollows in the length. Get the shape almost to size with a gouge. It is best to use a slicing action toward the thinnest part (Fig. 9-3F). Change to a chisel and slice toward the thinnest part from both directions. If you cut uphill, then stop the lathe and examine the surface. You will see that the fibers tear out and the general finish is rough.

Steps in using the tools to turn a shape are best seen with an example such as a spindle that might make a leg or be one of many in a frame (Fig. 9-4A). Start with a piece of wood an inch or so too long. It helps to have some waste wood at the headstock end. Turn the wood to a parallel cylindrical shape with a gouge. Finish almost to the intended maximum size. Use a rule or a strip of wood with the main measurements on it and a pencil to mark on the rotating wood where the key points are (Fig. 9-4B).

Have the tool rest fairly close to the wood. Use the chisel with the long point downward to cut straight in where there are divisions (Fig. 9-4C). The tailstock end can be trued by cutting straight in with the parting tool (Fig. 9-4D). This can also be used at the other end, but do not go too far or the wood will be weakened and might bend or break during other tool work. It is always best to deal with parts away from the ends first while the ends are large and able to resist strain.

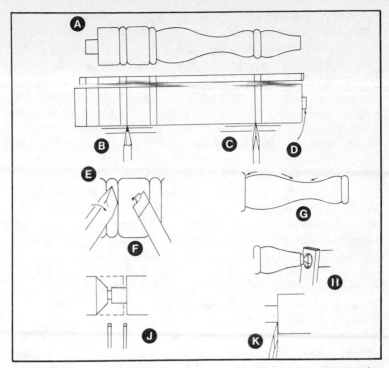

Fig. 9-4. Use a rod to mark marching parts (A,B,C,D). Cut in beads with the edge of a chisel and use it to pare surface smooth (E,F). A parting tool cuts straight in, but edges should be trued with a chisel (G,H,J,K). If a part has to fit a hole, drill a scrap piece of wood for testing.

Beads can be dealt with. Use the short side of the chisel and pare with a curving motion from the center of a bead into the cut (Fig. 9-4E). Do this both ways until you have satisfactory curves. Take off enough with the chisel to remove any of the rough gouge marks. Use the chisel on the parallel parts to smooth them (Fig. 9-4F).

Rough the tapered center part to shape with a gouge. Follow with a chisel and go from high to low (Fig. 9-4G). If the tailstock end is to fit into a hole, drill a test hole (with the bit to be used) in a thin piece of scrap wood and use this to try as you turn to size. If it is large enough, it can hang on the tailstock center (Fig. 9-4H). Otherwise, the tailstock must be withdrawn at intervals so that you can test with it. The dowel at the other end cannot be tested in this way. Instead, take the parting tool in some way at the shoulder and at its end. Then remove some waste with a gouge. Follow by paring with a chisel (Fig. 9-4J). Some of the excess at the end might have to be cut away to allow the chisel to be taken in at the correct angle.

A parting tool leaves a rough surface across the end grain. If it is important that a shoulder be smooth, cut on the waste side of the line with the parting tool. Then use a chisel with its long point downward and one bevel in line with the shoulder (Fig. 9-4K) to cut the end smooth.

Careful work with tools, particularly paring with a chisel that is really sharp, should result in a good surface that only needs a minimum of sanding with a fine grit paper. Much can be done to improve poor work by sanding with coarser grit, but a good turner gets results with his tools and only has a little use for abrasives.

When you are satisfied with the spindle, turn down the bottom to the center, or close to it, and take the parting tool in at the headstock end to cut off the surplus there. For the best end on something where it will show, use the long point of the chisel and reduce the wood progressively until it is quite small. Then remove the wood from the lathe and saw it off so that there is enough left to trim with a chisel and by sanding. For something of a large diameter, such as a bowl or base for a lamp standard, the wood has to be cut circular and mounted on a faceplate. A piece of scrap wood can be mounted with screws on the faceplate. Then the piece to be turned can be glued on with paper in the joint (Fig. 9-5A). After turning, a knife or chisel will prise away the work, then surplus paper can be sanded off. If screw holes in the base will not matter, the screws can go through a piece of plywood into the work (Fig. 9-5B).

Turn the outside of a true circle by scraping with a gouge (Fig. 9-5C). Because the grain will usually be across the disk, trying to cut by sloping the gouge up will cause it to dig in where the grain opposes it. On the face, use the gouge to rough the surface to the shape you want (Fig. 9-5D).

Ordinary turning chisels cannot be used on faceplate work. Instead, use scrapers that are sharpened to an obtuse angle (Fig. 9-5E). The edge should be keen and frequently touched up. Have the tool rest slightly above center and slope the tool downward (Fig. 9-5F), experiment with the angle until the tool takes off fine shavings (not just dust). For heavy work, there are very stout scrapers. For much turning, the ends of ordinary chisel section steel can be ground to shape. Much can be done with a moderately curved end (Fig. 9-5G) and one with a straight end having its corners taken off (Fig. 9-5H).

If a hole is needed at the center of a disk, it can be turned with a pointed chisel (Fig. 9-5J). There might have to be more sanding of a

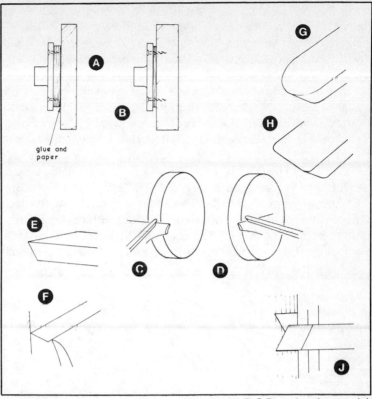

Fig. 9-5. Large discs are turned on a faceplate (A,B,C,D) and surface work is done with scrapers (E, F, G, H, J)

base or bowl because of the grain running across causing tearing up at two parts of a circle. If the lathe can be reversed, some of this roughness can be removed with a tool. Otherwise, sanding with progressively finer grits will be required.

CARVING

There have been times when furniture was carved extensively. In most fine cabinetwork today, carving is confined to borders or central panels and the covering of large areas with carving would only be needed in reproduction work based on one of the more flamboyant periods. Some carving can be done with ordinary knives and chisels, but for more decorative work, special carving tools are needed (Fig. 2-13).

Making molded edges can be regarded as a form of carving whether it is done with hand tools or by machine. The molding

145

normally goes right through, but it can be stopped and varied to form what is called *wagon bevelling*. The term comes from wheelwrights doing it on edges of parts of a cart or waggon. The basic design is a stopped chamfer (Fig. 9-6A). For hand work, the pattern should be marked in pencil. Then the ends are cut in and the waste is chiselled from between them. A spindle molder could cut a chamfer, leaving rounded ends (Fig. 9-6B), which could be altered to a bevel with a chisel. The end could step down (Fig. 9-6C). Small nicks could be made further along, but leave a short length of uncut corner (Fig. 9-6D) because a point would be too weak. Cuts could be curved and a bead shape cut (Fig. 9-6E). Edge bevelling should be with a 45 degree section (Fig. 9-6F).

Another form of decoration, sometimes worked near an edge, is done with a gouge sharpened on the outside. Patterns are built up from a series of basic cuts. The gouge is pushed straight in and then a scooping cut is made towards that cut (Fig. 9-7A). For a series of

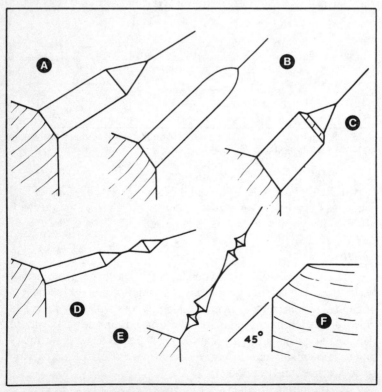

Fig. 9-6. Wagon bevelling can decorate edges: (A) basic design; (B) rounded edges; (C) stepped down end; (D) uncut corner; (E) 45 degree section.

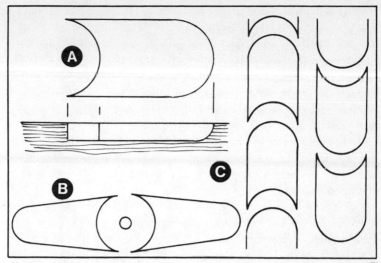

Fig. 9-7. A pattern of gouge cuts will make surface decorations: (A) scoop cut; (B) space evenly; (C) central pattern.

cuts, use pencil guidelines and space the parts evenly (Fig. 9-7B). The cuts need not have parallel sides and can be brought to a central pattern around a shallow hole (Fig. 9-7C). Gouge cuts can be arranged in other patterns, but they are usually most effective as narrow bands around a panel or parallel with an edge.

Another treatment that is not full carving is incising with a knife, a small gouge or a V parting tool. A pattern of lines are cut in to build up a border around a panel. When stained and polished, the lines tend to darken so they show up. A gouge or V tool will make a groove (Fig. 9-8A), but a knife cutting straight in does not make a very obvious mark. It is better to make two knife cuts at a slight angle to each other to remove a sliver of wood (Fig. 9-8B).

Incised patterns are usually made up of straight lines (Fig. 9-8C), but curves can be used to form stylized flowers (Fig. 9-8D). The best results are obtained with sharp tools used with good pressure to get the cut you want in one stroke. This is better than many light cuts which might not always coincide.

A further step in incising is to follow a pattern, such as the outlines of foliage, but keep it within a cut border. The pattern can then be made prominent by punching the background around it within the border (Fig. 9-8E). Punches with many designs on the end can be obtained, but what is needed is a generally matt finish and a suitable punch could be made by filing grooves across the end of a steel rod (Fig. 9-8F).

147

Most of the work so far described can be done with ordinary tools, if carving tools are unavailable, but what might be regarded as proper carving in relief needs a carver's gouges and chisels. The amount of relief on furniture will be quite shallow, but it gives the work a three-dimensional effect. The earlier methods are mostly surface decoration. Full three-dimensional carving of figures and similar designs are rarely used in cabinetwork. If they are, they would not be the work of a cabinetmaker.

A relief carving can be panels within borders. The background is lowered, then the actual carving is worked on its surface as well as around its edges. A modern aid to this sort of carving is a powered router. It can be used to lower the background, but this should not be done to the full depth so that the bottom can be given a tooled finish. Carved work in fine cabinetry should show only hand-tooled surfaces. Without a router, the background can be lowered by gouge work. A maple leaf is an example of low relief carving. Draw the outline of the leaf and its border (Fig. 9-9A). If a router is to be used, keep the cuts inside the lines. Leave enough wood along them for the use of hand tools. Cut around the border with a V tool or a deep gouge. Go around the outline of the leaf in

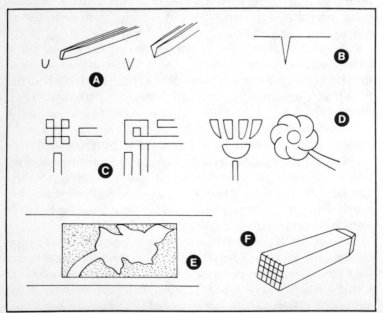

Fig. 9-8. Lines can be incised and the background punched in simple carving: (A) groove; (B) knife cuts; (C) incised patterns; (D,E) stylized patterns; (F) matt finish.

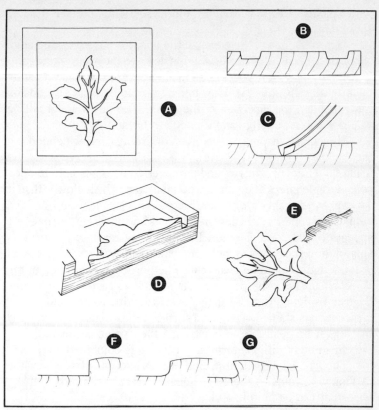

Fig. 9-9. For carved surface decoration the background is lowered (B,C,D,E) before the surfaces are cut with gouges (E).

the same way (Fig. 9-9B), but keep just away from the line at this stage. Finer details at the leaf edge can be left to trim later.

Use a gouge to lower the background. It might have to be a curved one to get into some parts (Fig. 9-9C). Make sure the corners of the gouge are always above the surface. There is less risk of splitting if cuts are across the grain. Remove waste in a series of short cuts that curve up to the surface. When a satisfactory depth is reached, use a gouge with a flatter curve to cut away high spots and get the background to an even depth. In most circumstances, leave tool marks showing. Do not try to scrape or sand them level.

No leaf is absolutely flat. The surface of the leaf has to be given a wavy surface with some points turned up and some turned down (Fig. 9-9D). Remove all flatness from the surface with broad shallow gouges. Mark on the veins and go around their outlines with a knife or V tool. Round them in section and taper the leaf surface in to them (Fig. 9-9E).

Cut to the line of the edges of the leaf. For strength, the edge should be a straight or curved section down to the background (Fig. 9-9F). However, it is possible to make a part of a leaf stand out by undercutting (Fig. 9-9G). How much this can be done depends on the wood and the direction of the grain. Too much undercutting would weaken the edge and cause it to break.

How much shaping can be given to a relief carving depends on the thickness of wood available as well as the skill of the carver. By using the effect of shadows and perspective, it is possible to get a considerable effect of depth in wood that is much shallower than it appears to be. Leaves, or other things, can be made to appear from behind each other by sloping the surfaces and undercutting one that appears to pass over another. In this sort of carving, all surfaces should show the marks of tools. It would normally be wrong to sand them. Edges should be clean cut. The border and outlines of the object should have sharp angles. Then shadows cast will emphasize the shapes. Backgrounds can be gone over with a patterned punch. If the wood is stained, a punched surface tends to finish darker and that might be desirable to emphasize the carved pattern.

In some traditional furniture, carving is combined with turning. The wood is turned first. Sometimes excess is left where the carving is to come. If there is a square part, as at the top of many legs, that can be held in a vise when you are carving.

VENEERING

Veneer is very thin wood which has to be attached with adhesive to solid wood or plywood. The attraction of veneer is that it can be made from wood that would be unsuitable for use in solid form and it will show the beauty of grain. A particularly attractively marked piece of wood can be cut into a very large number of veneers. The pattern will be available many times instead of just once as a solid piece of wood. Veneer can be used to give an attractive appearance to wood that is quite satisfactory structurally, but which does not produce a worthwhile furniture finish.

Plywood is made of veneers which are cut with a knife while the log is rotating in a sort of lathe. The veneer could be of a considerable length. However, the surface pattern would usually not be very attractive due to the circumferencial cutting. Some veneers for applying to furniture are cut in this way when their grain produces a satisfactory pattern. Another method of cutting uses a knife in a similar way, but the wood swings over it in an arc in a direction that takes advantage of the most attractive grain. Most veneers used in cabinetry are produced in this way and they are little more than paper thick. Some wood cannot be cut with a knife so veneers are sawn. They are thicker and more expensive because much wood is cut to waste due to thickness of the saw kerf.

Veneers should be stored flat between boards. They will absorb moisture quickly. Have them in the same atmosphere as the wood they will be applied to long enough for the moisture content to stabilize. Veneer is often applied with its grain across that of the base wood. It is important that it should be a wood that is not subject to much expansion and contraction. Most softwoods are unsuitable for veneering. However, yellow pine is a stable one that can be used. In traditional furniture, plain Honduras mahogany was used. Today it is generally better to use plywood or other manufactured board which will not move with changes in humidity.

If one side of a piece of solid wood is veneered, there is a tendency for it to pull hollow towards the veneered side. If it is built into framework that supports it, any tendency to warp is resisted. Otherwise both sides of the wood should be veneered to counteract the fault. The reverse veneer can be a cheaper plain one. As with other gluing, there would be an unsatisfactory bond for veneer to the end grain. If end grain or the edge of plywood has to be veneered, fit a solid wood lip there first.

Traditional veneering was done with natural glues that had to be heated before use. They were not waterproof and surplus glue could be removed with warm water. Modern glues are suitable, but they should spread evenly without lumps and not get tacky too soon so that the veneer can be moved as the joint is made.

The background wood should be flat and free from blemishes. Any flaws will show through the thin veneer. In traditional work, the background was roughened to give a better grip to the glue. The tool for this is a toothing plane. This is a small plane with a single iron having a finely serrated edge set almost upright. When used in crossing directions, it will break up the surface with fine scratches. A similar effect can be obtained by dragging a fine-toothed saw sideways across the wood. If the base wood is absorbent, it is advisable to put on a thin coat of glue first and let it dry. Then apply more glue and lay the veneer.

Veneers have to be pressed down tightly so that the glue makes contact all over and any air is squeezed out. This is done with a veneer hammer (Fig. 9-10A). It is made with a strip of brass about ⅛-inch thick let into the edge of a piece of wood and a rod attached as a handle. Despite its name, the "hammer" is pressed and not swung.

To lay a piece of veneer, spread glue evenly on the base and put the veneer in place. Stroke from the center outward with the side of your hand. Dampen the surface with warm water. Hold the hammer handle with one hand while pressing above the blade with the other. Use it with plenty of pressure from the center of the veneer outward in a zig zag motion toward the edges (Fig. 9-10B). This will push out air and surplus glue.

Thin veneer is best cut with a knife and metal straightedge. Do not use scissors. There are very fine veneer saws, but they are better for use with thicker veneers. If two veneers have to be cut to meet on a surface, one can be put over the other and both cut with a knife (Fig. 9-10C), then remove the waste and press the edges together.

Because veneers are cut in multiples from the same piece of wood, it is usually possible to obtain matching pieces so that patterns can be built up. The center of a panel can be divided so that one-half is a mirror image of the other (Fig. 9-11A). The grain of veneers does not have to follow the long way as it would in solid wood. Drawer fronts and the edges of plinths and other narrow parts can have the veneer with its grain the short way.

A panel can be arranged divided into four sections with each section cut diagonally. This could produce a border having its grain the short way (Fig. 9-11B). The veneers can be cut and assembled together before being glued to the back board.

Draw the intended pattern to the full size as a guide when cutting the veneers. A cardboard template of one panel can be used to mark the four diagonal pieces, but cut them slightly oversize. Plane the meeting surfaces for an accurate fit. Grip the veneer

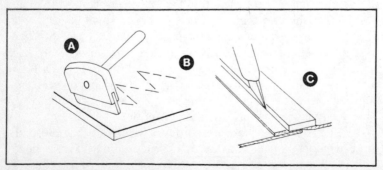

Fig. 9-10. Veneer is squeezed down with a "hammer" (A,B). Overlapping pieces may be cut together with a knife (C).

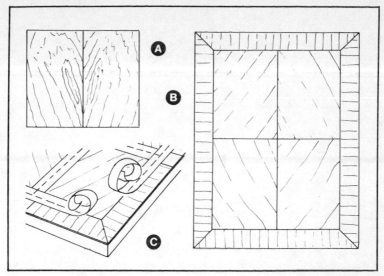

Fig. 9-11. Veneer allows a design to be built up using grain patterns: (A) center panel; (B) diagonal cuts; (C) tape the surfaces.

between two boards with only a little projecting and use a low angle block plane. Bring the central cross together, face upward and join the pieces with transparent tape of masking tape along the joints.

The border can be added after the central section is glued to the background, after trimming edges straight and scraping away glue, or it can be added to the veneer assembly first. Most woods will not cut very wide veneers, so there might have to be joints in the border. If they are cut straight and the grain matches, the joints will not show. The miters are best cut by putting one piece over the other and cutting through with a knife. Any error of angle should be cancelled out. Have the border slightly too wide so that it can be planed to match the background after fitting. Tape all parts together (Fig. 9-11C) and leave the tape on the surface until after the veneer has been pressed down. If it is carefully peeled off before the glue has set, any slight errors in joints can be corrected by sliding the veneers.

Other patterns can be built up over a drawing. If there are curves involved, some can be cut with a knife through two thicknesses or a fine fretsaw can be used. The waste removed by it would not be enough to matter.

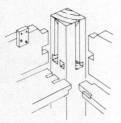

Chapter 10
Finishing

Almost all cabinetwork is given a surface treatment. Not many woods can be left bare or they will deteriorate, absorb dirt and moisture and become very unattractive in appearance. It is appearance which is usually the main concern in finishing furniture woods. A few woods contain oils that will preserve them, but it is unusual for any of these to be used in furniture without being given surface protection similar to other woods.

Some furniture is given an opaque finish so that details of the woods are hidden. Colored lacquers have been used and Oriental furniture, in particular, can be seen treated in this way. In general, painted furniture is considered inferior or at least utilitarian rather than of good quality. Much of the attraction of good furniture is in the way the beauty of the grain is brought out by the finish so that the wood shows through a transparent finish. Furniture wood is usually selected because of its grain appearance and some of the energy of the cabinetmaker is directed towards making the most of this.

The quality of a finish depends to a large extent on the state of the wood surface. It is a waste of time to cover wood with a transparent finish if the surface is rough and contains flaws that have not been treated. Any liquid finish will follow the surface underneath, undulating over inequalities and allow rough points to come through and sink into defects. The final finish cannot be expected to put right an unsatisfactory surface. Work applied to getting a surface as near perfect as possible will be repaid in the quality of the finish eventually obtained.

Finishing preparations really start with planing. Use a sharp plane properly set and the surface produced will need less treatment later than if a blunt plane is carelessly used. Planing must get the wood to the shape required (usually flat). When this has been achieved, sharpen a smoothing plane iron, set it fine and skim over the whole surface.

Some woods that should have involved grain patterns for their appearance might not finish absolutely smooth from the plane. Follow with a scraper to remove roughness, but also scrape surrounding parts to avoid a hollow forming where the roughness has been removed.

Follow by sanding. There are places where power sanding is acceptable, but the final sanding before applying a finish should be by hand. If there is a good surface after the plane and scraper, go straight into hand sanding. There are several abrasive papers available and most are in a large range of grits. Some manufactured grits are suitable, but avoid others that are better on metal or plastics. Garnet paper is suitable for hand work on wood. The methods of grading vary. A medium type might be marked "0" "F2" or "80." There should not be any need for a coarser grade. Finer grades are indicated by "3/0," "4/0" etc. in the first system. In the second system there are "1½," "1" and "0." In the third system, numbers get larger as the grit gets finer. For final sanding, 150 will do ("4/0" or "0" in the other systems).

Abrasive paper comes in sheets about 11 inch by 9 inch. For hand use, it is best torn into quarters (Fig. 10-1A). Never use it loose on a flat surface. There are cork rubbers available, but a block of wood can be cut to suit. For the best support, face it with rubber or soft plastic (Fig. 10-1B). Make it a size that allows the wrapped paper to be gripped. There are special sanders in which the paper can be clipped, but a plain block allows you to move the paper around and make the best use of it.

Most modern abrasive paper has the grit bonded to the backing paper with a waterproof glue. If you are unsure about this, warm the paper before use to drive off any moisture absorbed in a non-waterproof glue. Otherwise the grit might wear off the paper quickly.

It is important that any marks made by sanding should be in the same direction as the grain. Even with the first grit, cross-grain scratches that are invisible on the bare wood might show up through a transparent gloss finish. This means that if it is necessary to sand in any direction other than with the grain, there must be more sanding along the grain to remove those scratches. If an orbital or other sander is used, make sure that hand sanding removes the cross-grain marks.

Usually, two grades of grit are used. The second finer grade must remove all marks left by the medium grade. After using the medium grade, wipe off the surface to remove any particles of loose grit that remain. Otherwise they will be rubbed in to repeat larger scratches under the finer paper.

The tiny fibers which sanding is to remove might not always rub away, but some might bend. This depends on the wood. Moisten the surface with a damp cloth. Let it dry and feel it. If there are bent fibers, they will be standing up and felt as roughness. Further sanding should remove them.

Consider the situation of a part in the final assembly. Most sanding can be done after assembly and this might be the only satisfactory method when surfaces have to march. Other parts, such as some lower rails of a table, might not be easy to deal with when they are built into other parts. If something like the inner surface of a leg has a number of other pieces attached to it, its area would be broken down into parts and be difficult to sand cleanly without marking the attached parts. In these cases, sanding before assembly is advisable. If care is taken during assembly to avoid marking the surface and to avoid getting glue on the surface, only minor sanding will be needed there again.

Shaped parts will have to be sanded with the abrasive paper loose. For something like a long molded edge, a wood block shaped to the reverse of the profile will keep the paper in line. Pay

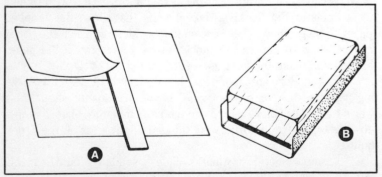

Fig. 10-1. Sheets of sanding paper are better torn than cut (A). For work on flat surfaces they should wrapped around a block (B).

attention to hollows. Roughness there will soak up more stain and finish darker than the surrounding wood.

FLAWS

Because wood is a natural material, its condition and appearance varies. This is one reason for the attractiveness of it, but sometimes there are blemishes and flaws that need treatment before you apply a finish. For the best quality furniture, choose wood that is free from flaws as far as possible. However, some flaws can be dealt with to still give a good appearance.

If wood has been knocked, the dent caused will be a compression of the fibers. Any treatment has to be directed towards expanding them again. Putting water in the dent might be all that is required. Cold water alone might not be enough. A method used by furniture restorers is to put water in the dent, then heat a spoon almost to redness and lower it into the dent. The steam produced will be driven into the wood to expand the fibers. Another way is to put a wet cloth over the dent and press a domestic iron, heated to its maximum, over it. Let the wood dry and sand it level.

If softwood is used and there are knots on the surface, they will almost certainly contain resin which will come to the top and break through many types of finish. This can be stopped by applying shellac over the knot. Use a thin shellac/alcohol mixture and apply more than one coat. Sand lightly. This is particularly important under paint, but some clear finishes might act like shellac in stopping the resin.

Cracks and holes will have to be stopped. There are several compounds available for stopping and it is better to buy one than to mix your own according to an old formula. Some stoppings can be used on bare wood and they will take stain or polish the same as the wood—but many stoppings would finish a different color. Some are made in many colors and are used after the wood has been stained. Follow the maker's instructions.

Water putty and wood compound are stoppings that might be suitable for use before staining, but stick shellac and plastic fillers (sometimes called beaumontage) are colored and must be used after staining.

Press in stoppings with a knife or screwdriver. Try to fill the space so that there is no air left in it. If it is a stopping that will contract as it hardens, leave it standing a little above the wood so that it can be sanded level.

The ordinary stoppings do no more than fill holes or cracks. They have little strength. Plastic Wood is a compound that set with some strength. If it is necessary to repair an edge that has splintered, or there is some other place where the stopping needs to be shaped at the surface, besides having to fill a space, it is possible to use Plastic Wood and cut or sand it to shape. If a joint fits badly and there is a gap where strength as well as filling is required, glue can be mixed with sawdust to a consistency of putty and pressed into the space. The sawdust causes the glue to bond without getting weakened by crazing (as it would do in a wide space if used alone).

If the color of wood varies it is generally better to darken a pale part with stain than to try to lighten a dark part by bleaching. However, sometimes bleaching is the only way of getting an even color. Laundry bleach can be used. Dilute according to instructions, but this will probably be about 12 parts water and 1 part bleach. Use with a cloth until the color is right. Wash off surplus bleach and allow the wood to dry. With this or any other bleach, wear rubber gloves and avoid getting on clothing. Avoid metal containers. They might cause the bleach to discolor the wood.

FILLERS

All wood is porous and has tiny cells breaking the surface. In many woods, these are invisible. In others, they are large enough to allow any finishing liquid to sink in. In some woods, such as oak, there are quite large gaps that look like cracks between grain lines. These woods need filling. Without a filler, any surface treatment would sink into the spaces and the finish would not be flat.

Fillers have something in common with stoppings and there are some stoppings that can be diluted to make fillers. Many hardwoods do not need filling, but if there is any doubt there are liquid fillers to use. The definitely open-grained woods need treatment with paste fillers. Some fillers can be used before the wood is stained. Others are colored and intended to be used after staining.

Filler can be bought already prepared or it can be a powder to mix with linseed oil or other binder. If it is colored, let it be slightly darker than the wood rather than lighter. To ensure an even color, mix thoroughly and have enough for the whole job. With paste filler, spread it all over the wood thickly. When the surface dulls, rub it with a coarse cloth across the grain to force the filler into gaps. Follow with a soft cloth along the grain to remove excess filler. Use a stiff-haired brush in corners or recesses. Leave the surface for a day proceeding. Sand it lightly.

Liquid filler can be bought or paste filler can be diluted with

Table 10-1. Wood Fillers.

Paste Filler	Medium Filler	Liquid Filler	No Filler
Ash	Butternut	Bass	Aspen
Chestnut	Korina	Beech	Cypress
Elm	Mahogany	Brich	Ebony
Hickory	Rosewood	Cedar	Gaboon
Lacewood	Sapele	Fir	Hemlock
Oak	Tigerwood	Gum	Holly
Padouk	Walnut	Maple	Magnolia
Teak		Poplar	Pine
		Sycamore	Redwood
			Spruce

benzene or turpentine. Brush it on and wipe it after it has dulled. Shellac can be used instead of a liquid filler. In both cases, more than one coat might be advisable and light sanding should follow drying. Many woods do not require filling and a varnish or shellac finish can act as its own filler on all but the more open woods. Table 10-1 shows the filling requirements of some woods.

STAINING

Wood does not always have to be stained. Many woods are quite attractive with a clear finish over their natural color. However, there are several woods that are normally stained. Oak is usually made a darker brown and mahogany has its redness increased. These are so much the usual treatments that many people regard the stained appearance as the natural color. For most furniture, staining should emphasize the original color. There are some examples of a complete change of color, but it is a safer choice to have a darker shade of the original color. It is possible to stain an inferior wood to look the same color as a better one, but this does not disguise the grain. Anyone familiar with woods could see that the wood was not what it was purporting to be. However, woods of an unattractive color can have their appearance improved by staining and it is sometimes necessary to use stain to match up parts of different colors.

Stain differs from paint in altering the color of the wood without obscuring the grain. Paints remain on the surface. A stain should penetrate the wood. It should flow on evenly. Some stains that are quick drying are different to get even.

A stain consists of a pigment in a solvent. The solvent can be oil, water or spirit (alcohol). Water stains are the least expensive, but oil stains are the most popular. Spirit stain dries quickly and is only for small parts or touching up.

The solvent in an oil stain is a light oil such as benzene, naptha or turpentine. A large range of wood colors are available. Brush on oil stain so as to cover the whole surface quickly. A cloth can be used to wipe off surplus and to get the color right. With any stain it is advisable to work from the least important to the more important parts. This usually means finishing with a top. Work so that you are looking towards a light. Move the furniture about so that the surface you are working on is horizontal and looks for runs from one surface onto another. Have a cloth ready for wiping away any excess. End grain will soak up stain quickly and become darker than a surface. Be ready to wipe away there. Thin shellac on end grain will prevent it from soaking too much.

Dried oil stain will look slightly darker than it will after a clear finish has been put over it. More than one coat can be put on, but there is no satisfactory way of lightening a color that has come out too dark.

Water stain comes as a powder to mix with hot water. Pour the powder in and stir and then let it cool. It should keep almost indefinitely. Concentrated stain can be mixed and thinned as required. Brush the stain on and use it plentifully along the grain. Two coats of a light stain will get a better result than one coat of a dark stain. Do all the staining of a piece of furniture at one time and quickly. Splashes on bare wood that dry are difficult to disguise.

Alcohol stain comes as a colored powder to dissolve. There are colors such as blue and green that are not usually associated with wood, but which can be employed in special effects. Spraying will give an even finish, but the stain dries too quickly for brushing on a large surface to give an even effect. Things like picture molding that can be brushed in a single action can be spirit stained. Try to always follow a wet edge when brushing this stain. Brushing against stain that has dried will show unevenly.

Some old furniture was given its color by chemical means. This is probably not worthwhile today as prepared stains will give similar results more conveniently. Rubber gloves and old clothes should be worn when you are experimenting with chemical finishes.

Oak and chestnut can be given a deep brown color with ammonia. This is done by using a box or cabinet in which the item could be enclosed while a tray of strong ammonia is allowed to evaporate in this confined space. This is a rather hazardous method because of the strong fumes. A similar effect can be obtained with very dilute ammonia brushed on in the open air. The "fumed oak" appearance is a warm brown different from anything obtainable with stains. It does not work with other woods.

Permanganate of potash is a safe chemical to handle. It is bought as crystals to dissolve in water. When brushed on, it will turn many woods to a medium brown. However, it is necessary to experiment with scrap pieces of particular woods to see what the result will be. Household lye and some domestic cleaning powders dissolved in water turn some woods brown.

For most furniture that needs staining, the best results today are probably obtained by using oil stain.

POLISHES

A protective film can be put over the surface of wood in many ways. Usually, appearance is improved by giving it a shine that can be anything from a slight sheen to a high gloss. The protective film is normally hard enough to withstand wear in ordinary use, but some have to be renewed periodically. Too hard a finish might also be brittle. There is a risk of knocks causing cracking, while expansion of the wood underneath might damage the finish. It is better for the finish to be a little softer and slightly flexible. Not all finishes will withstand heat or moisture. There have been many changes in wood finishes. Some modern ones used in quantity production are inappropriate to fine cabinetwork. Some older ones can be regarded as having been superseded, but they might still be the correct choice for some furniture.

A knowledge of many finishes will allow the correct one to be chosen for a particular piece of furniture. Some of the traditional hand applied finishes will give a more satisfying result on handmade furniture than a quick action modern sprayed finish. Some of the oldest furniture has acquired its sheen or patina with age. It might have started with animal or vegetable fat rubbed in and it might have been rubbed later with wax or oil, but the quality of the present surface is mostly due to handling. Natural fats from the skin and rubbing with clothing will have produced any quality of finish it now has. Obviously, the sort of finish that has taken centuries to develop cannot be reproduced quickly, but the nearest modern treatment is with wax or oil.

OIL AND WAX

Mahogany and similar close-grained furniture woods are better treated with one of the following methods. However, oak, elm and other coarser woods were given oil or wax finishes in Europe. Linseed oil, rubbed in with sufficient vigour, can eventually build up a good finish. There have to be several rubbings, with time between for drying. It might be a year before the result can be regarded as satisfactory.

For this treatment, mix linseed oil with a little turpentine and warm the mixture by standing the container in a bowl of hot water. Heating direct would burn the oil. Put on plenty of oil with a soft cloth. Let it soak in. Rub it hard to fill the grain. Wipe off any surplus oil. To get a luster, rub the surface with a fairly coarse piece of cloth or burlap. The coarseness helps to generate heat by friction and set the surface. For a flat surface it helps to wrap the cloth around the brick. Leave this for about two days before repeating the process and do this as often as necessary to get a good result.

The rather long overall time can be reduced if varnish is mixed with the linseed oil/turpentine mixture. One or two coats of this will seal the wood. Additional coats will remain on the surface and build up a polish more quickly. Up to 50 percent varnish can be used in the first coats, but at later stages it should be much less.

This is very similar to polishes sold as *teak oil* or *tung oil*. Follow the maker's instructions, but they are applied in a similar way and rubbed to produce a luster. No oil treatment lasts indefinitely and it has to be restored occasionally. For some furniture this treatment and the extra work will be considered worthwhile.

Polishing with wax might be as old as oil polishing. Beeswax was probably the original type used. Today, wax polishes are mixtures. Several paste polishes sold for use on furniture are basically wax mixtures. Turpentine is used as a solvent to soften them or make them into a liquid state. Paraffin is too soft for polishing, but it can be used to fill grain before polishing with other waxes. An important ingredient of prepared wax polishes is usually *carnauba wax*. This is a product of a Brazilian palm and is one of the hardest waxes known. *Cadelilla* is similar to beeswax and comes from a Mexican shrub. *Ceresine* is a modern wax derived from hydrocarbon that mixes with carnauba.

Starting from bare wood could take at least as long with wax as with oil. An equally good result can be obtained by preventing the wood from absorbing the wax first by filling the grain and following with a coat of shellac or varnish. Then lightly sand to remove any gloss, but not so much as to expose bare wood.

A paste wax polish can be rubbed on directly with a cloth. However, it is better to have the wax between several layers of wide meshed cloth. Rub in with a circular motion and finally in the direction of the grain. At first, keep the rubs light so that an even layer of wax is left. Leave this for about 10 minute so that the wax partially dries. Then rub it in a similar manner with a soft cloth. Repeat after at least an hour and subsequently as needed.

It is rubbing that produces a shine on wax. The harder waxes will produce a better shine, but they require more rubbing. It might help to use a soft scrub brush on the wax before using a cloth. Heat generated by friction is needed to harden the wax.

Polishing of wax and oil has been traditionally done by hand and this cannot be completely avoided. A polishing buff driven by an electric drill can be used to lessen the amount of physical effort. However, hand work is better while the wax is soft and the buff may follow when the surface is at least partially hard. Keep the buff moving and experiment with the amount of pressure. It is not always easy to ensure an even polish with power polishing.

In modern furniture finishing, wax is probably more useful in following other polishes. Wax can be used as the final coat in first polishing or be used to revive a finish after the furniture has been in use. If varnish is followed by wax in a first polishing, it is advisable to remove the gloss before waxing. It can be sanded with abrasive paper, but pumice or other abrasive powder could be used on a cloth. Some liquid or semi-liquid furniture polishes available today are intended to be used for reviving polished surfaces. Read what the makers claim they are for. Most would be unsuitable for a first polishing as they are only intended for use over an already built-up finish. Because of their chemical make up, some would be unsuitable for following with a conventional polish. A polish intended for use on a floor might be described as a wax, but most are unsuitable for furniture. Check the description. If furniture is not mentioned, avoid the polish.

SHELLAC

Shellac comes for India in the form of flakes and is dissolved readily in denatured alcohol. You can mix your own or buy it already in liquid form. It can be described by its "cut." The strongest concentration is 5-pound cut. This means that 5 pounds of shellac has been dissolved in a gallon of alcohol. Weaker cuts are down to a 2-pound cut. The strongest concentration can be diluted to make a weaker mixture.

Normal shellac has a transparent orange color. This is suitable for darker woods. If a lighter wood is not to be darkened by the finish, there is a white or bleached shellac. However, it does not store well. Orange shellac will keep better. Both are affected by dampness, but the white more than the orange shellac. Neither has a very good resistance to heat.

The best known furniture use for shellac is as *French polish*. This has to be applied with a shellac/alcohol mixture that is free from resin. Some denatured alcohol contains resin. This does not matter for brushed shellac, but if French polishing is intended it is better to buy a mixture described as "French polish" (about a 2½-pound cut without resin).

With alcohol as a solvent, shellac will dry quickly. It can be brushed on to fill and seal a wood surface and a second coat can follow in a short time. Brushed shellac is not really a good furniture finish. If it is to be used, many coats of a thin cut give a better finish than a few coats of a thick cut. As many as six coats can be applied in a day. Do not work the brush excessively or the rapidly drying shellac might pick up and become rough. Sand lightly between coats. Remove sanding dust with a cloth slightly dampened with alcohol. Hard shellac sands to a white powder. If it does not, that is a sign that sanding has been done too early. Put a brush in alcohol between coats and clean it at the end with alcohol.

Fine steel wool used in the direction of the grain will smooth the top coat. Brushed shellac alone might be a satisfactory finish inside a piece of cabinetwork, but for an exposed surface it would be better if finished by wax polishing.

FRENCH POLISH

There was a time when all good quality furniture in such woods as mahogany and walnut was French polished. Whether there was any special French connection is uncertain and the word is not always given a capital letter. The glowing surface obtained by French polishing is considered superior to any other gloss finish. There is a certain amount of labor involved and skill improves with practice. However, it is patience as much as skill that gets results.

French polish can be made from orange or white shellac to suit the color of the wood. It is possible to put coloring in the polish, but in most cases it is better to stain the wood to the color required first.

French polishing is done with a pad that is usually cotton batting wrapped in a piece of old cotton cloth. Use old cotton because it is then more likely to be free of lint. Have the inner piece a convenient size to grip, probably between 2 inches and 3 inches

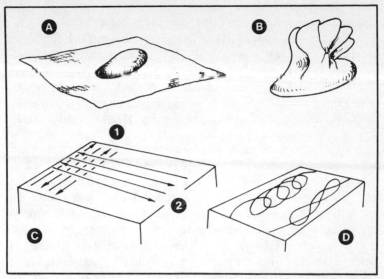

Fig. 10-2. A French-polishing rubber (A) is made to fit the hand (B) and used first straight (C) and then with a circular action (DS).

across, and use it with a cloth about 9 inches square (Fig. 10-2A). To make the pad, bring the cloth up around the batting and twist it (Fig. 10-2B). A pad can be made to last some time by keeping it in an airtight jar when not in use. Otherwise the polish hardens and the pad has to be discarded.

There are three stages in French polishing: bodying in, building up and spiriting out. Possibly more than any other clear finish, French polish emphasizes the quality of the wood surface underneath. Any imperfections will also be emphasized. The wood should have a good surface that is properly stained and filled.

Bodying in is the process that puts a skin of shellac on the wood. It is this that is polished later. You cannot polish if there is not a good coat of shellac already there. Sprinkle shellac on the inner pad and cover it with the cloth. Twist the cloth up so that the shellac oozes through. Rub across the grain and then with it (Fig. 10-2C). Cover every part of the surface (particularly the corners). Do not stop on the surface. If you want to lift the pad off, go over an edge first. Change to a circular or a figure eight action (Fig. 10-2D). Continue rubbing lightly until all the polish in the pad is exhausted. Let the surface harden, then recharge the pad and repeat.

Try to cover the whole surface with an even film of shellac. It is usually the corners that suffer. If you concentrate on them, the center of a panel will take care of itself. Recharge and repeat as often as necessary to give the whole surface a good protective coating. Leave the work in a dust-free room for a day.

Follow by examining the surface in a good light. Use fine steel wool to remove any unevenness. Charge the pad and apply more polish. If the pad sticks when moving over the surface, add a few drops of linseed oil to the outside of the pad. Be careful not to overdo this because too much will spoil the polish. Get an even coating of shellac and then wait another day. If flaws are still there, you should repeat the process.

Before the build up stage, lightly rub the surface with steel wool and wipe off the dust. Prepare the pad with polish, but not as much as for bodying in. The smaller amount of polish will cause the pad to drag and this has to be prevented with a few drops of oil. To check the pad, press it on paper. If oil is present, it will make a mark. If none is shown, the pad is ready for a few more drops of oil. The same test will show how wet the pad is with polish. If there is a definite wet trail when the pad is drawn lightly across the bodied-in surface, there is too much polish on the pad. If the pad marks are shiny, there is too much oil.

Work over the surface with circular figure eight movements in the same way as when bodying in. Stroke lightly. Do not rub hard. Make sure the whole area is covered. Do not pull down or take up the pad from the center of the surface. Slide on or off at an edge. Do not stop on the surface. It is the swift rubbing that produces a good polish, but there is no need to rush.

Recharge with polish as necessary and add spots of oil when the pad needs lubricating. Continue until there is a good layer of polish over the surface. At this stage, the layer need not have much of a shine or a very even gloss. Next, apply a coat of polish diluted with an equal quantity of alcohol. It does not matter if the work looks smeary at this stage. Leave it for at least five hours.

For the spiriting out stage, use a fresh pad with a double outer cloth. Dampen this with a little alcohol. Put the pad into an airtight jar for a short time so that the alcohol permeates the pad. Wipe the surface with very light strokes. This should remove smears. Change to a dry clean pad and go over the whole surface, first with circular strokes and then with the grain. This burnishing action should bring up an even glow to the surface. Be careful not to use too much alcohol. That would dissolve too much of the surface that has been applied. Leave the polished work for a few days to fully harden.

As can be seen, French polishing is a process for dealing with large areas. Many parts of furniture cannot be treated by rubbing with a pad. Simple molding can be rubbed lengthwise, but most fretted, carved and molded parts will have to be brushed on to give a thickness of coat to match any adjoining panels that are polished with a pad. Whether to deal with the brushed parts first or after polishing panels will depend on the piece of furniture. If the brushed parts are dealt with first, any excess that gets on a panel should be sanded off before you use a pad. Some brushed work around a framed panel might take care of parts the pad would have difficulty in reaching. However, avoid a hard edge to a brushed part, which should then be inconspicuous when polished over.

VARNISH

Varnish can be thought of as paint without color. Shellac has a similar appearance, but varnishes are tougher, more durable and have a better resistance to heat, moisture and solvents. Varnishes have been used for thousands of years to give wood a clear glossy finish. For all but the last half-century, they have been made with natural materials. Resins and lacs are used in an oil vehicle with thinner and drier. There has been a change to synthetic materials (either partially or completely). Some natural varnishes are still available, but modern varnishes are superior in many ways.

Some older varnishes took a long time to dry and tended to collect dust for several hours. They were affected by damp conditions as well as cold during application and setting. Most modern varnishes dry in about four hours and are dust-free in a much shorter time. They are still better used in warm dry conditions, but they are not so seriously affected by cold and damp. Older varnishes dried entirely by evaporation. There is some evaporation with synthetic varnish, but chemical reaction within the varnish provides some of the setting action.

Most varnish is one-part, but there are two-part varnishes. The two parts are mixed just before use and have to be applied in a limited working time. First setting is quick, then hardness builds up over several days to a point where some abrasives will not tough it. It also has a resistance to several solvents and liquids that might attack other varnishes or finishes. The obvious applications are bar tops and other places in contact with a variety of liquids.

Brushed varnish has uses in furniture. Because varnish has a much better resistance to abrasion, heat and moisture, it can be used on furniture in preference to any of the polishes. With careful application, brush marks should flow out. For a good furniture finish, the final varnish coat should be lightly sanded and the surface should be wax polished. The best synthetic varnish is often described as *boat varnish*. This has a special resistance to moisture. It is as good on furniture as on boats and it is particularly suitable for furniture that is to be taken outside.

Work in an area this is as free of dust as possible. Vacuum clean the room before work. Avoid drafts, but some change of air is advisable. Both the work and the varnish should be over 65 F, so have the wood in the work place some time before starting. If the varnish is thick, stand the can in a bowl of hot water (Fig. 10-3A). However, varnish at more than about 85F might become too liquid. Avoid extreme temperatures when storing varnish. Make sure the wood is clean. Grease from sweating hands might affect the finish.

Brush condition is important. They should be kept for varnish only. It is impossible to clean a brush previously used for paint so that it does not affect varnish. A brush could be stored temporarily in solvent, but it is better stored in varnish. Because varnish will oxidize if it is left in an open container, it is better to use a lidded container deep enough to enclose the brushes. To avoid bending the bristles, a wire can be put through them (Fig. 10-3B).

Most synthetic varnishes should not be stirred. Read the instructions on the can. Even a small amount of stirring could cause bubbles which will not disappear until they break on the wood surface and leave a rough spot. Much paint is spread first across and then along a surface and older natural varnish can be dealt with in the same way. If the instructions for a synthetic varnish say that

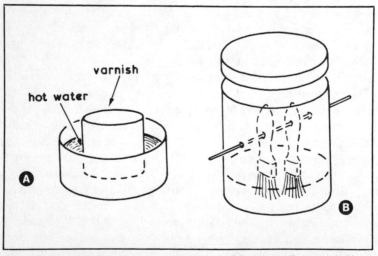

Fig. 10-3. Varnish (A) is better warm and brushes keep best if suspended in an airtight container (B).

it should be "flowed on," that means it should be put on with a minimum of brushing. Brush only enough to spread and cover the surface. Brush with the grain and do not continue after the brush is becoming exhausted. Try to avoid going back over varnish already spread. As you continue, make a last stroke each time back toward the previously done part and lift the brush off as it goes over that. Brushing over varnish too often will cause it to lift and leave a rough surface. If that happens, leave to dry. Then sand it level and varnish over it.

Varnish can be used directly on bare wood, but some makers recommend thinning the first coat with a thinner so that it will penetrate the grain better and bond it and further coats to the wood. Only a small amount of thinner is needed. Many synthetic varnishes are not compatible with shellac. Do not use that as a filler under varnish.

A first coat on bare wood might raise the grain (tiny fibers might stand up). Lightly sand them off. Further coats should be undiluted. Sand between coats. In some high quality coachwork there are as many as 20 coats, with careful sanding between coats, to produce a brilliant gloss. For furniture, three coats should be regarded as the minimum for a reasonable finish and there might have to be four or five coats.

The makers will indicate drying times. Do not try to rub down before a surface is hard. Rub down enough to remove the gloss, with abrasive paper, powder on a cloth or fine steel wool. Make sure any blemishes in a coat are sanded level before the next is applies. Some synthetic varnish makers specify a maximum and a minimum time between coats. These are mostly exterior or boat varnishes. It is better for furniture to have a varnish that will dry and can be rubbed down without having to rush to get another coat on in a specified time.

SPRAY FINISHES

Whether a sprayed finish is correct for a piece of fine cabinetwork is something the individual craftsman will have to decide for himself. Spray equipment was unavailable when most furniture was made by hand. Furniture users today tend to associate spray with mass production and they mostly expect a different finish on individually made furniture.

It is not impossible to spray some of the older finishing materials, but the usual sprayed finish is a lacquer specially prepared for the process. Furniture lacquer gives a clear transparent finish that should finish comparable to French polish or varnish.

However, anyone with a little knowledge of these treatments would be able to identify which has been used. There are lacquers that give a dull surface or anything between that and a high gloss. There are colored lacquers. Most lacquers will attack other finishes, so they cannot be used over or adjoining them.

Good spraying equipment is comparatively bulky and wasteful of lacquer, thinners, retarders and other things. For all-day spraying in industrial production, they obviously have advantages. When only one or two items of furniture are to be sprayed, there are a number of snags. Simpler small spray equipment, intended for amateur use, is mostly unsatisfactory on furniture.

If a cabinetmaker wants his work spray finished, it will probably be better to go to a specialist than to do it himself. If he decides to do his own spraying, more instruction should be obtained from the equipment supplier or a specialist book.

OTHER FINISHES

In traditional furniture of good design, the chosen finishes show up the qualities of the wood. Occasionally something unusual has been done, but special effects are more applicable to contemporary furniture.

Limed oak furniture has been featured in the past as well as today. The name comes from the original use of lime to fill the cracks that occur regularly in oak, chestnut and a few other woods. Today there are white fillers.

Prepare the wood fully, because the effect would be spoiled by sanding after filling the grain. It helps to seal the surface with a light thin shellac. Zinc white in paraffin wax can be used or there are some white fillers sold for the purpose. Flat or undercoat white paint can be used, but it should not be very liquid. Apply the paint or filler with a brush. Work in all directions to force the "lime" into all spaces. Wipe off any surplus. Leave it dry. If there is any white left on the surface, scrape it, rather than sand it. Cover everything with a coat of bleached shellac. Lightly sand and apply another coat. Sand that. The shellac will seal the lime in the grain. Any further treatment should be colorless to preserve the whiteness of the lime.

The wood can be stained before liming. It need not be the usual brown. Grey or a thinned black stain will show up the white better. Do any staining before sealing and filling the grain.

Shading stains have been used, so there are graduations of the same color. The best effect seem to be where the coloring varies as if it has been the effect of wear. A high spot would be lighter than surrounding parts. Recesses would be darker than open panel areas. A bulbous part of a leg would be lighter than the rest of the turning. Shading should not be done with geometric precision, but it should follow a pattern. For instance, a panel might be dark around the edges, shading to a lighter center, but the corners could be darker than along the edges and the grading of the shade should not be absolutely uniform all round.

Stain can be applied so that more goes on the darker parts. Spraying is a good way of controlling the amount of stain, but with oil stain it is better to rely on quick use of a cloth to remove stain from the lighter parts before much has soaked in.

Shading has limited uses. Most furniture looks better the same color all over. If woods are mixed and you are uncertain if you can stain them to match exactly, shading can disguise the differences.

There are special paint finishes to give unusual effects. Most are best avoided if you want your work to be described as fine cabinetwork. This also applies to the addition of machine made carvings, pyrography (pokerwork), flock spraying and other things that might be acceptable with mass produced furniture, but not with examples of good quality craftsmanship.

More detailed information on finishing processes can be found in TAB book No. 894 *The Do-It Yourselfer's Guide to Furniture Repair and Refinishing.*

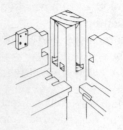

Chapter 11
Simple Cabinetwork

Not all pieces of cabinetwork are complicated or difficult to make, but to a beginner in search of a design the amount of difficulty of the work is not always obvious. It is always wise for any craftsman to tackle work within the scope of his ability, but it is good training to sometimes undertake work that stretches your skill. However, a beginner will find that quite simple work stretches his skill and if he picks a design with work of a difficulty he did not expect, he might become frustrated. The work in this chapter is representative of good cabinetmaking practice, but the skills required can be regarded as introductory.

Simple things are not necessarily small, although in many cases they are. Good quality hardwoods are not easy to obtain and many are quite expensive. You might have some fear of damaging and wasting wood. The smaller projects reduce the risk, so making a small thing can be regarded as a lesser risk. If work on larger pieces of wood is tackled systematically, there should be little risk of complete wastage. Quite often a larger part that becomes damaged can be cut to make a smaller part. In some cases if a joint is unsatisfactorily cut, the bad work can be cut off and the whole thing made slightly shorter without affecting the use and purpose of the completed piece of furniture. If the wood supplied is overlong, do not be in too much of a hurry to cut it to length. Then if a joint cut on one end is not as good as you would like, there for it to be cut off and still leave a piece long enough to finish to the intended size.

It is unlikely that you will be making one piece of furniture only. If a piece of wood cannot be used for what you intended, because of your lack of skill or just bad luck, it can go into stock and will almost certainly find a place in some later project. I do my typing at an oak desk that has one board in it with some unnecessary dado slots across its underside. This is due to making a bookcase with two sides the same instead of a pair. It happens to us all sometimes.

When starting a new piece of work, make sure that you understand how it is to be made. Try to follow through the description in relation to the drawings. If you want to make the thing a different size or if you have some wood slightly thinner than specified, make sure that you know where sizes have to be altered and mark out accordingly. In most pieces of furniture, slight variations in widths and thicknesses of wood do not matter. If wood is specified as 1 inch and yours finishes ⅞ of an inch thick, it will probably not matter. But what you have to do is make sure that you allow for the difference at appropriate points in the structure.

In any case, where two pieces of wood have to meet, it is always better to use the actual piece of wood than to rely on measuring when marking out. Get two lines at the same distance apart as the thickness of the wood that goes there. That is more important than conforming to some arbitrary measurement on a rule.

The drawings in this book give you most of the information you will need without the need for you to draw anything yourself. However, if there are several things to have matching measurments, mark the edge of a rod and mark from that rather than from a rule. If you are unused to a rod, it might be worthwhile to use one for the sake of practice even where it might not be absolutely essential. Some things, particularly shaped parts, cannot be drawn full size in a book. Therefore, it is then advisable to make your own full size drawing. In many cases, the drawing can be on a piece of cardboard or hardboard. Its outline can then be cut to use as a template. Full size drawings need not be very complex as long as you have the key lines in correct relation to each other and you know which is which and can take off measurements or angles from them. A workshop drawing might be better on a waste piece of plywood or hardboard than on paper. Some paper will expand and contract a surprising amount. There could be a difference of ¼-inch in 36 inches after a few days due to taking up or releasing moisture.

If you use paper and need certain vital measurements from your drawing, take off the information you want soon after drawing. Then any later variation in the paper will not matter.

Assemble all material you need before starting. If you mark out and cut some parts before obtaining other wood that has to join in, there could be small variations that cause poor joints or other alterations that would not have happened if all the wood had been there at the start. This is also important with hardware. If the furniture is to mount on casters or glides, you need to know what allowance to make in height. Hinge sizes can affect wood parts. Catches and fasteners will need particular sizes of wood if they are to be mounted easily. Metal handles need holes at certain positions and you may have to arrange to allow for this.

BOOK ENDS

Book ends (Fig. 11-1A) are simple things that might not be considered cabinetmaking, except that they provide a beginner with an opportunity to learn a joint without wasting much wood if it goes wrong the first time. There are many ways that the parts can be joined, using hand or machine-made joints, but the obvious one for the cabinetmaker is a through dovetail joint. If the first attempt is unsatisfactory, the joint can be cut off and the wood will still be long enough. Overall sizes are not critical, providing a pair of ends match.

Prepare sufficient wood in one length and mark on it the cuts to be made (including the dovetails, but not the pins). Separate the pieces and make the joints. At this stage, ignore the shallow recess to be made for the metal that will go under some books to hold the ends in place. See that the parts are exactly at right angles to each other.

Use sheet aluminum or other metal to go under the books (Fig. 11-1B). It need be no thicker than is necessary to hold its shape; 20 gauge should be suitable in stiffer metals. Cut off the extending corners and use a file and abrasive to remove any roughness around the edges. The metal has to be let into the wood. Clean up the dovetail joints so that surfaces are flat. Then cut a rabbet across the bottom that is just sufficient to let the metal in level (Fig. 11-1C). Drill for screws. After the metal has been attached, there should be a piece of cloth or thin soft plastic glued to the underside of the wood and metal so that the books ends will not mark the top of a table or desk.

The foregoing instructions deal with basic construction, but book ends offer scope for unlimited decoration. The joined pieces

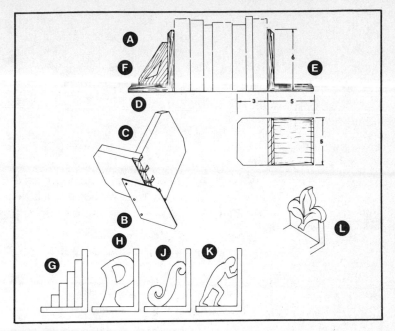

Fig. 11-1. Bookends (A) are dovetailed with metal (B,C,D,E) to go under the end books (G). Decoration can take many forms (H,J,K).

will be strong enough, so anything else will be done as decoration. The simplest treatment is to cut off the corners (Fig. 11-1D). The corners can have concave or convex cuts or combinations in molded form. Edges can be chamferred and preferably should be tapered from the corners (Fig. 11-1E).

Almost any form of wood decoration can be used on something to mount in the angle of a book end. It helps in the general effect if lines tend toward the books rather than away from them so that there is a feeling of support. A decorative piece might have its lines leading outwards, but this reduces the effect of solidity which might be desirable in the assembly of ends and books.

A triangular support is the obvious thing to build in (Fig. 11-1F). This is shown with a cutout. There can be several blocks of wood (Fig. 11-1G) and they can be pieces of contrasting colors. This would be an opportunity to display a collection of different woods.

The two book ends need not be the same although they should be complementary. An arrow might appear to enter at one end and project from the other. A fish might have its tail at one end and its head at the other and the body would be assumed to be in the books.

A pair of initials could be used (Fig. 11-1H), but much depends on the suitability of the chosen initials to fit into the angles. That shown is a simple cutout, but it would be possible to carve the letters in their thickness and decorate them with scrolls, based on medieval lettering. A further step in carving is to take some architectural detail, such as would be used on a bracket, and carve that (Fig. 11-1J).

A figure could be used. There could be a person or animal sitting with its back into the angle. They could be leaning against the upright or apparently pushing it to keep the books up (Fig. 11-1K). How the figure is dealt with depends on your skill. It could be an outline cut with a fretsaw from thin wood. It might be a little thicker and given some surface cuts to indicate detail. It could be a fully detailed carving.

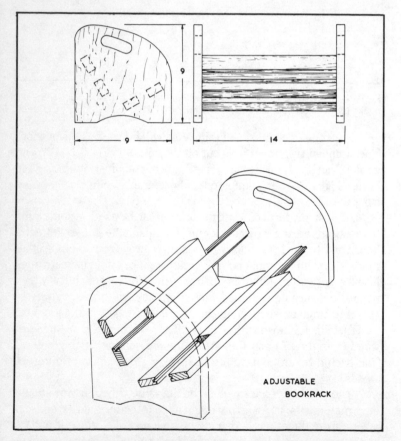

ADJUSTABLE
BOOKRACK

Fig. 11-2. An adjustable bookrack keeps varying quantities of books tidy.

Table 11-1. Materials List for Book Ends.

2 pieces	5 × 6 × ⅝
2 pieces	5 × 7 × ⅝
2 pieces (metal)	4 × 5 × 20g.

Most of the added things go with a fairly simple outline of the ends, but an alternative treatment is to shape the ends themselves (either on the upright part or in both directions). There might be the outline of a badge or emblem or this would be an opportunity to try carving a leaf (Fig. 11-1L) or other foliage.

Obviously, the type of decoration should be decided at the start and at least part of it done before the pieces are assembled. However, the joints are better cut while the wood is in plain parallel pieces. Most added things can be simply glued in, but some could be made with projecting tenons in one direction or screws could be driven into them. A screw through the base will be hidden by the cloth glued on. See Table 11-1 for a materials list.

ADJUSTABLE BOOKRACK

An adjustable bookrack (Fig. 11-2) allows different numbers of books to be held together without any of them falling over. This will happen if a rigid bookcase or rack is only partly filled. It is particularly suitable for anyone needing books for reference on the desk and these vary in their choice and numbers according to the work being done. Having the books kept together in this way is more convenient and tidier than leaving them scattered around the desk top.

Sizes will vary, but the rack suggested suits most sizes of books and can have its capacity varied from about 14 inches to 22 inches. The holes in the ends are to allow two or three fingers to be inserted to carry the rack. As a cabinetmaking exercise the skill comes in making good joints between the rails (which have to slide) and in securing them to the ends.

Start by laying out an end (Fig. 11-3A) either on the actual wood or as a drawing to be transferred later. Locate the rear corner of the books and draw a right angle with its rear leg at 60 degrees to horizontal. Mark the rail widths along these lines. Other shaping must be arranged to have enough clearance around these marks. There are many possible shapes for the ends, but simple curves are shown. Hollow the base so that the rack stands on four corner feet. The top edge can be a freehand curve. Mark out the pair of ends, but do not do any of the curving to the edges until after the joints have been cut.

The rails are cut from wood of the same overall section. Those with grooves and those with tongues can probably be made in long pieces. It is easier to adjust tongues than grooves, so plow the grooves first (Fig. 11-3B). Make the tongues on the other parts (Fig. 11-3C), but the sliding action has to be smooth. Allow for some sanding. It might be necessary to clean the insides of the grooves with abrasive paper wrapped around the edge of a narrow strip of wood. The grooves should be slightly deeper than the tongues so that the rails come close together. Take the sharpness off the edges of the tongues and sand them to run smoothly.

The rails join to the ends with mortise and tenon joints. They could go into the ends without protruding and be locked with fox wedges as well as glue (Fig. 11-3D). If this is done, make the saw cuts for the wedges approximately at right angles to the grain of the end. Alternatively, the tenons can go through and have their exposed ends rounded (Fig. 11-3E). In both cases, cut the ends down to solid wood by removing the grooves or tongues. Then make the tenons fairly thick to get maximum strength. On ¾ inch wood, they could be ⅝ of an inch.

Cut the ends to shape and see that they are accurately paired.

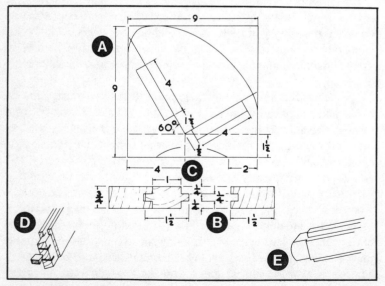

Fig. 11-3. Details of bookrack construction: (A) layout; (B) plow the grooves; (C) make the tonques; (D) fox wedges; (E) rounded ends.

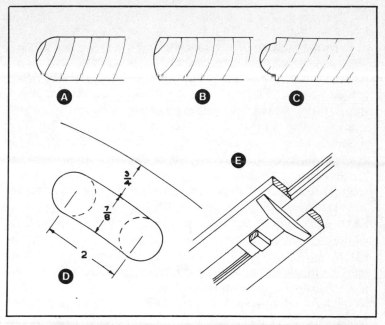

Fig. 11-4. The ends of the bookrack can have their edges decorated (A,B,C) and finger holes cut (D)Underneath,stops prevent the slides pullingapart (E).

The visible edges can be left square, made semicircular (Fig. 11-4A), given a more modest curve (Fig. 11-4B) or they could be given a more complex treatment (Fig. 11-4C) particularly if a suitable molding cutter is available. Make the holes by drilling the ends (Fig. 11-4D) and sawing between them. Round the hole edges similar to the simpler outer edge sections.

The sliding rails must have their movement limited so that the bookrack cannot be pulled apart. Assemble the rails to the ends and leave for the glue to set with the rails temporarily together and held either by light clamping, wrapping around with adhesive tape or by tying with cord. Make stop pieces to fit underneath (Fig. 11-4E). Those across the grooved pieces should be tapered to their ends so that they do not show. Screw the stops on so there are about 4 inches of the rails still overlapping when the rack is pulled out to its limit. After a trial assembly, remove the smaller pieces so that the parts can be disassembled for finishing. Do not get polish into the grooves. Rub the sliding parts with wax before the final assembly.

If the rack is to be used on a polished wood surface, put rubber feet below the ends or glue on strips of cloth. See Table 11-2 for a materials list.

TRAYS

In its simplest form, a tray is a shallow box. (Fig. 11-5). For some purposes, it is merely a nailed box, but that is not cabinetmaking. A cabinetmaking type of tray is one used to keep papers together on a desk. It can be a plain box or one end can be shaped to give easy access (Fig. 11-6A) or the whole end of the box be cut (Fig. 11-6B). These trays need to be of light construction and the simplest bottom is thin plywood or hardboard in a rabbet (Fig. 11-6C). It could be in a groove (Fig. 11-6D), but that reduces the capacity of the try for a given depth of sides.

The size of the tray should be related to the usual sizes of paper it will contain. With envelopes and some unusual size papers it needs to have plenty of clearance. The type shown in Fig. 11-7A is a reasonable proportion for desk use. The bottom is rabbeted ⅛ of an inch and this allows through dovetails at the corners. The bottom of the part with the tails is cut to fit into the rabbet (Fig. 11-7B), but the top is mitered (Fig. 11-7C). This makes a neat finish, although a normal through dovetail edge could be used. If the top edge is almost semicircular, a miter makes a better looking corner (Fig. 11-7D).

Fig. 11-5. A tray and a place mat enclosed and a desk tray.

2 ends	9 × 10 × ¾
6 rails	1½ × 14 × ¾
Stops from	1 × 12 × ¼

The bottom could be just the piece of plywood or hardboard. Because it will be hidden most of the time, that is satisfactory. For a good quality tray, there could be cloth or leather-like plastic on the plywood. Use glue in the rabbets, but also use thin screws or fine nails. These will have a better hold if driven at alternative angles in a dovetail fashion (Fig. 11-7E). If the bottom is to be given such a special treatment, it is advisable to leave the bottom out until after the staining and polishing of the rest of the tray has been done.

Very similar trays can be used for cutlery. The divisions should be as thin as can be reasonably made in the particular wood. In most hardwoods, ⅛-inch or 3/16-inch divisions are possible. Prepare the strips and round the top edges. The only way to cross pieces is with a deep halving joint (Fig. 11-8A). This is unsatisfactory because there is a risk of the deep unsupported ends moving, even when glued, because glue does not hold very well on end grain. It is better to stagger the joints (Fig. 11-8B). Around the sides of the tray there are stopped dado joints (Fig. 11-8C). Similar joints can be used where divisions meet, but this takes out enough to weaken the grooved member. An alternative is to make the groove V section (Fig. 11-8D). At the top this gives a miter effect. There is no need to stop the groove. Strength is improved if the divisions can be arranged almost opposite each other (Fig. 11-8E). Otherwise there can be a pin into the joint to supplement the glue. Hollowing top edges make removal of cutlery easier. The bottom can be faced with cloth before fitting.

A variation on this is a tray for displaying coins or other flat objects. A series of very shallow trays can be made to slide into grooves in a cabinet. Cut holes to suit the coins in thin wood and thoroughly sand the edges. Some things can rest directly on wood, but it is standard to put coins on cloth. Rather than cut disks to fit each place, it is easier and neater to sandwich cloth between wood (Fig. 11-9A). Glue can be used above and below the cloth, but this should only be in spot positions on top so that glue does not spread into the holes and spoil appearance.

With a valuable collection, or if the tray is to hang vertically, there should be glass over the coins. This means having a double rabbet. The glass slides into one and the other overlaps enough for screws to be driven (Fig. 11-9B). If opening will only be necessary at long intervals, the frame can be rigidly made and access is by unscrewing the base. If the owner will want to open the case fairly frequently, one end of the frame is screwed on. Sometimes elaborately molded picture frame molding is used, but the opening edge should be kept plain. If the tray is displayed vertically, it would be the base (Fig. 11-9C).

Trays for domestic use vary from the purely utilitarian types with a painted finish to those which are worthy of display when they are out of use. The tray can have comparatively plain outlines and depend on grain markings of the wood for its appearance. Or it might be made of plainer wood and include some shaping as decoration. The display feature might be veneering or other treatment of the central panel and the framing or other decoration should be

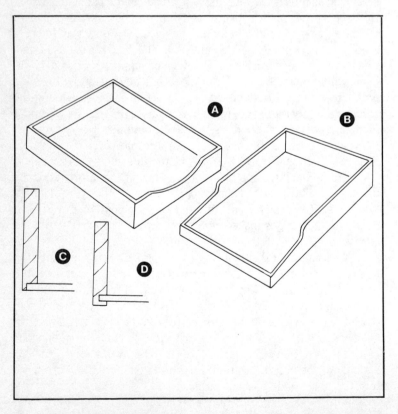

Fig. 11-6. Desk trays are boxes with cutdown edges: (A) plain box; (B) with end cut down; (C) rabbet; (D) groove.

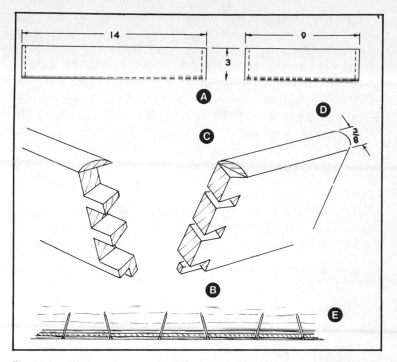

Fig. 11-7. Dovetails make the best tray corner joints (A,B,C,D). If the plywood bottom fits into rabbets, dovetail nailing adds strength (E).

subordinate to it. Whatever form the tray takes, it should be functional. It has to carry a reasonable number of plates, cups and other things. It has to be held with two hands at a resonable distance apart. There are some very large trays, but for general use the hands should not be spread so very much more than the width of the shoulders. There are two broad divisions in tray design: trays with handles and those where the framing itself provides hand grips.

A logical design is to make the tray like a desk tray, but shape the ends so there is enough width to allow a cutout for a hand grip (Fig. 11-10A). Although curves are standard, a modern treatment uses straight lines (Fig. 11-10B) with just enough rounding to take the sharpness off angles. In both of these cases, it is advisable to not make the shaping and hole too high (for the sake of strength). It is better if some grain lines go right through above the cutout. Raising too high brings short grain to each side of the hole and weakness that might fail when lifting a heavy load. The bottom of this tray could be let into rabbets or plowed grooves.

Sides of a tray with cutout handles can be straight or shaped, usually by stepping down (Fig. 11-10C), but be careful not to go so low that anything carried might slip off.

A piece of veneered plywood can be used as the bottom, bought with the veneer already applied, or veneer can be laid. This is a suitable place for a quartered design with or without a cross-grained border (Fig. 11-10D). This would also be a good place to display a marquetry picture. These veneered surfaces look best with a gloss finish, but a slippery surface is not what you want in a tray. For protection and to prevent slipping, it is best to use a cloth. To complement a high-quality tray, use a specially embroidered cloth.

There are some attractive place mats available. One of these can be used in the base of the tray. The advantage is that it will provide a surface on which crockery being carried is unlikely to

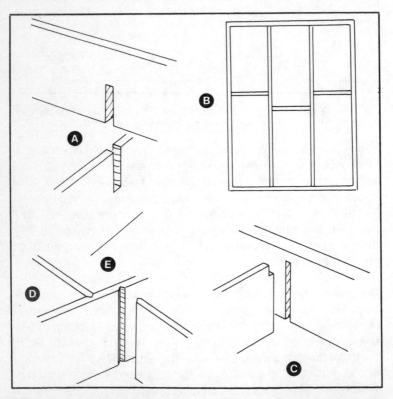

Fig. 11-8. Divisions in a tray would be weakened if cut to cross. Staggered notched joints are better:(A) deep halving joint; (B) stagger the joints; (C) stopped dado joints; (D) V sections (E) opposite divisions.

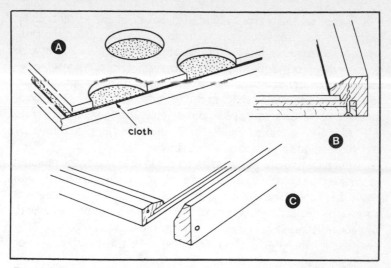

Fig. 11-9. A coin tray base is built up and could include glass: (A) cloth; (B) screw; (C) base.

slip. Because its size will determine the size of the tray, it should be obtained first and glued to the plywood that will make the bottom so that it is trapped in the rabbet (Fig. 11-10E). The bottom does not have to be let in level, but can project and have its edge painted black before fitting (Fig. 11-10F).

Another type of tray uses a frame that is molded to provide a grip anywhere along its length. Prepared molding can be bought or it can be made with a suitable cutter in a spindle molder or with planes. Some common shapes (Fig. 11-11A) have one or more deep hollows as finger grips. For hand work, it is best to make the molding on the edge of a wider piece so that it can be gripped in a vise or by clamping. If making all the molding in one length would be too long, it can be worked on opposite edges (Fig. 11-11B) with some of the waste first plowed out (Fig. 11-11C). The lower edge of the molding can be plowed or rabbeted (Fig. 11-11D) or it can be made to go on top of the tray base (Fig. 11-11E). Corners of this type of tray are best mitered like a picture frame. The bottom provides some security in the joint, but there can be thin nails driven each way, then punched and covered with stopping.

Another treatment of this sort of molding is to make the ends with sufficient shaping, but have the tray sides straight (Fig. 11-11F) or flat with curved edges. The handled ends can have a section for the full width or be cut down at the corners (Fig. 11-11G) where the joints can be dovetails, miters or other types.

185

There are many types of metal and plastic handles that can be bought. A plated or brass metal handle or a brightly colored plastic one draws attention. It is better if the tray is fairly plain, otherwise there is divided attention and the design is confused. Many of these handles are intended to be screwed to vertical surfaces. The ends of the tray should be upright on the outside and have enough wood to take the screws so that any molding must be inside only (Fig. 11-12A). A plain curved molded inside helps in cleaning if the tray has to be cleared of moisture or crumbs.

For a tray where the main feature is in the base or the molding of the frame, it would be better (if separate handles are needed) to make them of the same wood as the frame so that the prominence of a metal handle is avoided. Shapes can range from simple blocks to molded sections (Fig. 11-12B). Any handle or hole should be long enough for a finger grip (about 5 inches) while the thumb goes over the top.

The underside of a tray can be left as flat bare wood, but because the tray might be placed on a polished surface, it would be better to pad it. You could glue a piece of cloth on the bottom, but it is easier and probably better to have strips around the edges (Fig. 11-12C) covering the rabbeted joint. If the bottom goes into a plowed groove, there might not be enough width in some edges to take a satisfactory width of cloth. In that case, the corners can be

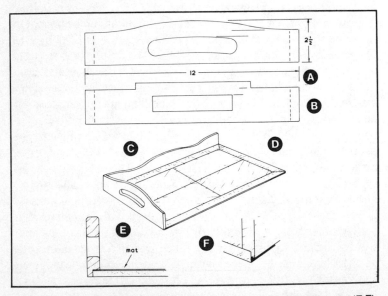

Fig. 11-10. A simple tray (A,B,C,D) might enclose a veneered panel or mat (E,F).

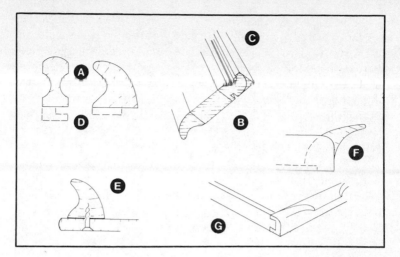

Fig. 11-11. A tray frame can be shaped (A,B,C,D) to provide hand grips (E,F,G).

packed out so that pads can be put there (Fig. 11-12D). There are other things besides cloth that can be used. Rubber or soft plastic strip can be used, but avoid any form of foam that will absorb water.

HANGING BOOKCASE

Shelves for books can take many forms and be in many sizes. They can be simple built-in shelves that are very practical or they can be arranged in a piece of furniture that has some decorative value. When designing accomodation for books, it is important to ensure that the books are fully on the the shelves and there is some clearance to allow them to be removed without damage. If the actual books can be measured, the finished case can be made to suit. Then the result is more practical and looks better than if the book accomodation is vastly oversize.

In general, it is better to have smaller books higher than larger books. Both for practical considerations and for the sake of appearance. Having deeper gaps low looks better than having them high. Even if the books on several shelves are all the same depth, appearance will be better if lower gaps between shelves become progressively slightly wider. Otherwise there is an optical illusion in a block of actually equal gaps where the lower ones seem closer.

This hanging bookcase (Figs. 11-13 and 11-14) is intended to be hung on a wall. It does not take up floor space and the sizes given will take many common sizes of books. They should be checked and modified for a particular collection of books. The wood is strong

187

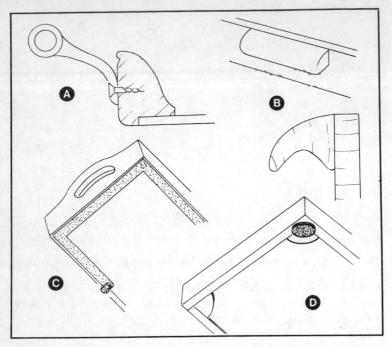

Fig. 11-12. Handles can be screwed on (A,B,C) or made by cutting hand holes (C). Cloth underneath protects table surface (D).

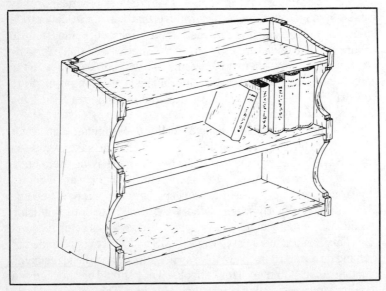

Fig. 11-13. A hanging bookcase does not take up floor space.

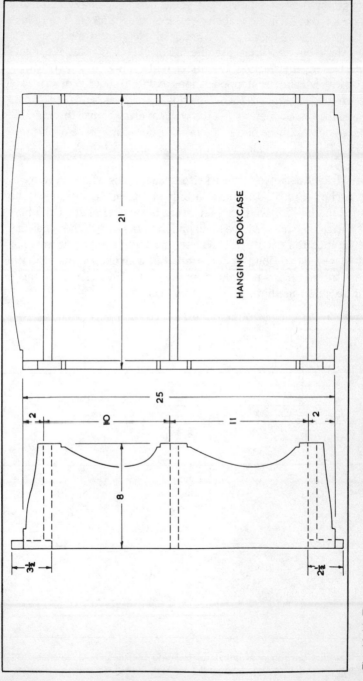

HANGING BOOKCASE

Fig. 11-14. These sizes suit average needs, but can be modified.

enough for the size shown, but books are very heavy and if the shelves are to be made longer, they should be thickened to reduce the risk of them sagging after being in use some time.

Mark out the ends together (Fig. 11-15A). Cut the joints before doing any shaping. Use the actual shelves as a guide to the slot widths. Take the stopped dadoes to within about ¼ of an inch of the front edge (Fig. 11-15C). The bookcase is shown with the part behind the books open so that the wall covering shows through. If a closed back would be better, rabbet the sides for a piece of plywood so that this can go halfway over the top and bottom shelves (Fig. 11-15D).

Make the shelves. Use a knife to cut across where they are to be notched (Fig. 11-15E) so that they are sawn cleanly and all the same length. The two back pieces are better left slightly too long until after the shelves have been joined to the ends. Then they can be trimmed to fit tightly. The shelves could be joined at the ends with dovetail dado joints for strength, but with plain joints, drill the ends for fine screws near the fronts (Fig. 11-15F). The rear edges will be held together by the back pieces.

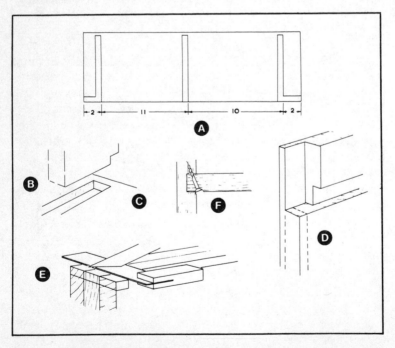

Fig. 11-15. Constructional details of hanging bookcase: (A) notches; (B,C) stopped dado; (D) rabbeted sides; (E) shelves.

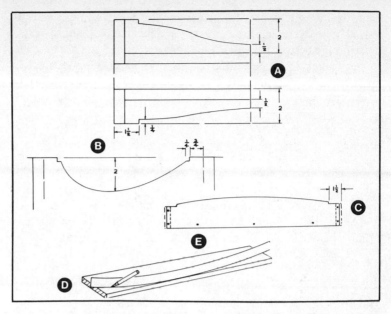

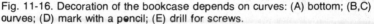

Fig. 11-16. Decoration of the bookcase depends on curves: (A) bottom; (B,C) curves; (D) mark with a pencil; (E) drill for screws.

The shaped edges are matched. Plain curves without the notched ends would be simpler, but having a step between a curve and a straight part is good architectural design. The top and bottom of the ends have similar curves, but the bottom is shallower (Fig. 11-16A). Measure the notches and the ends of the curves, then make a flowing freehand shape with pencil. Cut the curve on one piece and use it as a pattern to mark the other. Similarly, mark the notched ends of the shapes between the shelves and draw the curves between them. The curves can be parts of circles, drawn around a plate or other suitable circular thing, but curves with their greater depth lower than halfway look better (Fig. 11-16B).

The ends of the back pieces have their notches marked, then curves sprung to their greater widths (Fig. 11-16C). Mark the center of the edge and spring a straightedge through the points so that an assistant can run a pencil around (Fig. 11-16D).

Drill for screws through the back pieces into the shelves and ends (Fig. 11-16E). Take the sharpness off all exposed edges and sand the surfaces that will be difficult to get at after assembly. Join the shelves to the ends (including screwing from below). Check squareness and then trim the backs to length and add them.

The weight of the bookcase can be taken by two screws through the top back piece near its ends, but another central screw through the bottom back piece will share the load and prevent the case swinging from the wall in use. See Table 11-3 for a materials list.

FLOOR BOOKCASE

Books which are deeper in size also tend to be wider. If they are to be accomodated in a bookcase that will also hold small books, the shelves have to be different widths if the smaller books are not to be pushed to the back of wide shelves. Because the bigger books are heavier, they naturally have to be put at the bottom of a bookcase that is to stand on the floor. This bookcase (Fig. 11-17 and 11-18) has a wider bottom part to take a row of large volumes. Other smaller books are in the narrower shelves higher up.

The bookcase can have plain outlines or the edges can be given rounded decoration (like the hanging bookcase, but it is shown with more angular patterned edges). This is particularly suitable for the coarser-grained hardwoods such as oak, which gives an impression of solidity, and this further emphasized by the projecting plinth. Although the bookcase will usually stand against a wall, its back is closed with plywood. If it will have to stand in a room where it is viewed all round, the plywood should be veneered with similar wood to the solid parts (if possible). The plinth should then be taken around the back. If the bookcase will be standing against a wall, it would be better with the plinth only at the front and sides.

Mark out the 8-inch wide piece for the sides together with the positions of the shelves. Prepare the side extension pieces (Fig. 11-19A). Make sure all saw marks are removed from the tapered parts before gluing these pieces to the wide boards. Make sure the two sides match. It is advisable to leave some excess length at the bottom to trim level after gluing. It should be sufficient to glue and clamp the planed edges, but there can be dowels or secret screws to strengthen the joints. For the sake of a uniform appearance, the angle of the side extensions should be repeated at the top and on

Table 11-3. Materials List for Hanging Bookcase.

2 ends	8 × 24 × ⅝
1 middle shelf	8 × 21 × ⅝
2 shelves	7⅜ × 21 × ⅝
1 top back	3½ × 21 × ⅝
1 bottom back	2½ × 21 × ⅝

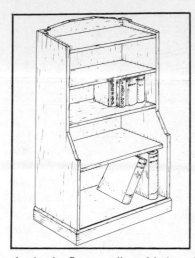

Fig. 11-17. In a floor bookcase, the broadened base for large books increases stability.

the back. Set an adjustable bevel to the angle and use this to mark the other bevels.

The shelves fit into stopped dadoes, similar to those on the hanging bookcase, with screws under the front edges. Although the bottom shelf must be the full width, the one above the wide compartment need not reach the front. It can be fitted without notching ½-inch back from the edge (Fig. 11-19B).

Shape the tops of the sides and prepare the back (Fig. 11-18C). Cut recesses for the back to come behind the top shelf, in the same way as in the hanging bookcase, but the back edges of the sides for the plywood and continue this across the solid top back (Fig. 11-19D).

Assemble the sides and shelves after sanding inner surfaces. Fit the top back. When the glue on these parts has set, cut the plywood to size and fit it into the rabbet with glue and fine nails. Do the same to the backs of the shelves and the rabbeted top piece.

Prepare the strips to make the plinth so that the width allows the top edge to come about ⅛ an inch below the shelf level (Fig. 11-19E). Give the top edge a plain bevel (Fig. 11-19F). Stepping it down (Fig. 11-19G) would give a section matching the other decoration, but being low and small it might not show. Miter where the plinth parts meet. If the bookcase is to go against a wall, cut the rear ends level with the back. If it is to stand away from a wall, make a rear piece of plinth and miter all corners. Attach the plinth with glue and a few screws from inside or with fine nails driven from outside and punched so that they can be covered with stopping.

193

Check the squareness of the bottom edges, otherwise the bookcase will not stand upright. It will help to take care of sight unevenness of the floor to plane each side of the bottom slightly hollow so that the weight is taken at the corners. See Table 11-4 for a materials list.

COFFEE TABLE

This small table (Fig. 11-20 and 21) is made in the same way as Tudor tables of many sizes, from small side tables to large dining tables, and the design could be altered in size to suit needs. As it is, the table is suitable for use as a coffee table or it might serve as a stool. Its legs could be lengthened if a greater height would be more convenient and the whole table altered in size and shape to suit available wood or particular needs. However, there are artistic considerations concerning proportions. So far as possible, avoid squareness in the view in any direction. It always looks better if any panel or view has one dimension greater than the other and there is a similar effect when viewed diagonally.

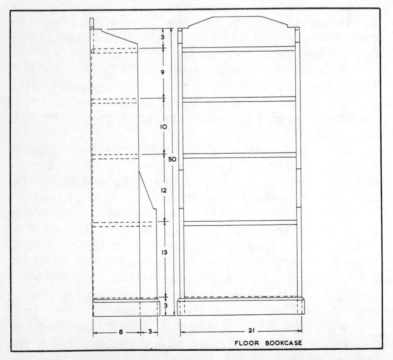

FLOOR BOOKCASE

Fig. 11-18. Besides taking different sizes of books, graduating shelf spacing gives a more pleasing appearance.

Table 11-4. Materials List for Floor Bookcase.

2 sides	8 × 51 × ⅝
2 side extensions	3 × 26 × ⅝
6 shelves	7¾ × 21 × ⅝
2 shelves	10¾ × 21 × ⅝
1 top back	6 × 21 × 5
1 plinth	2⅞ × 23 × ½
2 plinths	2⅞ × 12 × ½
1 back	21 × 48 × ¼ ply

The legs are shown turned (Fig. 11-22A), but they could be square with waggon bevelling between the mortised parts (Fig. 11-22B). Bevel the bottoms. Heaviness in appearance of square legs could be relieved by tapering on the two outside faces only (Fig. 11-22C). The inner surfaces should be kept upright for the sake of squareness in the joints. Alternatively, the legs could be kept square to below the rail joints and then tapered to the bottom (Fig. 11-22D).

If legs are turned, plane the wood accurately to a square section and allow just enough extra at the foot for truing there. There can be about an inch left at the other end. This allows for driving in the lathe and will not be cut off until after the joints have been cut. Carefully center the wood in the lathe so that the square section runs true. Be careful in turning so that tools do not catch in the parts that have to remain square and cause corners to splinter. Make all cuts away from the squares. Use the first leg as a pattern for the others and make a rod from it for marking and checking their parts. Pay particular attention to getting the overall lengths the same and the square-sectioned parts matching. Slight variations in the turned parts are less likely to show.

Prepare wood for the rails slightly over length. Plane all round to the finished sections. Do the shaping of the top rails (Fig. 11-23A). On the end rails the curves meet, but similar curves on the side rails are joined by straight edges. To get the curves the same, make a hardboard template (Fig. 11-23B). There need not be any decoration on these rails, but carving is shown in Fig. 11-23C, but there could be more elaborate scrolls or leafwork. If chip carving is used, make the apexes of the triangles sightly more than 90 degrees. Then cutting can be done with an ordinary paring chisel. If the angle is more acute, waste wood will have to be removed with a knife or a skew carving chisel. Cut in the outlines

195

with a knife, tapering to the apex, then pare down to it (Fig. 11-23D). There is no need to go very deep—between 1/16 of an inch and ⅛ of an inch—will do, but get all cuts the same.

Mark the shoulder length of all four rails in each direction together with a knife and the overall length with a pencil (Fig. 11-24A). Cut to length, gauge around and cut the tenons (including the haunches in the top rails). Mark and cut the mortises. Allow for the tenons being mitered in the legs (Fig. 11-24).

Take the sharpness off the angles of the bottom rails with bevels about 1/16 of an inch wide (Fig. 11-24C). Plow grooves on the insides of the top rails to take the buttons holding the top on (Fig. 11-24D). Sand the rails and legs. Assemble the long sides first. Check squareness with a try square and by measuring diagonals. See that there is no twist when viewed across and test one assembly over the other. It is better to allow the glue in these assemblies to set before going on to assemble in the other direction.

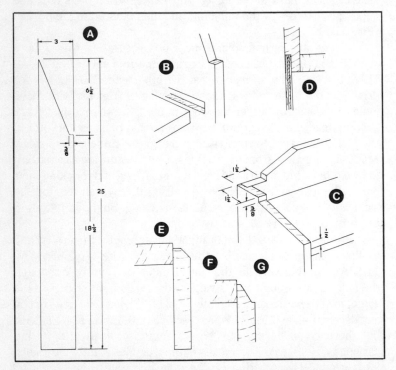

Fig. 11-19. Constructional details of the floor bookcase: (A) side extension pieces; (B) fit the shelves; (C) prepare the back; (D) rabbet the back edges; (E) below shelf level; (F) plain bevel; (G) stepping down.

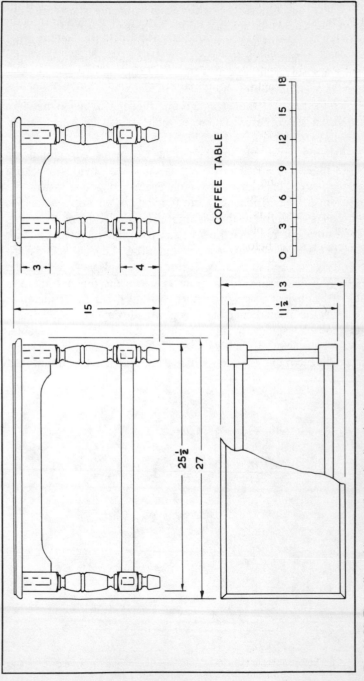

Fig. 11-20. The coffee table proportions give it a pleasing appearance.

Check squareness the other way when the short rails are added. Sight across to see that opposite ends match and there is no twist. Check squareness when viewed from above and leave the assembly standing on a flat surface for the glue to set. Cut off the top extensions on the legs. See that their tops and the top edges of the rails are flat and level.

For a table of the sizes given, there will be no need to strengthen the corners. In a larger table, triangular fillets can be glued in the top corners (Fig. 11-24E).

In many hardwoods, the top will have to be made by gluing two boards together. Because the top is the most obvious part to a casual viewer, take care to match grain and get an attractive appearance. Do any planing of the top and bottom surfaces before the wood is cut to size so that any marks from edge-holding devices will be cut off later. Check the final size over the framework so that there is an even overhang all round. Make sure the ends are accurately squared in relation to the sides and plane across the grain. Any discrepancy from squareness in the finished table is liable to be obvious to a viewer more than any other slight mistake.

How the molded edge of the top is made depends on available equipment. If a spindle or router with a suitable cutter is available, it can be machined. If that is done, allow for finishing by scraping and sanding to remove evidence of machine cutting. If a suitable old

Fig. 11-21. The coffee table, with its carved legs, is a miniature of a side or dining table.

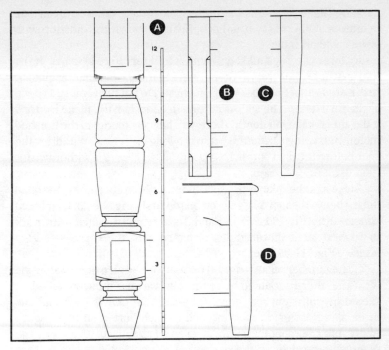

Fig. 11-22. Turned leg details (A,B,C) and alternatives (D) for other designs.

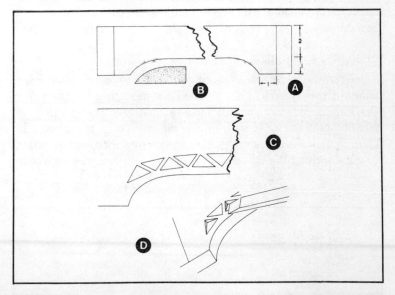

Fig. 11-23. The coffee table rails are shaped (A,B) and may be decorated with chip carving (C,D).

199

molding plane is available, the edges can be dealt with in one operation. Otherwise, it is not difficult to work this section with ordinary hand tools.

Lower the edge all round with a fillister (Fig. 11-25A). If the tool is fitted with a spur to sever fibers across the grain, use this for cutting the rabbets across the grain first. Do not plane quite as deep as the final level. The spur is cutting deeper than the plane iron and if the cut is made full depth, there will be spur marks in the finished molding showing across the cut in the long direction. Withdraw the spur before the final cuts across the grain and leave it withdrawn for cutting along the grain.

Use a rabbet plane, or the fillister without its guides, to round the rabbet to the molding section on top first (Fig. 11-25B) and then underneath (Fig. 11-25C). Sand to a smooth curve and work through at least three grades of paper. Get the corners to neat miters (Fig. 11-25D).

The number of buttons will depend on the size of the table and what risk there seems to be of the top warping if uncontrolled. It should be sufficient for there to be a single one at each end and three along each side. Cut the end of each button so that it goes easily into the rabbet, but when screwed to the top its upper edge draws the top tight on the framework (Fig. 11-25E). The buttons can be glued as well as screwed to the top, but it might be easier for staining and polishing if the top is left off until that is completed and then the buttons screwed on. See Table 11-5 for a materials list.

RUSH-TOPPED STOOL

A traditional method of seating used rushes or reeds that were gathered from riversides and dried. They were then twisted into a rope form as they were woven into a seat pattern. This is still done by a few craftsmen. Apart from the difficulty of gettilng suitable material, there is considerable skill in making the rope at the same time as working the pattern. There are alternatives available

Table 11-5. Materials List for Coffee Table.

4 legs	2 × 15 × 2
2 top rails	3 × 25 × ¾
2 top rails	2 × 11 × ¾
2 bottom rails	1¼ × 25 × ¾
2 bottom rails	1¼ × 11 × ¾
1 top	13 × 28 × ¾
buttons from	1¼ × 16 × ½

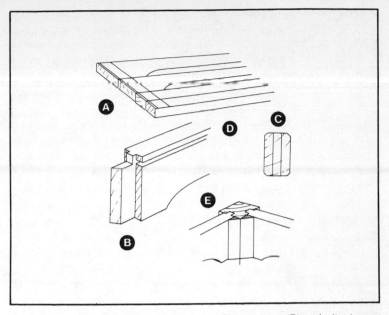

Fig. 11-24. Mark rails together (A) groove (B,C) for buttons (D) and miter tenons (E).

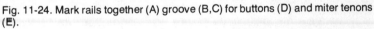

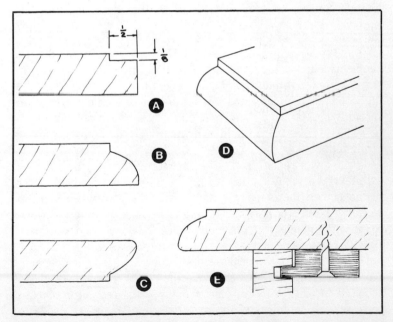

Fig. 11-25. Table edges can be shaped with ordinary tools: (A) use a Fillister; (B) top; (C) bottom; (D) corners; (E) use a screw to tighten.

already twisted into ropes. The one nearest to rush in appearance is seagrass. It comes from China and is bought as a sort of two-strand rope in the green/brown color very similar to dried rush. It is available in several diameters. The coarsest (about 3/16 of an inch) is quick and satisfactory, but the thinner (about ⅛ of an inch) gives a neater appearance. For an average chair, or the stool described here, 2 pounds should be sufficient.

Other suitable materials are described as *fiber rush*. This is a twisted cord made of paper and available in several colors as well as one that is comparable with rush. Also, there is a *Danish seat cord* which is a rope-like fiber material colored brown.

The stool frame shown in Figs. 11-26 and 11-27 has turned legs and bottom rails, but both of these parts can be square section and treated in the same way as the alternatives for the coffee table (Fig. 11-22).

Many other proportions are possible. The size shown makes a comfortable seat for an adult or child. If a much higher stool is made, the lower rails can be doubled with a second round of rails about 4 inches above the first to give extra resistance to the strain of rocking on two legs which some users might give. The smallest worthwhile stool is about 11 inches square and 9 inches high and that serves as a footrest or a seat for a child.

Turn the legs (Fig. 11-28A) with the aid of a rod to get them the same. Because the tops will be visible, take care to get them alike and smooth right to the centers. Have some waste wood at the headstock end and taper this down to allow final cuts to be made in shaping the top in a neat curve almost to the center. Then remove the wood from the lathe and saw off the waste with enough left to carefully chisel. Sand the center so that there are no torn fibers showing there as there would be if you parted right into the center in the lathe.

The lower rails (Fig. 11-28B) are turned so that the ends are parallel and drive fits in the leg holes. As a guard against chatter marks due to the wood vibrating under the tool when you are working the center part of the long rails, after turning the wood round with a gouge, turn the central bead and the shaped parts each side of it before reducing the sizes of the ends.

In the traditional rush pattern, the top rails are made deeper at the centers (Fig. 11-28C) and have the edges rounded. It is also possible to work a top in one of many variations on a checker pattern. The suppliers of the materials offer booklets on these methods. If you choose one of these methods, the top rails should be made parallel. However, such patterns are modern methods and

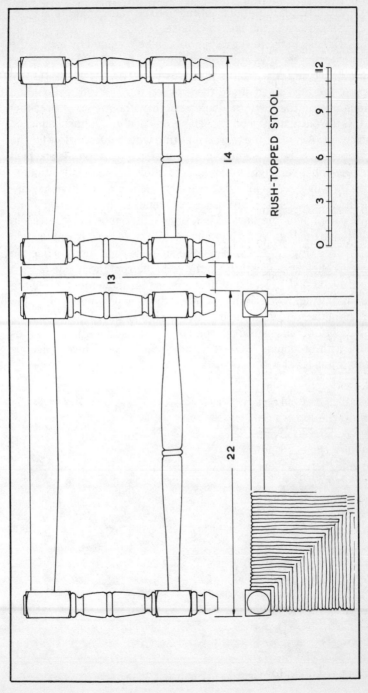

RUSH-TOPPED STOOL

13

14

22

12
9
6
3
0

Fig. 11-26. A rush-topped stool follows a traditional pattern.

very attractive. If the stool is intended to be of the traditional type, the rush pattern is the one to choose.

Stiffness in the lower rail joints can be obtained by having the rails entering the legs at different levels (Fig. 11-29A). Make the top mortise and tenon joints in the usual way (Fig. 11-29B). The tops of the legs stand above the worked top and there should be enough wood there to provide strength without risk of breaking out. If the particular wood chosen seems doubtful, short haunches can be cut. Allow for the tenons meeting with miters. Allow for the bottom rails to be the same overall lengths as the top rails and drill the legs for them slightly too deep to allow for some adjustment.

Do whatever sanding is necessary before assembly. Assemble the long sides first. To ensure squareness, clamp the top joints with pads under the jaws. Then adjust the angles of the top in relation to the legs with a try square. Allow the bottom rail to slide in its holes (Fig. 11-29C). When the shape is right, drive a fine pin or nearly headless nail through the rail end from the inside of each leg (Fig. 11-29D). This will prevent further movement while the glue is setting. If you wish to remove the clamps immediately, the tenons at the top rail can be locked in a similar way. Later, the nails in the bottom rails can be punched below the surface and the holes filled with stopping. However, they will be very inconspicuous even if left level with the surface.

Fig. 11-27. The rush-topped stool has turned legs and rails.

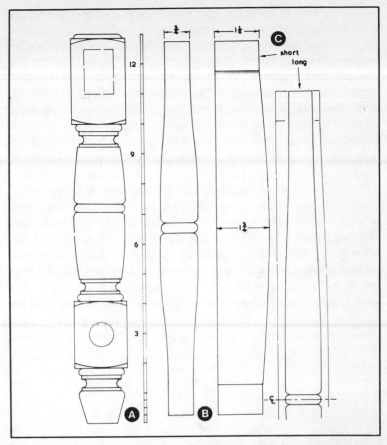

Fig. 11-28. Shapes of legs and rails (A,B,C) for the rush-topped stool.

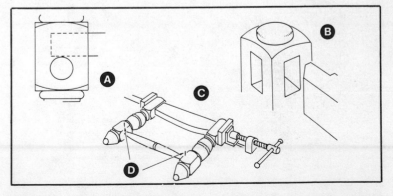

Fig. 11-29. Rigidity of the rush-topped stool depends on good joints (A,B) and carefully squared assembly (C).

Assemble the opposite sides and check to be sure they match each other and are without twist. When the glue has set, assemble the other way in a similar manner and check squareness from above and that the stool stands level.

Any finish the woodwork is to be given is best applied before working the top. However, there will have to be a final polishing later, because the woodwork will be handled in many directions while dealing with the top. The top rails will be hidden and any finish given to the rest of the frame will go just a short distance along each rail from the legs. It is better for the rush to grip if the rails are left bare.

For the purpose of instruction, it is assumed that seagrass will be used. However, the method is the same for the other materials as well. For working, the material from the hank should be wound on spools or shuttles. A spool (Fig. 11-30A) can be fashioned from scrap wood and need not be carefully shaped. You also need a pointed piece of wood. If you do not already have a pointed tool that can be used, whittle a point on a piece about 1-inch square.

Although the finished seat looks complicated and the method of construction is not obvious, the steps in working it are quite simple and merely a repetition of one action. Decide which way you

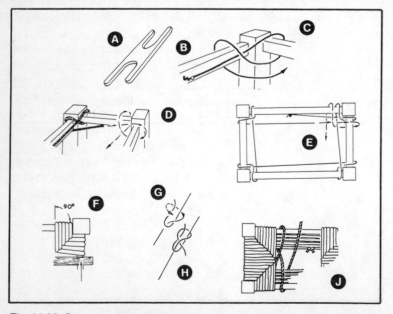

Fig. 11-30. Seagrass or similar material is worked with a spool (A) around the corners (B,C,D,E,F) to build up a pattern (G,H,J).

Table 11-6. Materials List for Rush-Topped Stool.

4 legs	1¾ × 14 × 1¾
2 top rails	1¾ × 21 × 1
2 top rails	1¾ × 13 × 1
2 bottom rails	1¼ × 21 × 1¼
2 bottom rails	1¼ × 13 × 1¼

will work around the stool. You will go around each leg the opposite way, but until you get used to the action it is possible to make a mistake and start going back.

Tie a knot in the end of the seagrass and tack it to a rail (Fig. 11-30B). Go over the next rail, under it and up through the center of the stool and back over the first rail (Fig. 11-30C). That is the complete action that has to be mastered. Subsequent work is a repeat of that. Take the line up through the center and do the same around the next leg top (Fig. 11-30D), then the third and the fourth. Pull tight as you go around each corner and hold that tight while you strain across and do the next corner. The whole top should be worked as tightly as possible. It helps to have an assistant. One person holds on to what you have done, while the other does the next step and tightens it.

After going around each leg, go to the one you started on and do the action inside the first round (Fig. 11-30E). Continue around like this, inside the previous step each time. You will see that the pattern builds up and the parts between corners will be hidden inside. As you progress, see that the turns at the points of the patterns do not ride up and see that you are working squarely and tightly (Fig. 11-30F). The square edge of a piece of wood can be used to push the seagrass along the rails (where necessary). If you have to join in a fresh piece, make the knot in one of the parts between corners and it will be hidden. The best knot is the sheet bend. Bend one end back and take the other end through the loop (Fig. 11-30G), around the back of it and across the front and under itself (Fig. 11-30H). Work it tight without altering its shape and do not cut off the ends too short.

Eventually you will have the short rails full. Further turns are put on in a figure eight pattern over the long rails (Fig. 11-30J). Continue doing this and pack tightly until you can get no more in. Then fasten the last turn with a tack driven through it into the underside of a rail. Cut off a few inches from the tack and tuck the end into the underside of the pattern. See Table 11-6 for a materials list.

UPHOLSTERED STOOL

A stool frame can be made with lower and upper rails and an upholstered top, but if the top rails are made deep enough, there will be enough strength in the joints for the lower rails to be left out (unless the stool is very tall). The one shown in Fig. 11-31 can be modified to a different shape and size top and the legs increased to chair height without the need for lower rails.

The legs are square, but tapered on the inner faces only from below the rail level (Fig. 11-32A). Bevel around their bottoms. Marking out of the tapers as well as the joints is most accurately done together while the parts are square. Mark opposite rails together with knife cut shoulder positions. Lower edges can be shaped in a similar way to the coffee table and they can be carved. The joints are best made with two-part tenons and haunched (Fig. 11-31B). However, four ⅜-inch dowels in each place would be satisfactory.

Assemble in the same way as the earlier stools, but be careful of squareness as there is no lower rail to help hold the shape. The top will be hidden, so it can be a piece of plywood that is nailed or screwed on. Drill a few holes in it to allow air through as the upholstery filling compresses and expands in use (Fig. 11-32B). Stain and polish the wood parts that will show before upholstering the top.

The top can be stuffed with traditional materials, but the simplest and more satisfactory way is to use a piece of plastic or foam rubber. It should be about 2 inches thick and cut to overhang the wood by about one-half inch so that it will be compressed by the covering. Most foam will cut cleanly with a sharp thin-bladed knife. Wetting the blade will help. Bevel the underside all round (Fig. 11-33A) to about half the thickness.

Use a piece of calico or other plain flexible cloth. Tack its center to one rail and then stretch over the foam to tack at the opposite side. Do the same centrally the other way. From these central tacks, work outward toward the corners. Pull each time against an opposing tack at the other side. Spacing will depend on the flexibility of the foam, but will probably be about 1 inch. Work a short distance down from the top of the rail (Fig. 11-33B). Aim to get the foam compressed and the bevelled under edge pulled down tightly.

At the corners, pull down diagonally to get a neat shape and fold the cloth as necessary to allow tacks to hold the shape. Use a knife to cut the cloth parallel below the tacks (Fig. 11-33C). Fix the

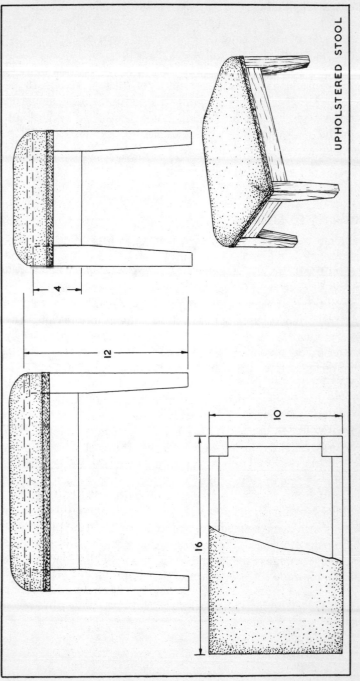

UPHOLSTERED STOOL

Fig. 11-31. The upholstered stool has its padded top made on the frame.

outer material in the same way. As far as possible, arrange tacks through that between and below the first tacks to level out any unevenness in the padding under the first piece of cloth. As the folds in the outer covering will show, make the folded arrangement the same at each corner. If it is a boldly patterned material, it will look best if a main motif comes centrally on the top. Make sure the row of tacks is parallel with the rail edge and at the same height all round. It might be necessary to lift some tacks and adjust the cloth to get the best effect. When it is satisfactory, trim the cloth below the tacks and cover the cut edge with a strip of *gimp*. Gimp is tape-like material that is available in many designs to match the covering cloth. Fasten it with small black nails called *gimp pins* (Fig. 11-33D). See Table 11-7 for a materials list.

LOOSE-SEATED STOOL

Many chairs have upholstered seats that can be lifted out. This stool is made in the same way and is at chair height (Figs. 11-34 and 11-35). It will serve as an extra seat at a table, piano stool or as a general purpose stool for adult use. It would be possible to give it enough stiffness by having deep top rails and no lower rails, but it is shown with moderate depth top rails and light bottom rails. The legs are square for their full length, but a taper effect is obtained by chamfering back from octagonal feet.

The top rails are the same thickness as the legs, but a rabbet is cut to take the top (Fig. 11-36A). Tenons at the corners have one face level with the rim and are haunched (Fig. 11-36B).

Mark out the four legs together, but make sure that the mortises for the bottom rails are paired. Include marking the chamfers, but leave planing them until after the mortises have been cut. The mortises for the bottom rails are kept reasonably thick for maximum strength (Fig. 11-36C). At the center of each rail, the mortise for the single rail is in the direction of the grain (Fig. 11-36D). Make this joint about three-quarters of the thickness of the end rail. Check the length between the shoulders of the central rail from the other parts. Allow for how much the cross rails are set back from the edge of the legs. The rail has to be that much longer than the top rails if the legs are to stand upright (Fig. 11-36E).

Table 11-7. Materials List for Upholstered Stool.

4 legs	1½ × 12 × 1½
2 rails	4 × 16 × ¾
2 rails	4 × 10 × ¾
1 top	10 × 16 × ½ ply

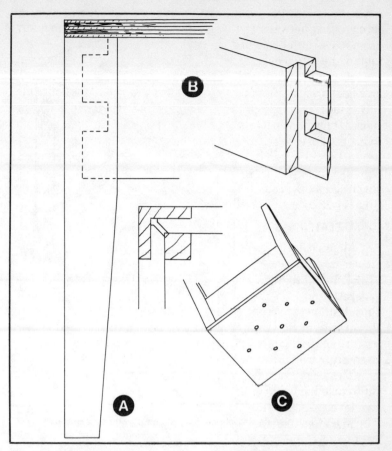

Fig. 11-32. Wide-tenoned rails (A,B) give strength. Holes in the top allow air to enter and leave the padding (C).

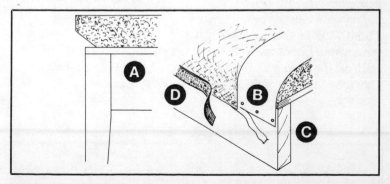

Fig. 11-33. A foam pad is cut and covered with two layers of cloth, then edged (A,B,C,D) with gimp.

211

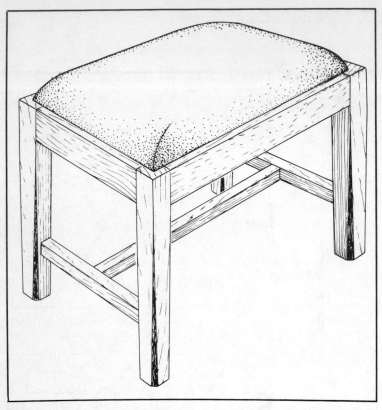

Fig. 11-34. A loose-seated stool has the padded part made separately.

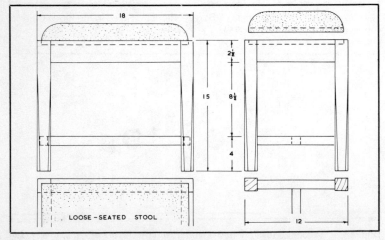

LOOSE-SEATED STOOL

Fig. 11-35. These sizes give a stool height about the same as a chair.

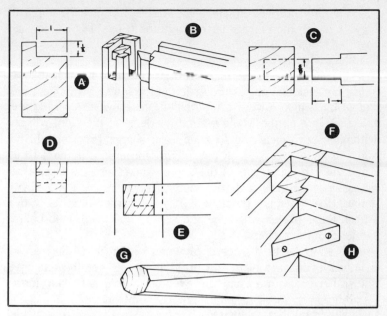

Fig. 11-36. The top is rabbeted (A) for the loose seat. Joints are tenoned (B) and legs are tapered (C,D,E). A reinforcing block goes into each corner (F,G,H).

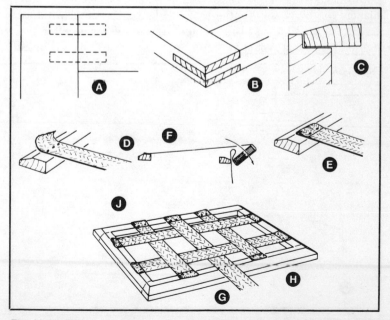

Fig. 11-37. The loose top is a frame, dowelled or bridled (A,B,C), with webbing stretched over it (D,E,F,G,H).

Cut the mortises in the legs. At the top of each leg, cut back to match the rabbets in the top rails (Fig. 11-36F), so that the loose top will have a level bearing all round. Plane the chamfers (Fig. 11-36G).

Assemble the short sides first, instead of the usual long sides, because this makes the fitting of the lower framing easier. Put in the single lowere rail when the lengthwise top rails are fitted. Square up the whole assembly. Because the stool will be without a permanent top to keep it in shape, there should be some stiffening gussets to put in the corners. Cut them from wood with the grain across the angle. Make sure the faces that go against the rails are true right angles. Allow for a small amount that does not go closely into the corner (Fig. 11-36H). Attach these pieces with glue and screws and keep them below the level of the rabbets.

The top can be a piece of plywood so that it can be treated in a very similar way to the previous stool, but the example shown here is with a frame and webbing. Giving the seat more flexibility in this way makes for greater comfort.

The frame has to fit into the recess so that is reasonably tight after the upholstery has been done. To make sure of this, both thicknesses of covering material should be obtained before making the frame so that the total thickness can be allowed for. It will be possible to plane something off the frame after it is assembled, but it would be better not to have to take off much.

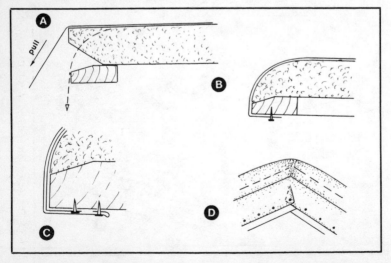

Fig. 11-38. The cut foam is pulled (A) over the top frame and the cloth tacked underneath (B,C,D).

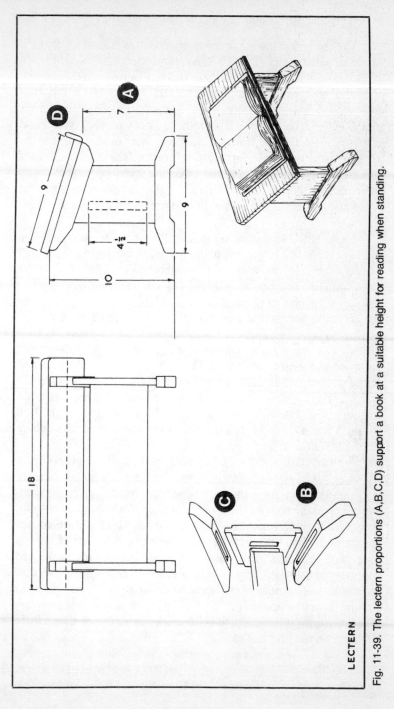

LECTERN

Fig. 11-39. The lectern proportions (A,B,C,D) support a book at a suitable height for reading when standing.

215

In any case, the frame cannot be adjusted after covering has begun.

The corners of the frame can be made in several ways. Dowels would be satisfactory (Fig. 11-37A). Haunched mortise and tenon joints can be used, but there is little strain. Open mortise and tenon or bridle joints are simple (Fig. 11-37). This is particularly true with a screw driven centrally. Make up the frame. Check its corner angles in the stool recess. If that shape is not perfect, you might have to settle for the frame fitting one way only. This can be marked on the underside for future reference. The frame is thicker than the lip on the stool and the covering will look neater if you taper around the top (Fig. 11-37C). Take any sharpness off the edges and corners of the frame, but do not round anywhere excessively.

Most upholstery webbing is about 2 inches wide. Space the webbing according to the size of the frame, but arrange spaces only a little more than the width of the webbing. Tack one end to the frame with two or three tacks (Fig. 11-36D). Then fold over the end and tack through that (Fig. 11-36E). Each piece of webbing has to be stretched across the frame with as much tension as can be reasonably applied. There are special webbing strainers, but for this stool a piece of scrap wood can be used. Fold the webbing over the wood and lever it down (Fig. 11-37F). On the first piece, pencil on the webbing where it comes after stretching. Use this as a guide to the amount of stretch to get into each piece. Tack the stretched webbing (Fig. 11-37G) and then cut it off with enough to fold back and tack again (Fig. 11-37H). Interweave the pieces of webbing (Fig. 11-37J).

A piece of plain cloth can be lightly tacked all round above the webbing or the piece of plastic or foam rubber can be put directly over the webbing. As in the previous stool, cut it slightly oversize and bevel its underside. Use a piece of plain cloth over it and strain it to curve the edges of the foam (Fig. 11-38A). Tack underneath far enough in for the line of tacks to come inside the edge of the top rails (Fig. 11-38B). The outer covering can be any patterned upholstery material. This is also a suitable place for a piece of embroidery. The inner cloth should be doing all that is necessary to pull the foam to shape, so the outer covering need only have enough tension to draw it close. On the underside, carry the cloth in a little further than the first line of tacks and turn under the edge as you go (Fig. 11-38C). If the covering cloth is thick, folds at the corners might build up the thickness so that the loose seat is held up there. Draw the cloth over a corner and then cut out some so that the

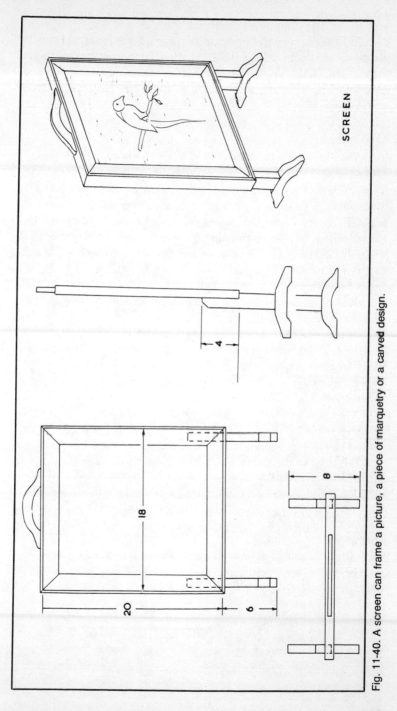

SCREEN

Fig. 11-40. A screen can frame a picture, a piece of marquetry or a carved design.

remaining parts can overlap without folds (Fig. 11-38D). The top should fit tight enough to stay in place in normal use, but a push from below should release it. If you find the frame was made too small, the cloth can be released from one side and a strip of cardboard can be put under it as a packing. See Table 11-8 for a materials list.

LECTERN

This is a reading desk (Fig. 11-39) to stand on an ordinary table and hold a book at a suitable height for reading when standing. It would also serve as a stand for a dictionary or encyclopedia. The size should suit most books, but can easily be modified.

The upper sizes and angles can only be obtained from a full size drawing, so start by drawing the end view to the size you want (Fig. 11-39A). Mark the wood sizes from the materials list and taper ends to about half thickness. The curves there can be drawn around a coin.

Make the pair of ends first. Cut away the feet underneath so that they stand without rocking. Mortises and tenons can all be ⅜ of an inch thick. The bottom joint is straightforward (Fig. 11-39B), but the top one is best made by cutting the tenon first so that the exact length along the slope for the mortise can be obtained from it. The ends of the mortise have to be chopped to suit the angle of the tenon (Fig. 11-39C).

Cut the top to size and make the lip. This can be the full length or be kept back a short distance at each end. A good glued joint should be strong enough, but a few fine nails or screws can be used into the edge of the top (Fig. 11-39D). Round all edges of top and lip.

Position the supports about 1½ inches in from each end of the top. Try them temporarily in position and this will give you the length to cut the front. Mark it between shoulders and allow about

Table 11-8. Materials List for Loose-Seated Stool.

4 legs	1½ × 16 × 1½
2 top rails	2½ × 17 × 1½
2 top rails	2½ × 11 × 1½
2 bottom rails	1 × 11 × 1
1 bottom rail	1 × 17 × 1
2 top frames	2 × 18 × ¾
2 top frames	2 × 12 × ¾
4 gussets	2 × 5 × ¾

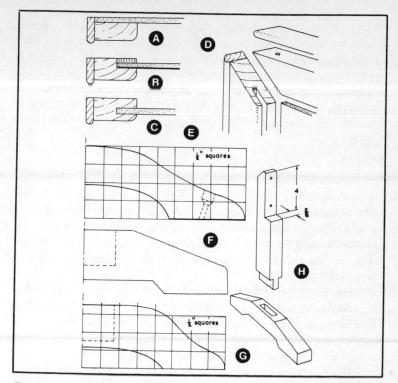

Fig. 11-41. The frame (A,B,C) is arranged to suit the panel (D,E,F,G,H) and there can be a handle. Feet are tenoned.

½-inch for the tenons. They can go right through with exposed ends if you prefer.

Clean and sand the parts before assembly. If excess glue is avoided when making the joints, there should be little further cleaning to be done after assembly. Assemble the ends and see that they match. Add the front and check squareness. Let the glue harden in this assembly.

If the top is a stable wood that is unlikely to expand and contract, it can be glued to the supports. It would be better to use

Table 11-9. Materials List for Lectern.

1 top	9 × 19 × ⅝
1 lip	1¼ × 19 × ⅜
2 feet	1½ × 10 × 1⅛
2 legs	4½ × 9 × ⅝
2 supports	1¼ × 10 × ¾
1 front	4½ × 16 × ⅝

secret slot screwing without glue. Then the screw heads could move in the slots if there is any difference in the width of the top. Invert the lectern and pencil around the positions of the supports under the top. Mark positions for screws on the center lines of the supports and opposite them under the top at about 1½ inches from the edges of the top. The screws are driven into the top and the slots made in the supports. See Table 11-9 for a materials list.

SCREEN

A screen has uses in standing in front of an empty fireplace, but it also makes a good display item. Its main panel can be an example of marquetry. It can be a piece of tapestry or decorative needlework stretched over a stiff backing. It might be a painting that is uncovered or mounted behind glass. The central area might be carved, just as a surface decoration, or anything up to prominent relief work.

The instructions are for making the screen with a plain panel that could be decorated in one of these ways. If there is an existing piece of some sort of art work, the sizes will have to be modified to suit. The panel can be hardboard or plywood and the rest of the screen solid wood to match other furniture.

The screen stands on two feet and has a handle for lifting (Fig. 11-40). In its simplest form, the frame could go on the surface of the panel (Fig. 11-41A). However, it is better craftsmanship to let the panel in, either as in a picture frame (Fig. 11-41B), if that suits the item to be displayed, or in a groove (Fig. 11-41C), which can be used for stretched cloth over the panel as well as for plain wood.

The mitered frame can have its corners screwed because they will be covered by the outer strips (Fig. 11-41D). The frame wood is shown with a rounded inner edge, but it could be molded. If the focal point is to be the decoration of the panel, it is better to have the frame more subdued.

Table 11-10. Materials List for Screen.

2 frames	⅞ × 21 × 1¾
2 frames	⅞ × 19 × 1¾
2 feet	⅞ × 9 × 1¾
2 legs	⅞ × 10 × 1¾
2 outer strips	¼ × 22 × 1⅛
2 outer strips	¼ × 21 × 1⅛
1 handle	2 × 10 × ½
1 panel	18 × 20 × ⅛ plywood or hardboard.

A graceful handle is part of the decoration. Make it with flowing curves (Fig. 11-41E) and well round all exposed parts. Attach it with glue and thin screws sunk below the surface and plugged or covered with stopping.

The feet can be angular (Fig. 11-41F) or given curves that complement those of the handle (Fig. 11-41G). Make the legs to hold the frame at the height required (Fig. 11-41H). Ensure that they stand upright. Any tendency to slope forward is liable to look worse than it is. Screw the legs into the back of the frame.

Because the screen is portable and the back is visible sometimes, finish there should be as good as the front. If the panel is covered with cloth at the front, plain cloth can be put over the back to hide the unattractive surface of plywood or hardboard. See Table 11-10 for a materials list.

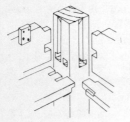

Chapter 12
Tables

Ever since man started making furniture, tables have been very important items. The basic table is a flat top supported at a convenient height for use when sitting or standing, but there are an endless number of variations. The usual shape is rectangular with a leg at each corner and the majority of tables are still made this way. Others have pedestals centrally or in parts at opposite ends. Tops can be almost any shape the designer likes, providing there is sufficient area for use, but practical requirements usually mean the majority of tops are close to rectangular.

Whatever its construction or details of its design, a table which is both satisfactory in use and pleasing in appearance follows the usual rules of design in giving a rectangular appearance whatever the direction of viewing. For normal sitting use, the height is about 30 inches. Other measurements should be somewhat more or less than this, but not close to that size. Usually the width is less than 30 inches and the length is more (unless it is a very large table).

A table should be stable. The location of the feet should not be far within the outline of the table when viewed from above. Much depends on weight. If there is plenty of weight in the lower parts, the legs need not spread as much. Coupled with this is the need to arrange the framing so that the legs of users are not cramped any more than is necessary if it is a table for use when sitting. This means keeping top rails shallow enough to clear the users knees and avoiding lower framing where a persons legs would come.

There can be considerable leverage on the joints of a table when it is pushed. The load must be spread with lower framing or the top framing should have joints wide enough to take the strain.

The tables described in this chapter are examples of several methods of construction. Many others can be found, but the techniques used in the examples can be adapted to most other types.

SIDE TABLE

This can be regarded as the classic table design (Figs. 12-1 and 12-2) on which there can be many variations. In itself, it serves as a small table with many uses. Primarily it is for use at the side of a room, for displaying flowers or ornaments, or for extra dishes when a meal is being served.

As a piece of cabinetwork, it serves as a good introduction for anyone without previous table-making experience and could lead to the making of more ambitious tables. In itself its attraction probably comes from its proportions and simple out-

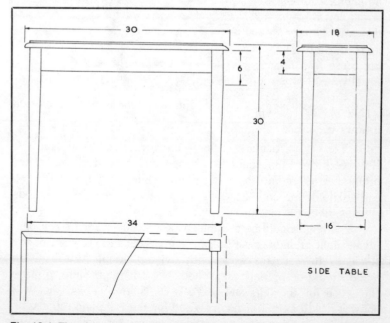

Fig. 12-1. The side table has the simple classic form basic to many tables.

Fig. 12-2. Proportions and a molded edge provide the attraction of the side table.

line. This is particularly true if an attractive wood is used. However, the rails could be shaped and carved if the maker prefers. The legs are best left plain, while the edge of the top can be molded in one of the ways described later. Two methods are described for making the top.

The legs should be made from wood chosen for its reasonably straight grain because there are no lower rails to restrict any tendency to warp for wood with twisted grain. Any furniture wood should be properly seasoned, but if it is possible to plane the wood for the legs and leave it for a few weeks, that will show if it will keep its shape. Wood for the rails and top can be chosen for its appearance without regard for straightness of grain. Prepare the wood for the rails and legs first (with a little extra on the lengths).

Mark out parts of similar length together. Use a knife where cuts are to come. The rails are mortise and tenoned centrally into the tops of the legs with double stubbed tenons (Fig. 12-3A). Alternatively, they can be cut exactly to length and dowelled (Fig. 12-3B). If the top is to be made of solid wood, plow grooves for the buttons inside the tops of the rails. If the top is to be framed plywood, there is not a need for the grooves.

Taper the legs carefully so that the tapers look the same from whatever angle they are viewed. Take the sharpness off the bottom edges, so as not to damage carpets, although metal glides could be used there.

Assemble the long rails to the legs first and carefully square them by measuring diagonals. Check the second assembly over the first and see that there are no twists. When that glue has set, assemble with the short rails and again check squareness in all directions. Cut the tops of the legs level with the rails.

The most appropriate traditional top is made from solid wood. It is unlikely that one piece of the full width can be obtained and two or more pieces might have to be joined by gluing. So far as possible, match the color and the grain patterns. Slight unevenness on the underside might not matter, but on top the surface must be finished smooth and flat in all directions. Check with a straightedge diagonally as well as parallel with edges. (Fig. 12-4A).

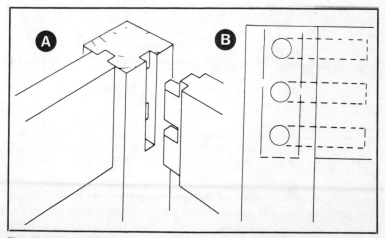

Fig. 12-3. The table rails can be tenoned (A) or dowelled (B).

225

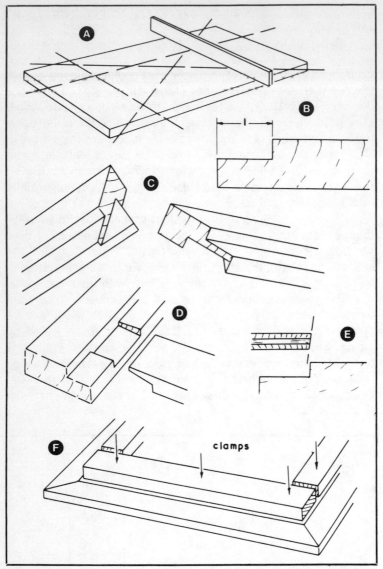

Fig. 12-4. The table top can be solid or framed plywood: (A) use a straight edge ; (B) cut a rabbet; (C) lap at the corner; (D) notch; (E) tapered edges; (F) clamp.

The top can be made with framed plywood. It is best if you use plywood that has already been veneered on the face with the same wood as it surrounds, but it might make an interesting effect to use a contrasting wood or even a plastic surface. Cut a fairly wide rabbet in the frame pieces (Fig. 12-4B). If this is just a little too deep, the frame can be levelled with the plywood after assembly. If it is too shallow, there is nothing that can be done to put it right. A wide rabbet helps to keep the whole assembly flat.

At the corners, the joints must appear as miters on top. But to provide stiffness, one piece can half lap in the other at each corner (Fig. 12-4C). Whether intermediate supports are needed depends on the thickness and stiffness of the plywood. If there is a risk of it flexing in use, put one or two crossbars underneath that are notched into the long sides (Fig. 12-4D).

The plywood panel should be a close fit in its frame. It is advisable to leave it oversize and assemble the frame first. Then carefully plane it to fit. If the edge is slightly tapered (Fig.

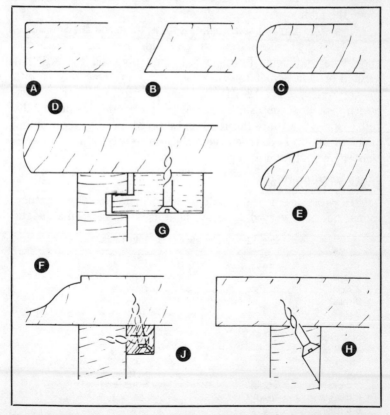

Fig. 12-5. Edge decoration can take many forms (A,B,C). A solid top should be attached with buttons, but a framed top may be screwed (D,E,F,G,H).

12-4E), the joints should finish close on top. Use glue only and spread clamping pressure with wood pads (Fig. 12-4F).

The simplest treatment of the edge is to leave it square with the sharpness taken off the angles (Fig. 12-5A). Giving it an angle is effective (Fig. 12-5B). Avoid 45 degrees because it looks better if more or less than this is used. Making the edge a full semicircle is not considered good design (Fig. 12-5C). It is better to use a larger radius so that there are angles between the curve and the surfaces (Fig. 12-5D).

The edge will look better if molded either with a spindle molder or by the use of planes. An edge similar to that described for the coffee table can be worked with a fillister and rabbet planes (Fig. 12-5E). More complicated shapes (Fig. 12-5F) will depend on suitable spindle cutters or molding planes. Avoid sharpness on the under edge where a hand will be placed to move the table.

If a solid top is used, make buttons to attach it to the rails (Fig. 12-5G). Three buttons at each side and one at each end should be sufficient. Because a framed plywood top will not expand or contract, it can be attached rigidly. One way is with pocket screws (Fig. 12-5H). Another way to get a very secure attachment is to put square strips all round the insides of the rails with screws into the rails and upward into the top framing (Fig. 12-5J). In both cases, glue the top to the framing as well. See Table 12-1 for a materials list.

TABLE WITH DRAWERS

Drawers are valuable additions to many tables, but they cannot be made very deep if the table is to be of normal height

Table 12-1. Materials List for Side Table.

4 legs	1⅞ × 30 × 1⅞
2 rails	4 × 34 × ⅞
2 rails	4 × 16 × ⅞
2 rails	4 × 16 × ⅞
1 top	18 × 37 × ⅞
or 2 pieces	3 × 37 × ⅞
and 2 pieces	3 × 19 × ⅞
and 1 piece	15 × 33 × ¼ × ⅜ plywood
buttons from	1½ × 18 × ¾
2 crossbars (if needed)	1½ × 16 × ⅝
2 top strips (if needed)	½ × 31 × ½
2 top strips (if needed)	½ × 13 × ½

and there is to be sufficient clearance underneath for the knees of a person sitting on a chair. A rail depth of about 6 inches, as in this table, gives a drawer of just over 4 inches internal depth. That is about the most that can be expected. The table (Fig. 12-6) is generally similar in construction to the side table. However, it is larger and there are modifications to allow for fitting the drawers. The top could be made up from solid boards glued together, but it is shown as framed plywood.

The legs are the same size as those of the side table and the mortise and tenon joints for the long rails are the same. But in the other direction, the bottom drawer rail uses pairs of tenons (Fig. 12-7A) and the top rail could have similar tenons. However, there is a slight gain in strength by using dovetails (Fig. 12-7B).

The section shows the relative positions of parts and how they are arranged to allow the drawers to slide (Fig. 12-8). If the table is being made to other sizes or wood of other sections is being used, it is advisable to make a full size drawing of this section to get the sizes of wood right.

The drawers slide on runners which are glued and screwed inside the long rails (Fig. 12-8A). At their ends, they could merely butt against the bottom drawer rails. There would not be a risk of movement in relation to each other and interference

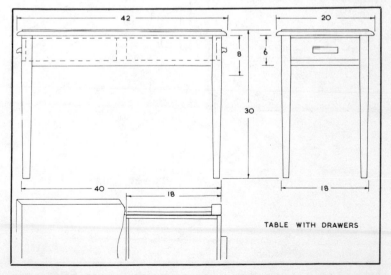

Fig. 12-6. Drawers add to the usefulness of a table. This one has drawers at then ends.

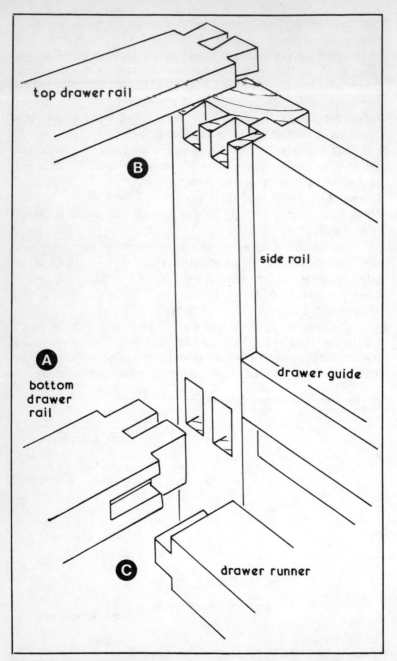

top drawer rail

B

side rail

A
bottom
drawer
rail

drawer guide

C

drawer runner

Fig. 12-7. Rails above and below the drawers meet tenons (A,B,C) in the other rails.

with the smooth run of a drawer if the end of the runner has a short tenon into the rail (Fig. 12-7C).

Make up the two long sides by gluing the rails into the legs and see that they are square. Attach the drawer runners

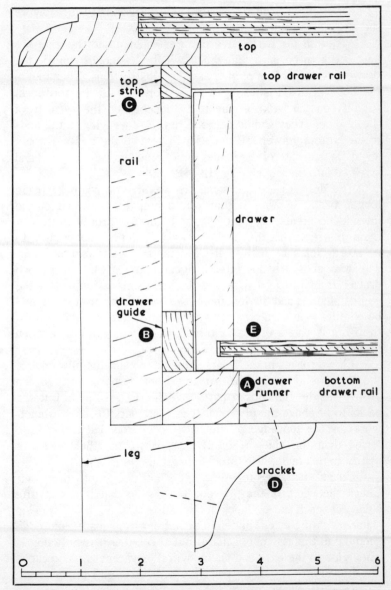

Fig. 12-8. Section through the table, showing how the drawer fits.

with glue and screws. The drawer guides make up the width between the side rails and the inner edges of the legs (Fig. 12-8B). Glue them and use a few fine nails to prevent movement while the glue is setting. Put the top strips, that will be used to screw on the top, along the top edges of the side rails (Fig. 12-8C). Holes for the top screws will be easier to drill before the strips are put in position.

When all the parts have been assembled and the glue has set, check to be sure that there will be a smooth run for the drawers with no blobs of glue or other obstructions. Then join in the bottom crosswise drawer rails. Follow with the top ones. Rigidity on the width of the table depends on the security of these joints. They should be good fits. Fox wedging in the ends of the bottom drawer rail tenons will help. If there is any doubt about the strength of the joints, small brackets can be glued and screwed into the angles (Fig. 12-8D).

The drawers are the same. However, one could be made longer than the other if that would help the stowage of the intended contents. Cut the wood for drawer fronts first. Get them to size so that they make an easy fit in their openings with no more clearance than is needed for trouble-free movement. The two ends are not interchangeable, so mark where each drawer front is to go. Use the drawer fronts as guides to the widths of sides and the lengths of the back. Drawer sides should be parallel with each other or very slightly closer at the back. If the front is narrower than the back, a drawer will not function properly.

Plow grooves in the fronts and sides to suit the plywood for the bottoms (Fig. 12-8E). At the front corners, include the groove inside the bottom part dovetail (Fig. 12-9A). Cut the backs to fit above the plywood. It is customary in some cabinet-work for the top edge of the back to be rounded and a little lower than the sides (Fig. 12-9B). However, that does not matter in this table. Use through dovetails (Fig. 12-9C).

To put a drawer together, glue both sides into the front. Check the width of the plywood bottom so that it has a little clearance each side. Check to be sure that its front edge is square with the sides. Slide in the bottom. Its square front edge should pull the assembly square, but check that it is fully home. Then glue in the back and check overall squareness. Also check the drawer in the table. When the drawer is slid in, the front surface of it should match the opening made by the legs and

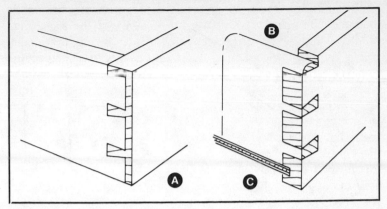

Fig. 12-9. Dovetail details at front (A) and back of drawer (B,C).

rails. If there is a slight error in the squareness of these, push the drawer to a shape that matches. Then carefully remove it and screw through the bottom into the drawer back to lock it in shape before the glue sets.

Clean off surplus glue and plane level any extending pins or dovetails at the back of each drawer. Try the drawers in place. Make stops from small blocks of wood screwed to the runners. Adjust them so that when the drawers are pushed fully home their fronts come level with the table end.

There can be metal handles on the drawer fronts or wooden pulls can be made from the same wood or from a contrasting wood. Although the handle shape shown is contained in a 1-inch square, it is easier to make handles together in one piece on the edge of a wider board so that there is something to hold in a vise or under a holdfast (Fig. 12-10A). The hollow could be worked with a curved molding cutter or it could be plowed and opened out. The rounded outside can be shaped with ordinary planes and plenty of sanding. Cut the handles to width, to length and round their ends. Attach them with glue and screws from inside the drawers (Fig. 12-10B).

The top is made in the same way as the side table top, but with the greater width the crossbars will almost certainly be needed (unless it is a very stiff plywood). Any of the edge sections suggested for the side table could be used, but a curve compatible with the handle shapes would be a feature of good design. Attach the top by screwing from below through the top strips at the sides. At the ends, drill through the top drawer rails and countersink the screws enough to clear the drawers.

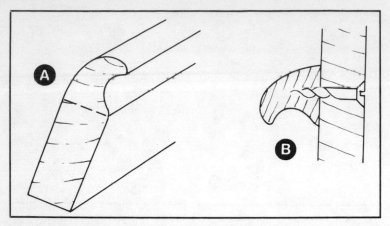

Fig. 12-10. Handles can be worked on the edge of a board and then cut off: (A) round the ends: (B) secure with a screw.

Joining the top to the framework is best done with everything inverted so that an even overhang all round can be checked and the screws are easier to drive downward. See Table 12-2 for a materials list.

WRITING TABLE

Construction of this table (Figs. 12-11 and 12-12) is kept light so that it is easy to lift and move about. It is intended for use as an occasional table, particularly for writing, with one

Table 12-2. Materials List for Table with Drawers

4 legs	1⅞ × 30 × 1⅞
2 rails	6 × 40 × ⅞
2 bottom drawers	1⅞ × 18 × ⅞
2 top drawer rails	1⅞ × 18 × ⅜
2 top frames	3 × 43 × ⅞
2 top frames	3 × 21 × ⅞
1 top	18 × 38 × ¼ or ⅜ plywood
2 drawer guides	1 × 38 × ½
2 drawer runners	1¼ × 38 × ⅞
2 drawer fronts	4¾ × 15 × ¾
4 drawer sides	4¾ × 18 × ⅝
2 drawer backs	4¼ × 15 × ⅝
2 drawer bottoms	15 × 18 × ¼ plywood
2 drawer handles	6 × 1 × 1
2 crossbars (if needed)	2 × 16 × ½
2 top strips	½ × 38 × ½

large drawer that can be divided for the storage of stationary and writing materials. The top is made of veneered plywood that is framed around with solid wood. It could be in contrast to its frame or matching wood. For writing, the surface could be plastic imitation leather.

The front has the drawer opening and the rail below it is cut away to give leg clearance. Back and sided match externally, but internally the sides differ from the back. The corner joints are different with the front legs as one pair and the rear legs as another. Mark them and the parts that join them to avoid confusion.

There is no lower framing to control the legs. Use straight grained wood. Mark the lengths and leave some surplus at the ends until the joints are cut. Each leg is square to below the top framing and the inner surfaces only are tapered to the bottom (Fig. 12-13A). Prepare the parts for back and front. Check that distances between shoulders are all the same. Shape the lower front rail (Fig. 12-13B) and well round the outer edge. It has a tenon into the leg, but the shallow top rail is dovetailed (Fig. 12-14A). At the back, the wide piece has bareface tenons to fit into the legs (Fig. 12-14B). The lower piece can have a wide tenon (Fig. 12-14C). It and the front rail will be notched to take the ends of the side piece, but leave cutting this until the sides

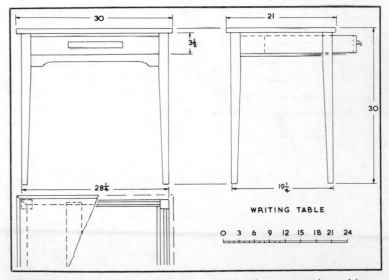

Fig. 12-11. This writing table has a good working area and good knee clearance.

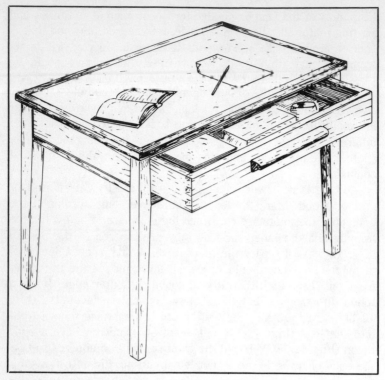

Fig. 12-12. A broad drawer provides good storage space in the writing table.

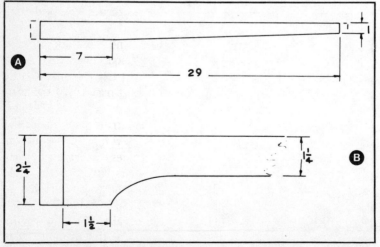

Fig. 12-13. Leg (A) and rail (B) shapes for the writing table.

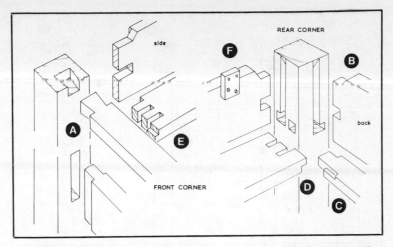

Fig. 12-14. Front corner joints (A,E) and rear corner joints (B,C,D,E) differ to suit the drawer fitting.

are made. Put the front and back pieces aside until the other parts are made.

Prepare the side pieces. The wide ones fit into the legs in the same way as the back. The lower piece is wider (Fig. 12-15A) and supports the drawer. Its end notch into back and front parts (Fig. 12-14D and E). Allow enough wood past the shoulder for this. Make the mortise and tenon joints into the legs and notch the joints into back and front lower parts. Be careful to get all top surfaces level because the drawer will slide on these. Round the exposed outer edges of the side and back lower pieces.

When all of the joints have been cut and the wood cleaned up, start assembly with the back. Check squareness and leave this clamped for the glue to set. Check that there is no twist by sighting across the legs. Assemble the front parts over the back so that they match.

Join these parts with the sides. The narrow parts under the wide pieces at back and sides can have a few fine screws driven upward, but otherwise it should be sufficient to glue all parts together. Check squareness in all directions and view the table from a distance to check for twist. This is shown by legs that do not appear in line when sighted across.

The top has to be made to overlap equally all round, but its controlling dimension is the inner edges of the framing. This should be level with the inner surfaces of the sides and backs

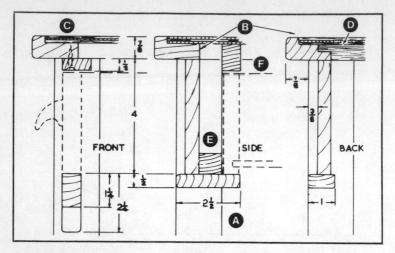

Fig. 12-15. Sections through the edges of the table showing the arrangement of parts: (A) lower piece; (B) sides and back; (C,D) front (E) side; (F) kickers.

(Fig. 12-15B) so that the top can be attached with buttons (Fig. 12-14F). Allow a comparable amount at the front, but the attachment is with screws (Fig. 12-15C).

Make the top framing with a broad rabbet (Fig. 12-16A) with the depth to suit the plywood insert. Ideally the match is exact, but it is better to have to level the frame to the plywood than to find that the plywood stands high in the final assembly. At that point, little can be done to put it right.

Use plain miters at the corners. Other parts will strengthen these joints, but corner fillets will help (Fig. 12-16B). Unless the plywood is very thick and stiff, there would be a risk of it flexing after the table has been in use some time. To prevent this, put stiffeners equally spaced from back to front (Fig. 12-15D and 15E) notched into the frame.

Glue the miters and stiffeners. Pull the corners together with picture frame clamps or put a rope around the frame with padding under it at the corners and twist it right. Fit the plywood insert closely by first matching two adjoining edges to the frame. Then plane the other edges to match. If the plane is tilted so that the underside is slightly smaller than the top surface, that can be fitted first and a little more taken off to get the top in.

Glue the plywood in. Have strips of scrap wood to put near the edges and plenty of weights over them while the frame is supported level. Use newspaper under the frame and scrap wood to prevent excess glue sticking where it is not wanted. Round the corners of the top and take the sharpness off the outer angles.

At the sides, fill the space between the wide parts and the thickness of the legs with strips to act as drawer guides (Fig. 12-15E). Above them, put strips with their lower surfaces level with the front rail that comes above the drawer. These act as drawer kickers (Fig. 12-15F) and prevent the drawer from tilting downward as it is pulled out.

Make the drawer in the usual way (preferably with dovetails). Include any divisions or compartments during construction so that dividers can be notched into the sides. Make a wooden handle or use a metal one. If the drawer is made slightly undersize back to front, packing pieces can be put inside the table back to act as stops when the drawer front closes level with its framing. Check the action of the drawer and make any adjustments before attaching the top.

Unless there is any tendency to warp or twist, it should be sufficient to have three screws upward into the top along the front top rail and three buttons at the back and one certainly at each end. Center the top and attach the buttons with the table inverted and the drawer removed. See Table 12-3 for a materials list.

Table 12-3. Materials List for Writing Table.

4 legs	1¾ × 30 × 1¾
2 sides	4 × 21 × ½
2 sides	2½ × 21 × ½
1 front	1⅛ × 30 × ½
1 front	2¼ × 30 × ¾
1 back	4 × 30 × ½
1 back	1 × 30 × ½
2 top frames	1¾ × 31 × ⅞
2 top frames	1¾ × 22 × ⅞
2 top stiffeners	3 × 20 × ⅝
1 top panel	21 × 30 × ¼ plywood
1 drawer front	3½ × 27 × ¾
2 drawer sides	3½ × 20 × ⅝
1 drawer back	3 × 27 × ⅝
1 drawer bottom	20 × 27 × ¼ plywood
2 drawer guides	⅞ × 20 × ¾
2 drawer kickers	1⅛ × 20 × ¾
buttons and fillets from	1½ × 24 × ½

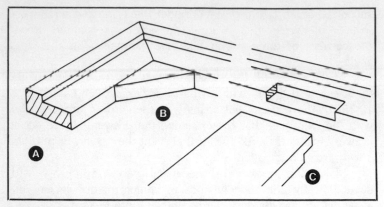

Fig. 12-16. The frame for the plywood top is rabbeted (A) and reinforced underneath (B,C).

SIMPLE GATE LEG TABLE

The idea of a table with a narrow fixed top and broad flaps that can be extended from it to make it a much larger size has been used for many centuries. There are many example of fine cabinetwork that include complications in decoration and method of functioning. A simple table of this type has many uses. It can be stored in a small space, yet it can be opened to become a dining table. The usual supports for the flaps are gate-like frames that swing out so that there is a leg to the floor at each side to ensure stability. Hence the name of *gate leg table*. A simple version of good proportions and made from attractive wood can be very attractive and functional without the need for much decoration. This example (Figs. 12-17, 12-18) is basic in

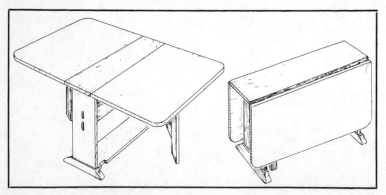

Fig. 12-17. A simple gate leg table folds compactly, but opens to give a large top area.

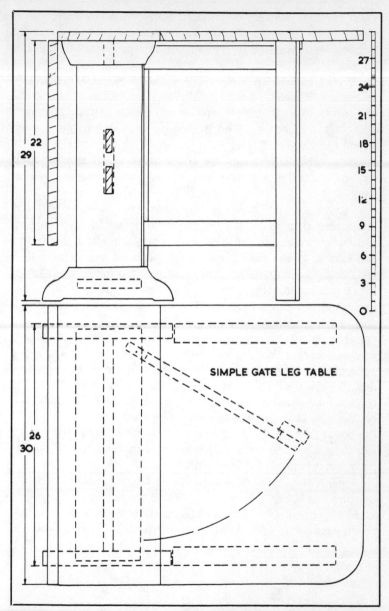

Fig. 12-18. The parts of the simple gate leg table are uncomplicated.

form and simple to make. The sizes given allow for a fully open top size of 30 inches by 55 inches, a partly open size 30 inches by 33 inches and a closed top size of 30 inches by 11 inches. The wood sections suggested suit close-grained hardwoods, but it can be made in good softwood. Thicknesses should be increased by about ⅛ of an inch to compensate for the lesser strength of the wood.

There is a choice of assembly with mortise and tenon joints or dowels. The list of materials allows for tenons. Some parts can be shorter if dowels are used. Dowels with a ½-inch diameters and about 1½-inch centers should provide enough strength if they penetrate each part about 1 inch where that is possible. The instructions are for mortise and tenon jonts. If dowels are used, cut and square the ends at the shoulder lengths.

The main part, which governs the sizes of other parts, is the central pedestal. It should be made first, although its final assembly can be left until the other parts are fitted. There are two similar gates. They pivot on the pedestal and swing into it for storage and out to the centers of the flap for an open table. The top is made with a central narrow piece and two wide flaps that hang down until required. If only a small table is required, only one flap need be raised.

The flaps are too wide to be made from single boards unless you are exceptionally lucky at the lumber yard. They are prevented from warping by battens, but if the wood for joining to make up the flaps can be selected quarter-sawn, with the annual rings on the ends of the boards across (Fig. 12-19A), there will be less risk of warping than if the lines are more in the width of the board (Fig. 12-19B). If you have to use boards of this sort, join them alternate ways so that any overall tendency to warp is particularly cancelled (Fig. 12-19C).

Make the ends of the pedestal (Fig. 12-20). Tops and bottoms are blocks 1½ inches thick and the legs are arranged on them level with the inner surfaces. Use double mortise and tenon joints (Fig. 12-21A) between the legs and blocks. The feet

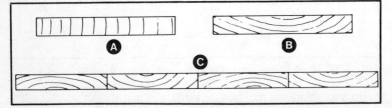

Fig. 12-19. Parts to make up the broad tops (A,B) are joined to reduce warping (C).

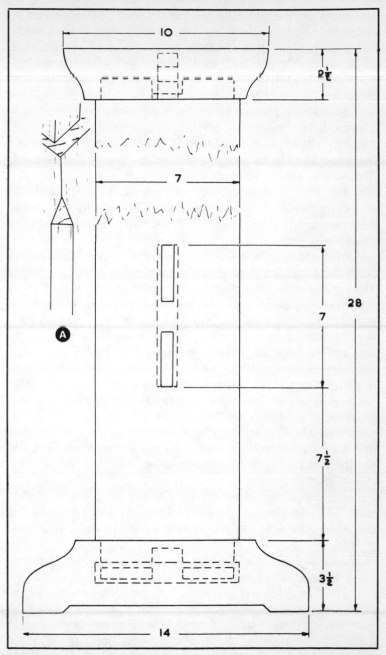

Fig. 12-20. End assemblies (A) are tenonned and can have wagon-bevelled edges.

will need mortises to take the bottom rail and these can be marked at the same time (Fig. 12-21B). Shape the ends of the feet (Fig. 12-21C). It is advisable to make a cardboard template of the curve. Or one end can be shaped and used to mark the others while one on the other piece can mark the end of the first piece.

So that the feet stand firmly, even if the floor is slightly uneven, it is advisable to cut away the bottom edges to leave supports only at the ends (Fig. 12-21D). Alternatively, leave the bottom of the blocks straight, but make squares about ¼-inch thick to attain below the ends.

The top is similar to the feet, but shorter and should be given comparable curves on the ends. The top rail tenons into the top supports (Fig. 12-21E) and the mortises come between those for the legs.

At the center of each leg, the center rail has its tenons taken right through to give maximum rigidity to the assembly. Mark the mortises on both sides and cut from both sides so that there is no risk of the grain breaking out and spoiling the appearance of the pedestal. The tenons can be planed off flush outside, but they will look better if they are made slightly too long and the projecting ends are rounded (Fig. 12-21F).

The edges of the legs can be given stopped chamfer wagon bevelling on all four corners or the outer ones only (Fig. 12-20A). If this is done, the center rail should be made to match by treating in the same way.

Make the lengthwise rails. Assemble the parts of the ends first and clean off the inner surfaces level if necessary. Then add the three rails. Check for squareness and see that the pedestal stands level.

The center part of the top joins to the top rail with dowels (Fig. 12-22A), but to allow for expansion and contraction it should be joined to the top supports with buttons. A groove plowed through would disfigure the ends. Cut short slots, like mortises, but a little wider than the buttons to allow for movement (Fig. 12-22B).

The two gates are the same, but they pivot from opposite ends of the pedestal. Allow for two small pads (Fig. 12-23A) to take ½-inch dowels that act as hinges. The top dowel can go partly into the table top, but the hole for the bottom one will go right through the pedestal bottom rail (Fig. 12-23B). This allows the frame to be brought into the pedestal and the dowel to be

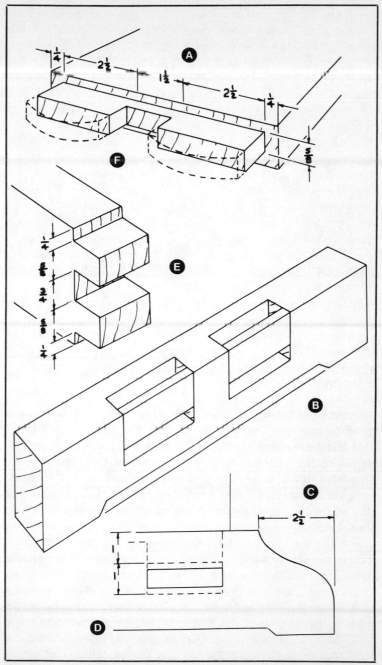

Fig. 12-21. Tenons are cut (A,B,C,D) to get the maximum strength (E).

245

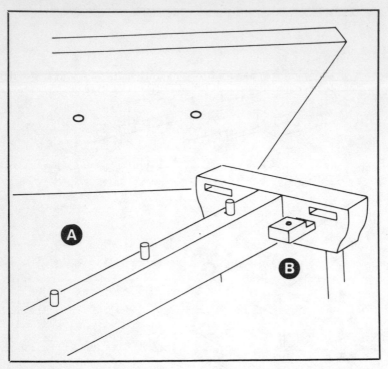

Fig. 12-22. The center of the top is dowelled (A) and buttoned to the framing (B).

inserted from below. Otherwise, leave the table top off until the gates are inserted.

Make sure that each gate leg length is the same as the height of the pedestal under its top. Then the flaps will be supported level when the gates are turned out. The inner uprights will fit directly between the drilled pads, but wear will be reduced if you allow for a thin metal washer at each place (Fig. 12-23C).

Assemble the gates with mortise and tenon joints (Fig. 12-23D) or by dowelling. When the gates close, they should notch into the bottom pedestal rail. There might be enough clearance for the flaps to lower without notches. Drill the gates for the dowel pivots and make a trial assembly. Swing each gate to the bottom rail and mark from it where the notch has to come (Fig. 12-23E). This is wiser than relying on measurements, as there can be slight discrepancies that do not matter, but which might cause a measured notch to be slightly out of line. Mark

246

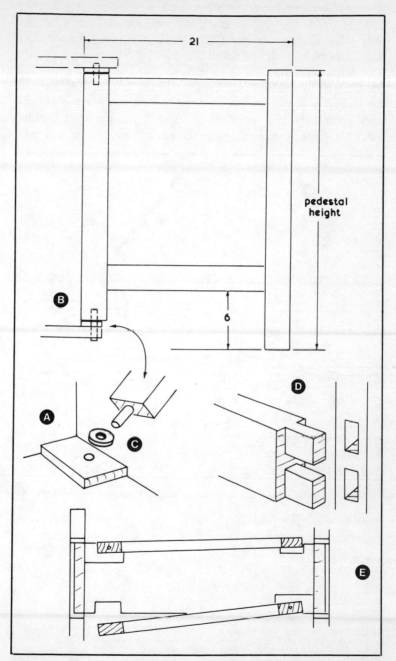

Fig. 12-23. Gate parts are tenonned together (A, B, C, D) and swing on dowels (E).

and cut the notches. Also mark the side for each gate in case they differ slightly. Do not fit the gates permanently until after flaps have been made and fitted.

After sufficient boards have been glued up to make up the flaps, carefully square the shapes and round the outer corners. If the hinged edge and the ends are out of square, the table will not open so that the long sides are straight. If you have any doubts, hinge the flaps temporarily to the center top and try the action of

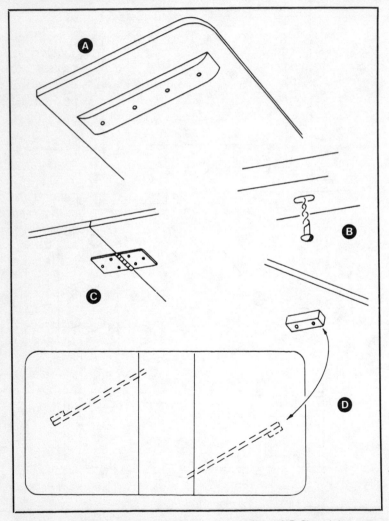

Fig. 12-24. The parts of the table top hinge together ((A,B,C) and the gates swing against stops (D).

the flaps before planing their ends to size. Round the outer corners. The table is shown with the edges squared, but they can be molded or rounded in any of the ways suggested for other tables.

To resist any tendency of the flaps to warp, put battens across underneath, in line with the pedestal ends, but far enough away not to touch them when the flaps are down (Fig. 12-24A). Round the edges and taper the ends. Attach the battens with slots nearest the hinged edge (Fig. 12-24B) so that the screws can slide with any movement in the width of the flaps.

The hinged meeting edges are cut square and not made into rule joints, as they are in more advanced gate leg tables, so there is no need for backflap hinges with their knuckles set into the wood. But they are still a good choice, because they spread the screws away from the edge (Fig. 12-24C). Strap hinges, which are similar but longer, are also suitable. Use three hinges on each edge with the knuckles downwards. To ensure a close joint when each flap is up, screw on the hinges with the table inverted and the top flat. There is no need to let the hinges into the wood.

When all parts have been made and you are sure that there is no more tool work to be done on them, remove the flaps and thoroughly sand all parts in preparation for the finishing process. Any staining and polishing finishes can be used. Because the top will probably have to support hot dishes, make sure that is has a heatproof finish even if a different finish is used elsewhere.

While the table is inverted, put the gates in position and make sure that their dowels are securely glued into the inner upright while free to turn in their own supports. Smooth movement will be helped if the holes and dowels are smeared with wax or candle fat. Move each gate so that the leg comes to the center of its flap. Then screw on a stop there (Fig. 12-24D). Turn the table the right way up and test its action. Take off any sharpness from the bottoms of the gate legs to avoid marking floor coverings. See Table 12-4 for a materials list.

LARGE GATE LEG TABLE

This table (Fig. 12-25) differs from the simple gate leg table. It has the pedestal mounted on four legs and higher rails so there is more leg room when people are seated all round the fully extended table. The gaps in the top have rule joint hinges to give a more attractive appearance when the table is folded.

Table 12-4. Materials List for Simple Gate Leg Table.

Pedestal

1 top rail	2½ × 26 × 1
1 center rail	7 × 28 × 1
1 bottom rail	7 × 26 × 1
2 legs	7 × 25 × 1
2 feet	3½ × 15 × 1½
2 top supports	2½ × 11 × 1½

Top

1 center	11 × 31 × 1
2 flaps	19 × 31 × 1
4 battens	2 × 18 × 1
buttons from	1½ × 10 × ¾

Gates

2 legs	2½ × 29 × 1
2 inner uprights	2½ × 27 × 1
4 rails	2½ × 20 × 1
2 stops	1½ × 4 × ¾
pivots from	10 × ½ dowel rod

All the legs are shown with casters. The gates move easily and the whole table can be moved about. If casters are used, they should be obtained first so that the correct allowance can be made for their height.

The table can be made in any of the usual furniture hardwoods. The legs should have a reasonably straight grain and the boards for the top should be quarter-sawn or joined alternate ways to minimize the risk of warping.

The pedestal is made like a plain table and it would be possible to complete it without the flaps for use as a side table. Any decoration in the table is mainly in the legs and the edges of the top. Other parts are rarely visible, so they can be plain. The legs (Fig. 12-26A) have the rails joined with the usual type of mortise and tenon joints, with haunched tenons at the top tail (Fig. 12-26B) and double tenons for the lower rails (Fig. 12-26C). At both levels, the outer edges should be the same distance from the outsides of the legs so that the gates will be upright when they pivot. Mark out the positions of the joints on all the legs together.

Leaving the legs square and unadorned might be satisfactory in some circumstances, but they are usually better decorated in some way. They could have wagon bevelling in the form of stopped chamfers (Fig. 12-26D) between the joint areas. Leaving the parts near the joints square and turning the rest gives a lighter and attractive appearance. A great many forms of turning are possible. The one shown in Fig. 12-26E is based on a 17th century spindle.

If some decoration is required on the square parts between turnings, they can be carved. Reading is shown (Fig. 12-26F) on the outer surfaces only. This can be done with a suitably shaped molding plane or it is possible by cutting in with a knife along a straightedge between the reeds and then shaping them with a rabbet plane followed by sanding.

Make all the pedestal rails. Groove the top rails for buttons (Fig. 12-27A). Arrange two cross rails between the long lower rails (Fig. 12-27B) with tenoned joints (Fig. 12-27C). Assemble the pedestal framing and legs and check for squareness and level standing.

Cut the top of the pedestal to size. Make it up from narrower boards if necessary, but do not attach it to the framework yet. Make the two flaps, but form the rule joints between them and the center before finally trimming them to size and doing any molding to the edges. Have the backflap hinges ready so that they can be measured to locate the point on

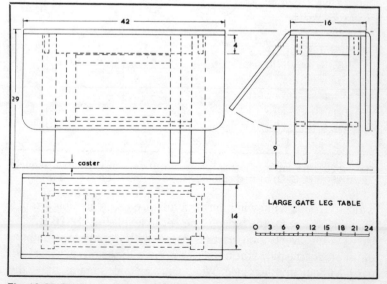

Fig. 12-25. The large gate leg table has four legs and rule joints in the top.

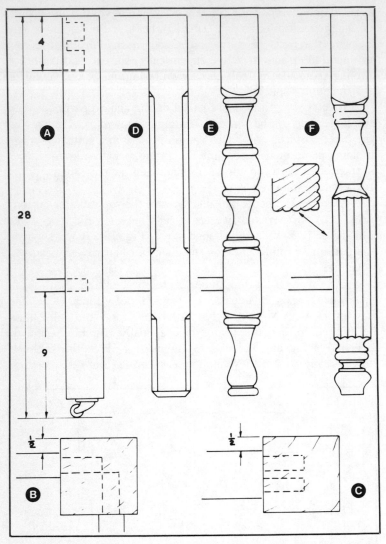

Fig. 12-26. The table legs can be made in several ways, with square sections (A, B, C, D) turned spindles (E) or turned and reeded (F).

which the flaps will swing. Draw a full size cross-section through the joint. Allow for the hinge to be set in level (Fig. 12-28A). The curve of the overlapping parts is drawn with the compass point at the center of the pin of the hinge. This gives the same curve on both parts without any clearance. When you assemble the top, move the flap outward very slightly (Fig. 12-28B) so that the concave curve in the flap edge does not rub on the convex curve of the center part.

It will help to get the curves right if templates are made for testing (Fig. 12-28C). When planing the edges, work along the full lengths so that any shaping is the same all the way and unevenness is avoided. On the center edges, first cut a rabbet (Fig. 12-28D). Then shape to the template with rabbet and other planes (Fig. 12-28E). It is this part which shows when the flap is down. Sand it to a good surface. The other part can be cut with a spindle molder or it can be started with rabbets (Fig. 12-28F). Follow this with a round-bottomed plane, a curved scraper or coarse abrasive paper around a shaped piece of wood. Except at the ends, this part does not show. Therefore, a good quality finish is not as important.

Let in the hinges and make a trial assembly with one screw in each flap of each hinge. Three hinges along each joint should be sufficient. See that the parts swing over each other without binding and that the edge of each flap comes close to the curved edge of the center part when the flap is hanging down.

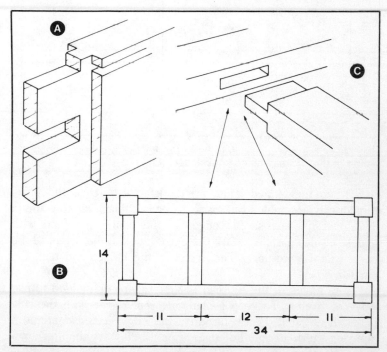

Fig. 12-27. There are deep top rails (A,B) and shallow bottom ones (C).

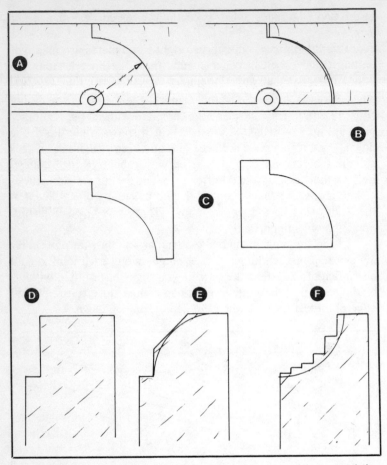

Fig. 12-28. The rule joint has to be cut (A,B,C) with curves around the center of the backflap hinge knuckle (D,E,F).

When the hinged joints are satisfactory, leave the parts temporarily assembled and mark the ends of each flap to come in a straight line across the edges of the center part and with opposite sides parallel. Mark the extremities of the flaps and the curves for the corners. Then remove the hinges and trim the parts to size.

The edges of the top can be left square or molded in any way you prefer. To keep a matching appearance with the rule joint when the flaps are hanging, the edges could continue a similar pattern around the edges (Fig. 12-29A). A simple rounding is effective (Fig. 12-29B) or this could be combined with a bevel (Fig. 12-29C). Edge molding should not be too wide or this could cause something to fall off if brought too close to the edge. It should not be cut in on the surface (Fig. 12-29D), because that would trap dirt and make cleaning of the top difficult after a meal.

The gates are of light construction (Fig. 12-30A) and all the joints are tenoned or dowelled. The inner upright fits between top and bottom rails. There is a washer at the lower position. At the top, the pivot is made from an iron rod (piece of stout nail) (Fig. 12-30B) driven into the upright and inserted in a hole in the top rail. The bottom pivot is made from a screw, but it should be long enough for the plain neck to extend through most of the nail (Fig. 12-30C). If a shorter screw is used, counterbore so that the head goes below the surface.

At the top of each leg there can be clearance under the top, for ease of movement, then the stop is arranged for the leg to slide into it (Fig. 12-30D). If the bottom of each frame leg is not thick enough to take the caster, thicken it on the inner surface (Fig. 12-30E).

The top of the pedestal overhangs to give some clearance for the folded gate legs. But this is not quite enough to allow the flaps to hang down. Make shallow recesses in the legs and the rails, similar to those cut for halving joints, but only deep enough to get the gates far enough under the pedestal top to clear the flaps when they are hanging (Fig. 12-30F).

Put all the screws in the hinges and have the table inverted while attaching the center part with buttons (Fig. 12-29E). Test the action of the gates and locate the positions for the stops under the flaps. Use a straightedge across the top and see that the flaps are supported level with the center part. If necessary, cut the tops of the gate legs to suit or pack out the stops to raise the flaps. When a trial assembly shows that all parts are right, any finishing treatment will be easier to do if the table is disassembled as far as possible again. See Table 12-5 for a materials list.

REFECTORY TABLE

In medieval homes, from cottages to castles, a main item of furniture was the table. It was often large enough to accomodate large families and retainers. In many places, particularly castles and monasteries, narrow twisting access meant having a table that could be assembled in place. Otherwise it could not be

Table 12-5. Materials List for Large Gate Leg Table.

Pedestal

4 legs	2¾ × 29 × 2¾
2 top rails	4 × 34 × ⅞
2 top rails	4 × 12 × ⅞
2 bottom rails	1¾ × 43 × ⅞
4 bottom rails	1¾ × 12 × ⅞

Top

1 center	16 × 43 × ⅞
2 flaps	21 × 43 × ⅞
4 battens	1¾ × 20 × ⅞
buttons from	1¾ × 24 × ⅞

Gates

2 legs	2 × 29 × 1
2 inner uprights	2 × 15 × 1
4 rails	2 × 22 × 1
2 stops	1¾ × 4 × ⅞

brought into the room. Hence this type of table was assembled with wedged tenons. In a monastery, food was eaten in the *refectory* and that provides the name. However, the type of table can also be described as *trestle*. *Wedged tenons* are sometimes used just as decoration and their take-down feature has no value if other parts cannot be disassembled. There is still some advantage in having a substantial table that can be separated into its components for convenience in storage or transport—even if it is not taken apart very often. This example (Figs. 12-31 and 12-32) is a strong dining table, but the top and rails can be removed from the end legs for packing flat. Height and width should suit normal use, but the length can be varied to suit needs without affecting the type of construction.

The key parts are the leg assemblies, made in three pieces, but with outlines that flow into each other. Mark out the parts (Fig. 12-33). The feet are shown extending to the width of the top (Fig. 12-33A), but they could be brought in a little without affecting stability. The top (Fig. 12-33B) is narrower. For maximum strength in the bridle joints, keep the horizontal center parts thicker (Fig. 12-33C). Get these parts as good a fit as possible as rigidity depends on their joints. Make sure the meeting surfaces are flat to give a good bond to the glue. Test across the surfaces of the inner parts with a straightedge.

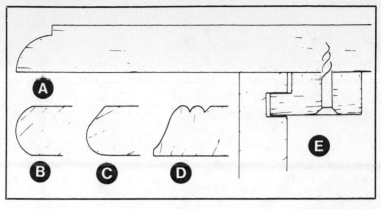

Fig. 12-29. The table top edges (A,B,C) can follow the pattern of the rule joint or be molded (D,E) in other ways.

Mark the outlines and cut close to the shapes. Leave final shaping until after assembly so that the curves can be worked to blend into each other smoothly. Assemble the leg parts. Clamp while the glue sets. Simple glued joints should be satisfactory, but dowels could be put right through each joint and the pattern they make could be regarded as a design feature. Four in each place should be sufficient. See that the legs make a matched pair. Get the outlines true, but leave finishing the edge surfaces until after other work has been done. Draw centerlines on the legs and mark on these the shapes and positions of the rails.

Mark out the lower rail so that the legs will be 6 inches in from the ends of the top. Let the tenons be overlong (Fig. 12-34A) until after the wedge holes have been cut. Mark the shoulders with a knife and cut carefully to the line for a good fit against the legs (Fig. 12-34B). Mark the mortises on both sides. So that no grain breaks out and spoils appearance, check squareness through the hole when trimming to size. The tenons should make a good push fit in the mortises. Try an assembly.

Mark the thickness of the legs on the tenons. Go back about ⅛ of an inch so that the wedge can draw the joint tight (Fig. 12-34C). It is unlikely that both joints will be exactly the same. Mark the mating tenons and mortises inconspicuously as a guide for later assembly. Mark the sizes of the wedge hole on each side of a tenon. Also mark the sizes on the wood that will make the wedge at the same distances apart and draw through these marks on a piece that will be overlong at this stage (Fig. 12-34D). Cut the wedges to the lines.

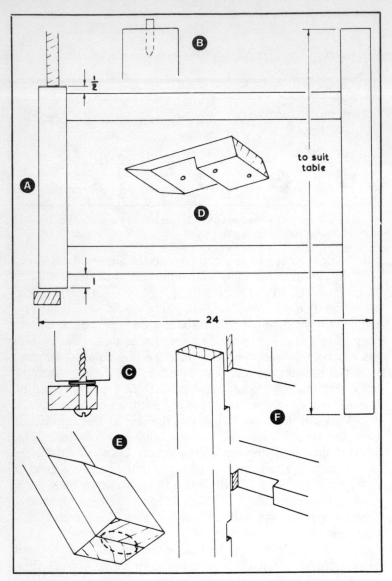

Fig. 12-30. The gates pivot on screws (A,B,C,D) and close into notches in the frame (E,F).

Drill out some of the waste from the wedge holes. Work from each side and be careful not to let the drill wander. Cut the hole first to size at the straight inner edge (Fig. 12-34E), then taper close to size at the other edge (Fig. 12-34F). Try a wedge

Fig. 12-31. This refectory table is a modern version of a traditional form.

through the hole to check the taper. Then cut fully to size. Do not cut the wedges to length yet.

The top rail joins the legs with a dovetail dado joint. It tapers so that it can be entered from the top and will draw the legs tight when it is fully down (Fig. 12-35A). Mark the rail to

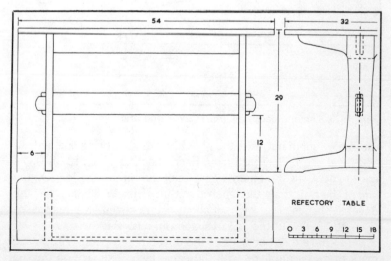

Fig. 12-32. These proportions give a good dining table area, but they can be modified.

259

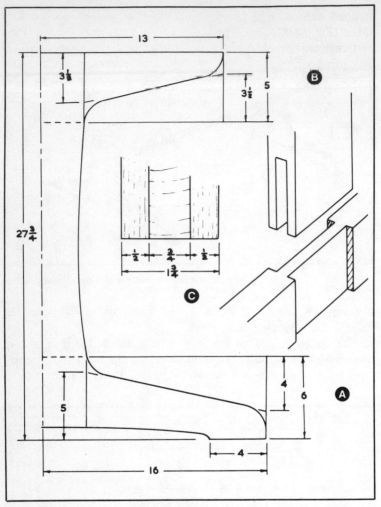

Fig. 12-33. The end pedestals (A,B) have large bridle joints (C).

the same length between the shoulders as the lower one and cut and level the end ½-inch from each shoulder (Fig. 12-35B). At each joint, draw the tapered outline of the rail on the leg. On the end of the rail, draw the tapered outline (Fig. 12-35C). Draw the dovetail shapes at an angle of about one in seven on the surfaces (Fig. 12-35D). Cut the end to shape (Fig. 12-35E).

Measure the root sizes of the dovetail at top and bottom and mark these on the leg—with the same bevel and size on the top (Fig. 12-35F). Cut away the waste in the same way as a straight stopped dado with the closed end chiselled before sawing the sides (Fig. 12-35G). Adjust the fit of the joint so that top surfaces come level.

Join boards to make up the top. Use dowels or secret slot screwing If you want to strengthen the joints. Alternate curves

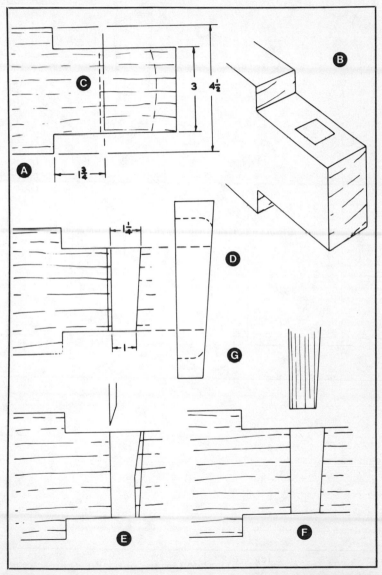

Fig. 12-34. A tusk tenon (A,B,C) takes the rail through each end (D,E,F,G)

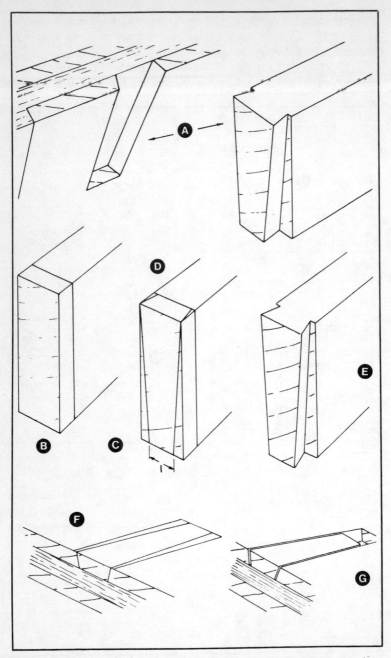

Fig. 12-35. The top rail (A,B) drops into a tapered dovetail dado in each end (C,D,E,F,G)

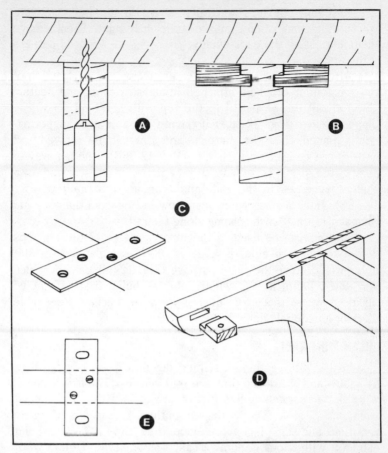

Fig. 12-36. The top can be screwed or buttoned (A,B) and the extensions buttoned or screwed through plates (C,D,E)

of end grain to minimize the risk of warping. The top is shown without shaping of the edges except for rounding corners. If the wood has an attractive grain, there might be no need for decorated edges. If it is plain, there can be molding.

Table 12-6. Materials List for Refectory Table.

1 top	32 × 56 × 1¼
1 top rail	4 × 42 × 1½
1 lower rail	4½ × 48 × 1½
2 leg bottoms	6 × 32 × 1¾
2 leg posts	6 × 28 × 1¾

Assemble the legs and rails. Drive in the wedges. Note where they come when they are sufficiently tight. Then remove them and cut off the ends evenly, rounding the exposed corners (Fig. 12-34G).

Allowance has to be made for expansion and contraction of the top, but it could be attached immovably along the center. The top rail can be joined to the top with glue and screws in plugged holes (Fig. 12-36A) if having the top and rail permanently joined does not matter. The rail can be plowed and buttons can be used on each side (Fig. 12-36B). Another way of joining the parts is to use metal plates, first screwed into shallow recesses in the rail, and then up into the top (Fig. 12-36C). Have plates or buttons a few inches from the legs and then at about a 12-inch spacing along the rail.

Buttons can be used in the inner surfaces of the leg tops with two on each side (Fig. 12-36D). Metal plates with slot holes would serve the same purpose (Fig. 12-36E). Mark which way the top fits as the whole table is being first assembled upside down so that equal overlaps can be checked. See Table 12-6 for a materials list.

QUEEN ANNE TABLE

In the 18th century, a fashion developed for cabriole legs for tables and chairs and they are still with us. The name means a leg shaped something like that of an animal with a pronounced knee and a foot. The S-shaped outline is capable of many variations and some legs were elaborately carved. The claw and ball foot, with talons gripping a ball, was one type. Others were carved in the length, but much furniture was, and still is, made with the legs given smooth sweeps.

This table (Fig. 12-37 and 12-38) is a small version of the cabriole leg style popular in Queen Anne's reign. It is intended as a coffee table—which it would not have been then—but it could be regarded as a miniature version of a dining table or side table. Sizes can be altered and there could be a drawer fitted if the rails are deepened. Except for the legs and the shaping of the top, constructional work is similar to that in some of the tables already described.

The original cabinetmakers did all of the shaping of the legs by hand and that could be done again. However, a bandsaw lessens the labor and ensures cuts that follow curves while being square to the surface. After sawing, the rest of the shaping will

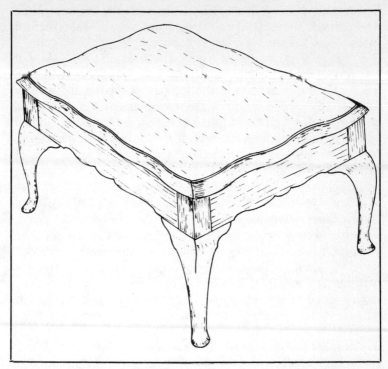

Fig. 12-37. A Queen Anne Table has curved edges and cabriole legs.

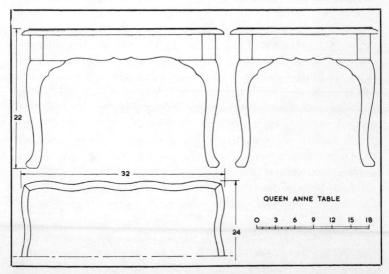

QUEEN ANNE TABLE

0 3 6 9 12 15 18

Fig. 12-38. A Queen Anne table is of basically the same construction as other tables (with allowance for the many curves).

have to be done by hand. If the making of a leg is tackled systematically, the skill involved is not as much as the final shape would suggest.

The best legs are made from solid wood (Fig. 12-39A), but this results in much cutting to waste. It is possible to start with a square piece of the size of the top part of the leg and glue on other pieces to make up the width for the curves. However, it is difficult to match grain. A glue line plus different grain could spoil the finished appearance. With the outline to be marked at least eight times, draw the shape and make a hardboard or stout cardboard template to ensure uniformity. Use this to mark the shape both ways on the wood (Fig. 12-39B).

Saw the outline in one direction (Fig. 12-39C). Careful cutting close to the line will reduce the amount of further work. This will remove some of the marking out of the shape in the other direction. It would be possible to use the template to mark the lines again on the shaped part. However, it is better for bandsawing to have flat surfaces so that the waste pieces can be lightly nailed back in place (with the nails into what will be cut off). Then the cuts are made in the second direction (Fig. 12-39D).

Get the top part of the leg truly square and straight. Use a spokeshave or Surform tool on the other parts. At the bottom, the foot is made circular. The narrow part above it is also circular in section, but as you shape further up the leg the outer corner is allowed to remain progressively more angular (with just a slight rounding) so it meets the square top sharply. However, leave final shaping of the top few inches until after the ears have been glued on (Fig. 12-39E). Dowels into the legs are advisable. Shape the surfaces of the ears with the top of the leg to matching curves, but make sure its top surfaces are square to match the lines of the rails (Fig. 12-40A).

So that all four legs match, it is advisable to do similar work to all legs at the same time. They move towards completion together in steps and progress and shapes can be compared.

Assembly of the table framework is the same as for tables with simpler legs using buttons to hold the top (Fig. 12-40B). The top can have straight molded edges, but it is shown here scalloped or with a pie crust edge. To get an even pattern around a top that is not square, it is necessary to make each side a multiple of the intended size of scallop (in this case 4 inches). But the point should be noted if a different size of table is planned.

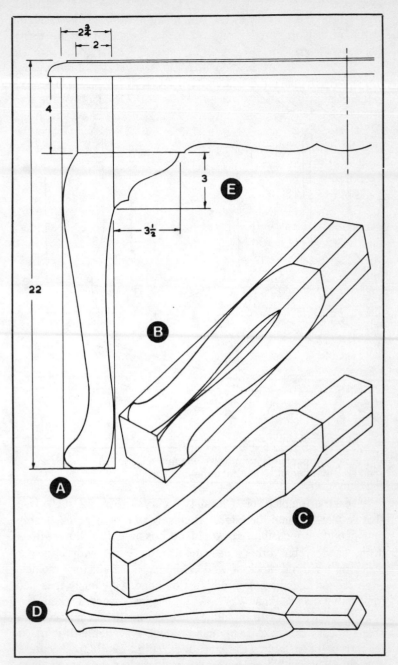

Fig. 12-39. A cabriole leg is cut from solid wood (A) in stages: (B) mark the shape, (C) saw the outline; (D) make the secondary cuts.

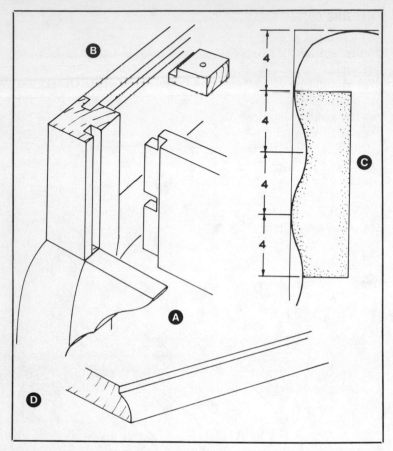

Fig. 12-40. Corner joints are mortise and tenon (A,B,C). Top edges can be marked with a template and then molded (D).

Make a template of at least two curves (Fig. 12-40C). Use that to mark around the edges. Bandsaw to the shape as closely and evenly as possible. It would be possible to follow with a drum sander, but otherwise smooth the edge with abrasive paper on a curved block of wood. Making a satisfactory molded edge around the shaping is difficult by hand. Obviously it is not impossible because that was how the originals were worked. If a spindle with a suitable molding cutter is available, an accurate shape is easy to work. If only hand tools are available, it is much less trouble to mold straight edges (Fig. 12-40D). Accurate straightedges will look better than scalloped edges showing inaccuracies. See Table 12-7 for a materials list.

NESTING COFFEE TABLES

A block of three tables, in which two tables fit inside the other and can be lifted with it, will provide unit storage in the minimum space. It will also allow tables to be used in three different positions when required. For the tables to fit together, it is necessary to make the two larger tables without front rails at top and bottom. The smallest table can have rails all round in the usual way. This should not weaken the two tables enough to matter if the other constructional work is done properly. But obviously the tables should not be expected to stand up to use as seats when a user might try to rock on two legs.

The small table slides on to supports under the top of the second table and hangs from it. The second table does the same inside the outer table. The legs of the hanging tables are cut so that they do not quite touch the floor when they are nested. Then the large outer table can be moved without fear of the other tables catching in the carpet and pulling out.

The general drawing (Fig. 12-41) shows sizes that should suit most purposes, but it is advisable to experiment with possible sizes before getting wood cut. To allow clearance for fitting the tables together, the smallest table has to be about 8 inches less in length and about 4 inches less in width than the largest one. The other is midway between the two. Of course, a nest of two tables only can be made, but it is customary to have three.

When viewed from the front (Fig. 12-41A), the tables assemble symmetrically. Reduction in size for nesting is the same for both sides. When viewed from the side (Fig. 12-41B), the rear legs have to be brought in in a similar way to the sides. But at the front, all legs are level. The view from above (Fig. 12-41C) shows the relative sizes and positions of the legs at the back, but at the front all table edges are level and the legs are in the same plane.

Table 12-7. Materials List for Queen Anne Table.

4 legs	2¾ × 22 × 2¾
8 ears	3 × 4 × 1½
2 rails	4 × 27 × ¾
2 rails	4 × 20 × ¾
1 top	24 × 33 × ⅞
8 buttons	1½ × 3 × ¾

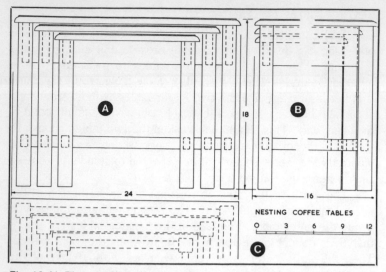

Fig. 12-41. Three coffee tables can be arranged to fit into each other for storage: (A) front view (B) side view; (C) top view.

Although the general drawing (Fig. 12-41) should be understood, it is a section through the three tables nested that shows how they fit into each other (Fig. 12-42A). This should be drawn full size on a piece of plywood or hardboard and used for reference as the various parts are made. Draw it with the actual sizes of wood you have available because wood only slightly larger or smaller in section than drawn might affect smooth assembly. Note that the table tops are given clearance between the front legs. Then they rest on supports which hold and guide them at the sides. There is no need for supports at the back, but there the top sizes have to be arranged so that they go against the rails (Fig. 12-41C) when the front edges are all level.

Parts for all the tables can be made to their sections at the same time. But for the sake of smooth fitting, it is best to make one table at a time. In its basic form, each table is shown with square legs. They could be decorated, as described later, although this should be done before assembly.

Make all legs in the same way and with all of the lower rails level. The top rails are different widths so that their lower edges are level when the tables are nested. Mark out four legs for the large table (Fig. 12-43A). Remember that there are no rails across the front. The back legs have holes or mortises both ways, but the front legs have them paired one way each.

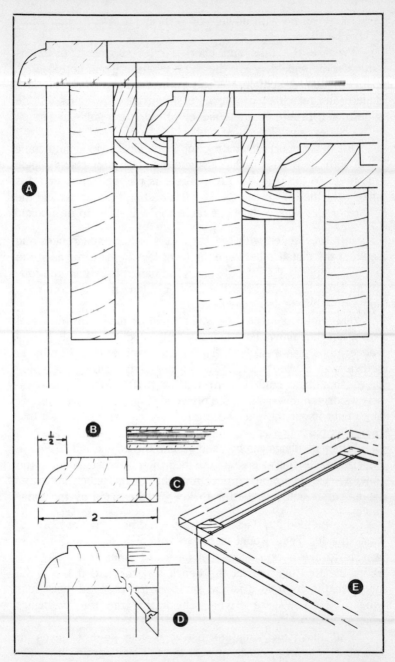

Fig. 12-42. Sections show how the tables nest (A,B,C,D) and the top is built up (E).

Assembly can be with dowels or with mortise and tenon joints (Fig. 12-43B).

Prepare the rails and check to be sure that distances between the shoulders are the same where top and bottom rails should match. Assemble the end frames. Be sure that they are square and match each other. Put them under weights for the glue to set if there is any tendency to twist. Irregularities might affect the easy fit of the next table.

Fit the supports inside the top rails. One strip should come level with the insides of the legs and the other projects as a slide for the table top (Fig. 12-43C). There is no need to extend this slide over the leg surface. Take off any sharpness and round the front corners where the next table top will have to be hooked on.

Join the frames with the back rails. Check squareness and see that the distance between the front legs is the same as at the back. A temporary strut of scrap wood nailed lightly on the tops of the front legs will keep the assembly true if it has to be left some time before doing the next step.

The table tops could be solid wood or made up in several ways, but that shown here is framed plywood which could have a veneered or plastic surface. The frame section (Fig. 12-42B) is shown with a wide rabbet. The corners are simple miters and there should be sufficient strength with the joints glued and screws driven upward into the plywood (Fig. 12-42C). If there is any doubt about the joint strength, they can be altered so that the lower parts are lapped.

Other moldings can be used around the edges, but leave the under surfaces flat to give a good bearing on the supports in the inner tables. The molding design might not matter on the outer table, but it will look better to keep it the same as the inner tables.

The method of attaching the top must not leave any projections inside. They would interfere with nesting. The simplest way is to use pocket screws at back and sides (Fig. 12-42D). Have the top inverted on the bench and check that the width between the front legs is the same as between the back legs when the screws are driven. Check that the top overhangs evenly.

With one table complete, use it as your guide to sizes for the next table in conjunction with the full size section drawing. Make the top of the second table. Note that it has to fit between the legs at the sides and reach the inside of the back rail while

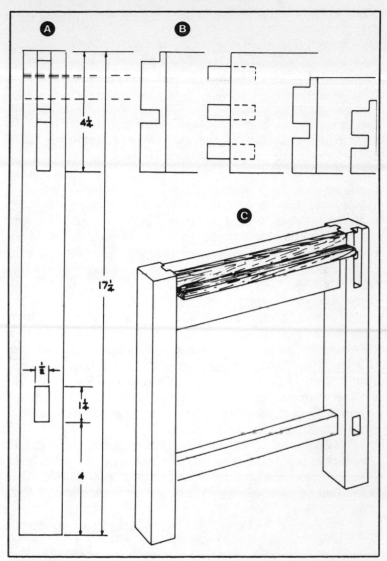

Fig. 12-43. Legs (A) and rails may be joined with dowels or mortise and tenon joints (B,C). The supports fit inside the top rails.

its front edge is level with the outer table top (Fig. 12-42E). When you are satisfied with the fit of that top, use its underside to mark out the layout of the under framing. Use this as your guide to rail lengths between shoulders on that table.

Make the legs. Check that the rail widths will match those on the first table when nested. At this stage, it is simplest to

273

leave the bottoms of the legs level with the outer ones. They can be trimmed to give clearance later. Make up the second table framing and attach it to the top in exactly the same way as the outer table. Besides checking squareness independently, check that the legs will be hanging parallel with the outside ones when nested.

Making the inside table is almost a repeat of the second one, with its size reduced to suit, except that it is given a full set of rails because there is no need to leave a clear space at the front. Check that the rail positions match the others as you mark out and assemble. With the three tables at the nesting stage, check levels of the bottoms of the legs. See that the large table stands level. If it does not, do whatever trimming is necessary to its legs. Cut the legs of the second table about ⅛ of an inch shorter when they are hanging. However, it might be advisable to take off more than that if the nest is to be used on deep pile carpet. When the table will stand level independently, cut the legs of the small table a similar amount less than that. Bevel around the edges of the leg bottoms.

If wood with an attractive grain is used, the nest will look quite attractive with square legs. Appearance can be lightened by taking the sharpness off the outer corners with a simple chamfer (Fig. 12-44A) or by working a bead (Fig. 12-44B). Chamfers could be stopped to give wagon bevelling (Fig. 12-44C) on all four corners of all 12 legs. The legs could be tapered below the bottom rails (Fig. 12-44D) whether the legs are left square or chamfered.

All legs could be turned, leaving the rail positions square. This could be confined to the part between the rails (Fig. 12-44E) or continued below the bottom rails (Fig. 12-44F). The bottom might be mainly square and just a ball turned as a foot (Fig. 12-44G).

There are several designs for turned legs given elsewhere in the book. One problem if turning is chosen is the need to keep 12 turned parts matching (instead of the usual four). Turn one leg to your satisfaction. Then make a rod to use with a pencil to mark the important parts on subsequent legs (Fig. 12-44H). Keep calipers set to key diameters. If there are any slight discrepancies, they will be less obvious at the back than at the front. It may be advisable to turn the legs and select their positions before cutting mortises.

Besides turning or otherwise decorating the legs, the wide upper rails could be decorated. Undersides could be shaped, but

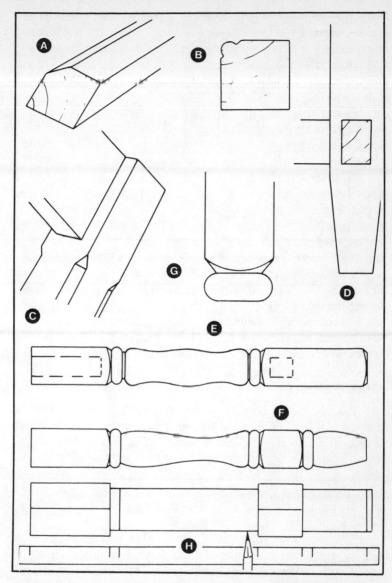

Fig. 12-44. Legs can be decorated: (A) chamfers; (B) bead; (C) wagon beveling (D) tapering; (E,F,G) turning: (H) mark the subsequent legs.

you have to allow for the different lengths. Start with the small table rails and repeat that shaping without lengthening it on the other rails (Fig. 12-45A). This is best kept simple and could be just a reduction in depth. The lower edges of the top rails might

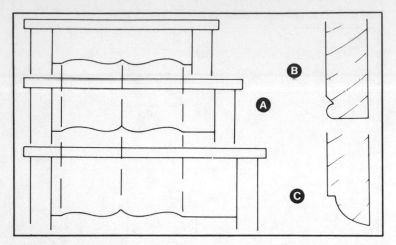

Fig. 12-45. Top rail edges can be shaped (A) beaded (B) or molded (C).

be beaded (Fig. 12-45B) or they could be given a matching shape to the table tops (Fig. 12-45C). These rails are also suitable places for carving. It could be an all-over pattern or just a border of chip carving done on the outside table only or on all the tables. See Table 12-8 for a materials list.

MAGAZINE TABLE

A table with a storage shelf can have many uses. This is particularly true in allowing for such things as magazines and books to be kept in quantity underneath, while only those wanted currently are put on top. Sizes can vary considerably, so the design can be adapted to suit the particular needs or situation in which the table is to be used. Sizes on the drawings and in the materials list are offered as suggestions. A smaller table can be made with thinner wood.

The top is shown as solid wood. This is a good place to display wood with an attractive grain that is possibly made up to width with several pieces glued together. The availablitiy of suitable wood will govern the size the table is to be made. Alternatively, a top can be made up from framed plywood or assembled as described for other tables.

This table has sloping legs (Figs. 12-46 and 12-47) with the long top rails going through them. The bottom framing can be fitted with plywood as a tray bottom, but it is shown with a number of slats across. The key parts that determine how

Table 12-8. Materials List for Nesting Coffee Table.

Outer table

4 legs	$1\frac{1}{2} \times 18 \times 1\frac{1}{2}$
1 rail	$1\frac{1}{4} \times 23 \times \frac{3}{4}$
2 rails	$4\frac{1}{4} \times 15 \times \frac{3}{4}$
1 rail	$1\frac{1}{4} \times 23 \times \frac{3}{4}$
2 rails	$1\frac{1}{4} \times 15 \times \frac{3}{4}$
2 top frames	$2 \times 25 \times \frac{3}{4}$
2 top frames	$2 \times 17 \times \frac{3}{4}$
1 top panel	$14 \times 22 \times \frac{3}{8}$ plywood
2 table supports	$\frac{7}{8} \times 15 \times \frac{1}{2}$
2 tabe supports	$\frac{7}{8} \times 15 \times \frac{3}{8}$

Second table

4 legs	$1\frac{1}{2} \times 17 \times 1\frac{1}{2}$
1 rail	$3\frac{3}{8} \times 21 \times \frac{3}{4}$
2 rails	$3\frac{3}{8} \times 14 \times \frac{3}{4}$
1 rail	$1\frac{1}{4} \times 21 \times \frac{3}{4}$
2 rails	$1\frac{1}{4} \times 13 \times \frac{3}{4}$
2 top frames	$2 \times 21 \times \frac{3}{4}$
2 top frames	$2 \times 15 \times \frac{3}{4}$
1 top panel	$11 \times 18 \times \frac{3}{8}$ plywood
2 table supports	$\frac{7}{8} \times 15 \times \frac{1}{2}$
2 table supports	$\frac{7}{8} \times 15 \times \frac{3}{8}$

Inner table

4 legs	$1\frac{1}{2} \times 16 \times 1\frac{1}{2}$
2 rails	$2\frac{1}{2} \times 19 \times \frac{3}{4}$
2 rails	$2\frac{1}{2} \times 13 \times \frac{3}{4}$
2 rails	$1\frac{1}{4} \times 19 \times \frac{3}{4}$
2 rails	$1\frac{1}{4} \times 13 \times \frac{3}{4}$
2 top frames	$2 \times 14 \times \frac{3}{4}$
2 top frames	$2 \times 14 \times \frac{3}{4}$
1 top panel	$7 \times 15 \times \frac{3}{8}$ plywood

several other parts are cut are the legs. Draw the end full size (Fig. 12-48A). The jointed part of the top of each leg is parallel, so the parts can be slid together (Fig. 12-48B). Use this drawing as a guide to the taper of the legs and the angles to which their ends have to be cut.

For the best construction, the lengthwise bottom rails should be tenoned, but all crosswise rails are dowelled (Fig. 12-49A). Use the full size drawing as a guide to the long rail length and angle. The end of the tenon need not be cut sloping.

The long rails can be parallel, but the top edge of the lower rails and the lower edge of the top rails might be hollowed slightly (Fig. 12-47). Leave the ends of the rails parallel for a

Fig. 12-46. A magazine table provides storage below.

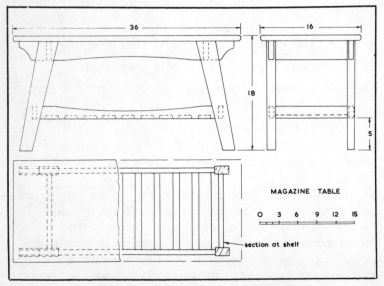

Fig. 12-47. The table has sloping legs and a slatted shelf.

278

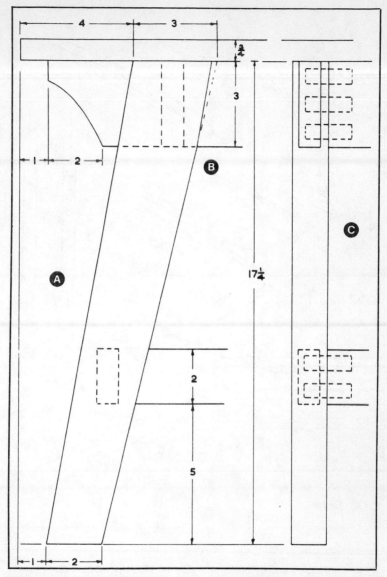

Fig. 12-48. A drawing of a leg (A) shows the angles (B) and construction of joints (C)

short distance and get the curve by springing a lath to draw around (Fig. 12-49B). The slats to form the shelf are given barefaced tenons at their ends. The easiest way to accomodate them in the rails is to plow grooves (Fig. 12-49C), but it would

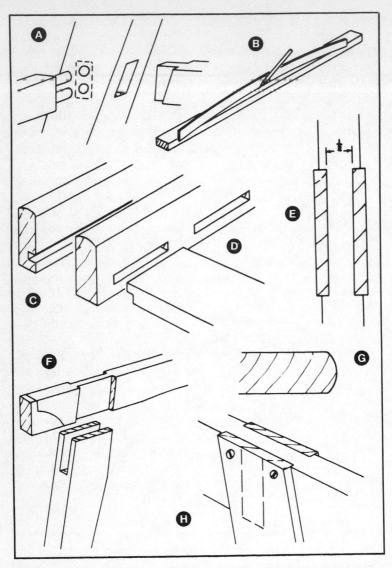

Fig. 12-49. Joint details of the table parts: (A) rails; (B) curve; (C) plow grooves; (D) separate mortises; (E) cut; (F) bridle joints; (G) round exposed edges; (H) reinforce with screws.

be better craftsmanship to make separate mortises (Fig. 12-49D).

Mark out the top rails together, but do not cut or shape their ends at this stage. Mark on the positions and shapes of the tops of the legs. Mark the rail positions on the legs. A bridle joint is to be used at the top of each leg. Because the legs are thicker than the rails, there is no need to cut much out of the rails (Fig. 12-49E). Mark the joints all round the wood and use a knife where the saw cuts on the rails. These parts of each joint will show in the finished table.

Cut the bridle joints (Fig. 12-49F). Mark on the inner surfaces of the legs where the ends of the top crosswise rails will come. Have the lengthwise bottom rails ready to assemble. Then make up the long sides after the ends of the top rails have been shaped. All wood can be left with square edges, but a neat finish is obtained by rounding all exposed edges (Fig. 12-49G)—including the top. If this is to be done, deal with the edges of the bottom rails and the lower edges of the top rails before assembly.

The bridle joints are fairly wide and it is advisable to reinforce them with screws near the top driven from inside at positions that will clear the crosswise rails (Fig. 12-49H). Assemble the opposite sides over each other to check that they match and see that they are without twist when left for the glue to set.

Make the crosswise rails and the shelf slats. Check lengths carefully. Because of the difference in thickness of the legs and rails, the slats have to be longer between shoulders than the rails (with extra for the tenons). After assembly, the joints must come tight without any tendency to bulge or hollow the side rails. Make the dowel joints at the ends of the rails. Let the dowels go as far as possible into the lengthwise joints (Fig. 12-48C), but be careful that the point of the drill does not break through the outside. Level the tops of the legs with the rails.

Table 12-9. Materials List for Magazine Table.

1 top	16 × 37 × ¾
4 legs	3 × 20 × 1¼
2 top rails	3 × 36 × ¾
2 top rails	3 × 36 × ¾
2 bottom rails	2 × 30 × ¾
2 bottom rails	2 × 13 × ¾
9 slats	2 × 14 × ½

Give the edges of a solid top similar rounding to the edges of the legs and rails. Pocket screws or buttons can be used to attach it. Buttons are preferable if it is the type of wood expected to expand and contact. Trim the bottoms of the legs, if necessary, so that they stand level. Then take off sharp edges. See Table 12-9 for a materials list.

Chapter 13
Stools and Chairs

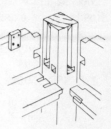

Early man sat on simple stools and benches. These developed into chairs with increasing regard for comfort by shaping the parts of the chair to suit a person's anatomy. With this came the development of upholstery, which started as skins and rugs thrown over the chair, followed by cushions and fitted padding. Often the woodwork was almost entirely hidden by the upholstery. This is still so, but the framework of a fully upholstered chair is not really a cabinetmaker's work. He is more concerned with furniture in which the wooden parts are the dominant theme.

Stools usually have rectangular lines and can be made with the aid of squares and the usual methods of getting such shapes true. The simplest chair might have squared angles in some place, but as the design gets adapted to increase comfort by shaping, the parts and their assembly become more complex. The front of a chair seat will be wider than the back, so side rail angles are not square. Legs will taper and are not always upright. Joints have to allow for this. The back usually curves and the supports between the uprights are curved to suit a person's back. The seat can be treated in several ways. The wood can be shaped, as in the popular Windsor chair, but it is more common to provide it with flexible support, such as rush, or give it padding in the form of lift-out or built-in upholstery.

Coupled with the complication of shaping is the need to provide adequate strength at key points, while other parts are reduced in size to lighten and improve appearance. If a good chair is examined, it will usually be found to have parts that started with squared sections. These keep their shapes at the joints and are tapered or shaped and the edges rounded away from the joints. A chair can by pushed about or tilted on to two legs while a person's weight is on it. That puts considerable strain on joints that are not very large areas. They have to be a good fit and properly secured to withstand the strains. Greatest loads can be expected to be front to back. Any rails between the legs provide strength as well as decoration. Arms provide extra members and joints to strengthen the assembly.

DRESSER STOOL

This is a piece of bedroom furniture (Fig. 13-1). However, it could be used as a seat elsewhere and might be adapted as a piano stool. There are two end frames joined by lengthwise rails

Fig. 13-1. This dresser stool has shaped edges on all rails and hand holes in the ends.

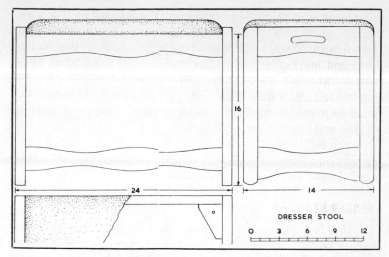

Fig. 13-2. This stool is made with end frames joined with lengthwise parts.

and a padded seat screwed to the top. All the frame joints can be mortise and tenons, but where the lengthwise rails have to be joined into the comparatively thin legs, a stronger joint can be obtained with dowels. This is particularly true if a drill can be used with a short point so that the dowels can be taken as far as possible into the legs. Mortise and tenon joints can be used throughout, but the stool is described with all dowel joints. In this example, ½-inch dowels in the ⅞-inch wood should be satisfactory.

The sizes shown (Fig. 13-2) can be varied to suit needs. If the length is to be increased, make the long rails deeper for stiffness. Other sections can remain the same.

All rails are shown with shaped edges. The curves on the undersides of the top rails are the same as those on the bottom rails. Draw half the length of a rail and make a card or hardboard template of the curve (Fig. 13-3A) so that it can be turned over to mark the other way symmetrically. If a bandsaw or jigsaw can be used, allow a little more for further work. Clean the curves with a Surform tool or a spokeshave and follow by sanding. The stool looks best if all exposed edges are rounded in cross section (Fig. 13-3B). This can be done with a suitable spindle molding cutter or by careful work with hand tools and abrasive. Leave edges square at the joints and a short distance each side of them.

Mark out the legs (Fig. 13-3C) together. The curves at the bottom can be cut, but leave trimming the tops to shape until

285

after joining in the rails. Mark rails that should be the same length together. Then square around with a knife and cut the ends to size. Finish by planing to the knife-cut lines. Do all edge shaping. The top end rails are shown with hand holes (Fig. 13-3D). Although not essential, they provide a grip and can be regarded as decorative. Drill holes at the ends and saw out the waste between them. Get the outlines correct before thoroughly rounding the section through the holes.

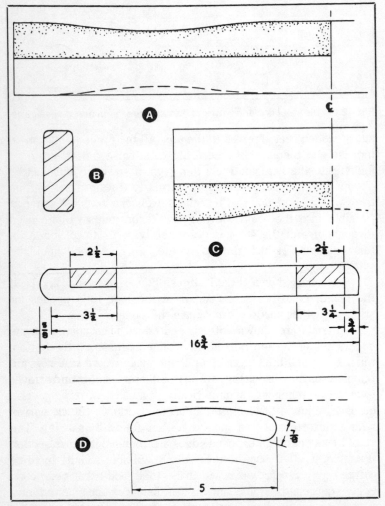

Fig. 13-3. Use templates (A) for frame shapes: (B) cross section; (C) legs; (D) hand holds.

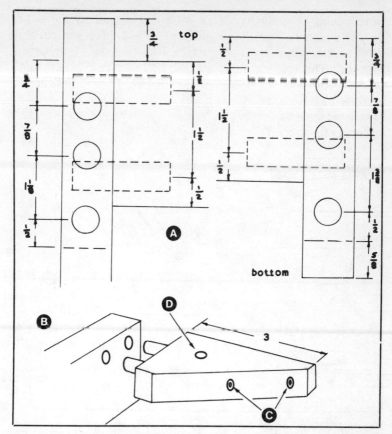

Fig. 13-4. Corners of the stool are dowelled (A). Corner blocks dowel (B,C,D) to the sides and screw to the ends.

So far as possible, stagger the dowel holes each way into the legs. It does not matter if dowel ends have to partly overlap, but avoid getting dowels exactly in line. The lengthwise rails are narrower than the end rails. Mark their dowel holes and arrange the others to come in different places (Fig. 13-4A).

Make up the end frames first (Fig. 13-5A). Check squareness and flatness and try the second one over the first. It will be easier to bring the end frames to a good finish at this stage than after the stool is assembled. Trim the tops of the legs to shape and round the top edges of the frame (Fig. 13-5B). If necessary, plane and sand the frame surfaces inside and outside to match.

To keep the stool square and provide attachment points for the top, there should be brackets in each corner. They could be

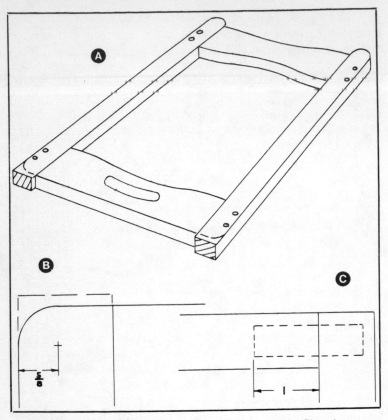

Fig. 13-5. Square the end frames (A), round their corners (B) and prepare for dowels the other way (C).

merely glued and screwed, but the whole thing will be made more rigid if each bracket has two dowels into the long top rails (Fig. 13-4B) where it can be attached and checked for squareness before assembling to the ends. When the whole stool is assembled, screws are taken through to the top end rails (Fig. 13-4C).

The holes for dowels in the thickness of the frame should be taken as deep as possible without the bit center breaking through. If a *Forstner bit* is available, it can take the holes to within ⅛-inch of the other side because it does not have a projecting center point. Take the dowels about 1 inch into the end grain of the rails (Fig. 13-5C). Dowel joints rely on closeness of fit for strength and appearance. Clamp them while the glue sets.

The top is a piece of plywood upholstered in a similar way to that described next for the piano stool. An exception is that it will be screwed down and the edges of its end will not show. When the top is in position, its ends should fit closely inside the wooden ends and long sides should be level with the rails. Have the upholstery material ready so that the size to cut the plywood can be judged to give the correct final dimensions. Put a few holes in the plywood to allow air movement and take sharpness off all of its edges.

Drill holes for screws in the brackets so that four screws can be driven upwards in to the plywood (Fig. 13-4D). Make a trial assembly. Then remove the upholstered top while the framework is finally sanded, stained and polished. See Table 13-1 for a materials list.

PIANO STOOL

This is a stool of traditional design (Figs. 13-6A, 13-6B and 13-7) that is suitable for construction in most hardwoods. The sizes given provide a seat at a suitable height for most pianos. There is plenty of space inside for storing sheet music. The top is large enough to allow for the movement of the player, but sizes can be reduced for situations where compactness is needed. For use with an organ, it would be better to increase the length. The legs are fairly stout to withstand the pushing and levering loads they will have to withstand. Heaviness could be relieved by stopped chamfers or other decoration on the edges. Whether there is to be any carving or not depends on the piano and other furniture the stool is to be used with. Much decoration would be out of place in a room where the other furniture is fairly plain. In any case, the turned hand rails probably provide all the decoration needed in most modern setting.

Table 13-1. Materials List for Dresser Stool.

4 legs	1½ × 18 × ⅞
2 top rails	2½ × 24 × ⅞
2 top rails	3¼ × 13 × ⅞
2 bottom rails	2½ × 24 × ⅞
2 bottom rails	3½ × 13 × ⅞
brackets from	2 × 14 × ⅞
1 top	14 × 22½ × ½ plywood

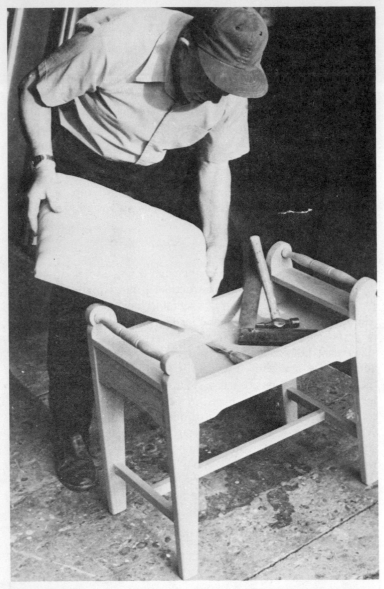

Fig. 13-6A. The piano stool has an upholstered top and lifting handles.

The legs are the key parts and should be marked out first after all the wood has been planed to size. Mark lengthwise measurements across the four legs together. Then mark on the shapes and positions of other parts (Fig. 13-8A). Watch that the

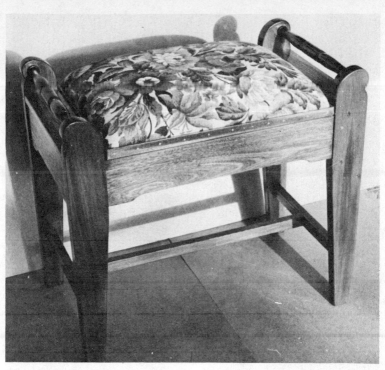

Fig. 13-6B. The finished stool.

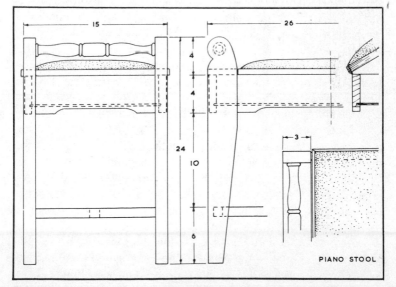

Fig. 13-7. The center of the piano stool is a box with a hinged lid.

legs are marked in pairs. Do not cut the outlines until after joints have been cut. Assembly can be with tenons (Fig. 13-9A) or dowels (Fig. 13-9B). If tenons are used, those on the rails can be single ones to the full width of each rail in most hardwoods. But if you believe that the long mortises would weaken the chosen wood too much, they can be divided with a gap between two tenons. All top parts going into the legs can have barefaced tenons. The shoulders are outwards and the faces are set back about ⅛-inch from the legs. Make the mortises or dowel holes about ¾ of an inch deep.

Mark the tops of the legs (Fig. 13-8B). The curved outline is drawn around the hole center before it is drilled. Drill the holes ¾ of an inch deep and be careful that the point of the drill does not break through at the other side. Any differences between the shapes of the tops of the legs will be rather obvious when the stool is finished. Be careful that they match. Mark them all independently, but shape one first and use it as a pattern to test the others as they are cut. Remove tool marks on the curves and round the edges by sanding.

The top rails can be left with their lower edges straight across, but their appearance is improved if they are cut back slightly. Do this at the same distance from the ends of the rails in both directions (Fig. 13-8C). Groove the rails to suit the plywood (Fig. 13-8D). If there is no cutter to exactly match the plywood, it is better to cut the grooves slightly too narrow, so that the underside of the plywood can be planed around the edges, than to have it loose in the grooves.

Across the ends, the top pieces are the full width of the legs. The top rail is set back below each of them (Fig. 13-8E). Round the outer edges of the top. The bottom rails have plain mortise and tenon joints (Fig. 13-8F) at their ends and centers.

When turning the hand rails (Fig. 13-10A), use one of the other rails as a guide to shoulder length (Fig. 13-19B). Turn the dowel ends to fit the holes in the legs, but slightly shorter than the hole depths so that the shoulders are not prevented from pulling tight. Use a rod to check that each hand rail is symmetrical and that they match (Fig. 13-10C). Turn to maximum diameters of about 1⅛ of an inch.

Assemble the two ends first. Glue the tops to the top rails as they are brought to the legs and the joints glued there. Check squareness and lack of twist in the first end assembled. Then use it to test the other end which is assembled to face it. Let

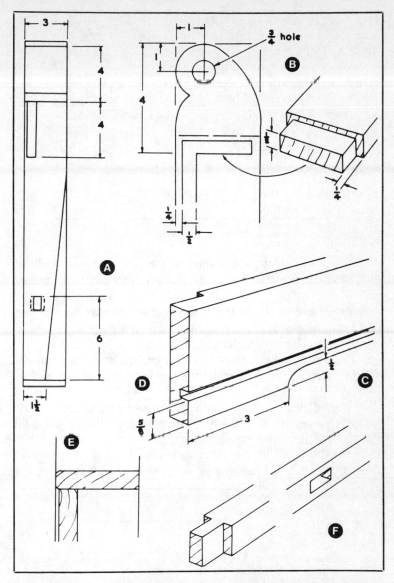

Fig. 13-8. Construction details of the piano stool: (A,B) mark shapes and positions; (C) cut back ends; (D) groove the rails; (E) set back the rail; (F) joints.

these joints set before joining the ends with the other parts. Check for glue that might have gotten into the grooves and remove it.

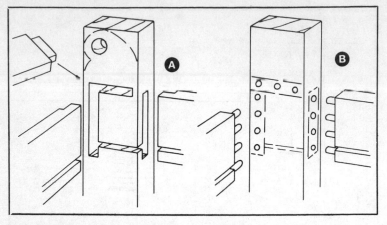

Fig. 13-9. Corners may be tenoned or dowelled.

Check the fit of the plywood bottom into the ends and see that it will fit into the long top rails when they are introduced partially into their mortises. The plywood need not go to the bottoms of the grooves. It is more important that the mortise and tenon or dowel joints pull tight so that a little slackness in the fit of the plywood is acceptable.

Complete the assembly. Check that the legs stand upright and see that the opening for the top had to be made out of square to fit it.

The lid overhangs the width of the box by the amount of the lid edge pieces. It will be satisfactory to make the plywood lid the same as the width of the box part. The other way there has to be an allowance for the covering material and the edge pieces (Fig. 13-11A). A clearance of as much as ⅛ of an inch might not

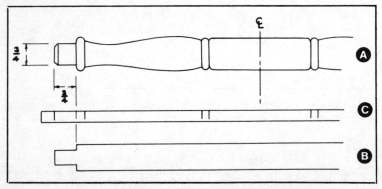

Fig. 13-10. Details of the handles (A) and rails (B,C).

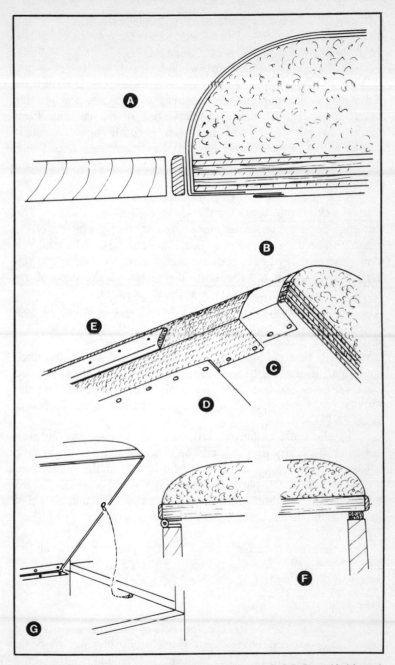

Fig. 13-11.The upholstered top has wood edges (A,B,C,D,E) and is hinged at one side (F,G)

matter, but it is better craftsmanship to make the fit closer than that. The covering materials as well as the edge strips should be ready before the plywood is cut to length.

Drill a few holes in the plywood to let air out and in as the padded part is sat on. Plastic foam 2 inches thick should be satisfactory. It could be 2½ inches or 3 inches for greater comfort. As in the earlier upholstered seats, cut the foam slightly oversize and bevel the lower edge all round so that it can be pulled to a rounded edge with the inner piece of calico or other light cloth (Fig. 13-11B). Have the line of tacks far enough in to miss the top rail.

Have the outer covering material wide enough to go to a line of tacks inside those for the inner cloth (Fig. 13-11C). The cut edge need not be turned under, but another piece of cloth is used to line the underside of the lid. Fold this under and rub down the fold so that it comes a short distance inside the top rails (Fig. 13-11D) and the same distance from the ends of the lid to give a neat appearance when the lid is raised.

Stain and polish all the woodwork before fitting the lid. Get the lengths of the lid edges from the upholstered lid. Cut them mitered at the corners. Stain and polish them as well. Fit these strips with thin nails driven into the plywood at about 2-inch intervals. If the nails are brassed or blacked, they will be inconspicuous because their heads will have to remain on the surface of the wood which is too thin for punching and stopping. (Fig. 13-11E).

The lid could be hinged with two 2-inch hinges and let into the top rail slightly. But it would be neat and appropriate to have a long piano hinge which need not be let in. At the other side, the wood can be left bare. However, it would be better padded slightly. This could be a strip of felt glued on, although a strip of self-adhesive foam draught excluder makes a good pad (Fig. 13-11F).

So that the lid cannot go back too far, put screw eyes in the lid and the underside of one top strip so that a cord can be attached (Fig. 13-11G). See Table 13-2 for a materials list.

SIDE ARMCHAIR

This is a chair of basic construction with its shape giving reasonable comfort, but without the shaping of parts found in more advanced chairs. The front legs extended to the arms provide strength with the extra joints. This type of chair looks

Table 13-2. Materials List for Piano Stool.

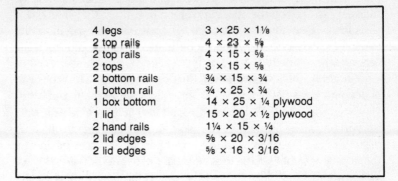

4 legs	3 × 25 × 1⅛	
2 top rails	4 × 23 × ⅝	
2 top rails	4 × 15 × ⅝	
2 tops	3 × 15 × ⅝	
2 bottom rails	¾ × 15 × ¾	
1 bottom rail	¾ × 25 × ¾	
1 box bottom	14 × 25 × ¼ plywood	
1 lid	15 × 20 × ½ plywood	
2 hand rails	1¼ × 15 × ¼	
2 lid edges	⅝ × 20 × 3/16	
2 lid edges	⅝ × 16 × 3/16	

best in oak or similar coarse-grained wood. The more delicately marked hardwoods are better for more slender construction. The chair can be made in softwood if it is to match other pine furniture. The overall sizes shown (Fig. 13-12) suit side chairs or dining chairs. They could be increased slightly if it is to be an individual carver chair.

Start by marking the back legs (Fig. 13-13A) together. The front edge is straight for the joint at seat height. Then there is a taper to the foot, but the back edge is straight to the seat. A suitable curve can be drawn around a sprung batten. Shape the

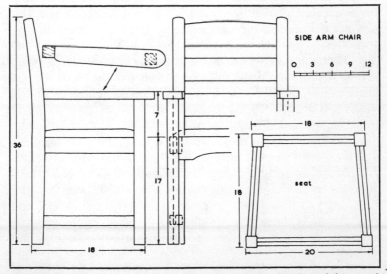

Fig. 13-12. The side arm chair provides comfort with the minimum of shaping.

297

front edge of the back legs, but it is more convenient for cutting the joints if the rear edge is left for shaping later. Prepare the wood for the seat rails. Draw the plan view of the seat (Fig. 13-12) full size. This gives the angles for the sides. Set an adjustable bevel to this and use it instead of a try square for marking the shoulders of the tenons at the sides.

Joints in the crosswise rails are cut squarely. The front rail is deeper to get the benefit of strength in a wider joint. Cut away its lower edge (Fig. 13-13B) and round it. The two-side seat rails have to be paired because of the taper of the back legs. You could make a full size side view of the lower part of the chair or make a temporary assembly of the legs and seat rail to get their length. Cut away outside the rabbet parts of the seat rails and use mortise and tenon joints (Fig. 13-13C). These and the lower rails can have tenons ¾ of an inch thick.

The back slats are curved across and tenoned into the uprights (Fig. 13-14A). It would be possible to steam thin wood around a former, but they are shown sawn from solid wood. This usually results in an attractive grain pattern. Draw the curves around a sprung batten and bandsaw to shape. The outside of the curve can be smoothed with a Surform tool. Follow by scraping and sanding if a plane with a curved sole is unavailable.

Give the upper slat a curve on its top edge and round all slats in cross-section (Fig. 13-14B). Cut down the ends to clear the rounding and slightly shoulder the front of each joint. The distance between shoulders should match the rear seat rail. The ends then go into tapered mortises (Fig. 13-14C).

The angles and shape of the arms can be found by drawing one over the legs in the full size drawing of the seat. To get maximum strength at the front, use double tenons with fox wedging (Fig. 13-13D). At the back, curve the outer edge in and use a single tenon (Fig. 13-14D).

Finish cutting the back legs to shape. Round their tops. All of the exposed parts of the finished chair should be well rounded. Be careful to leave the areas where the joints come with square edges. However, where the legs are thicker than the rails that join them, the curves can follow through. Round the upper edges of the arms more than the lower edges and give the front ends—which will be prominent—smooth sweeps and curved sections.

Assemble the sides first. Check that the horizontal parts are square with the front legs and the two sides make a matched

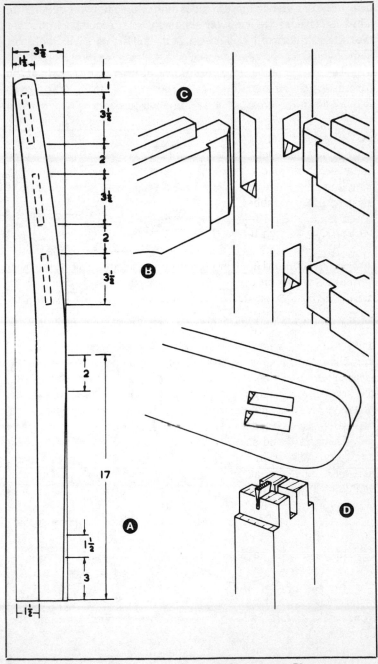

Fig. 13-13. Details of the back (A), arms (B,C) and seat (D).

pair without twists. Join the sides with the crosswise members. Check squareness that way at slats and rails. Also check that the seat is symmetrical, by measuring diagonals, and that the chair stands level.

The seat is an upholstered piece of plywood that fits in, in the same way as described for earlier stools, using fabric over foam. The only complication is the need to notch the corners to

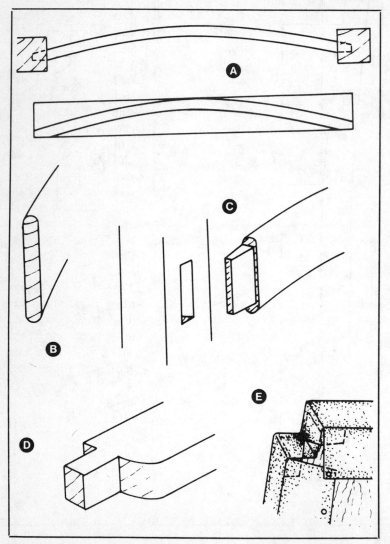

Fig. 13-14. Shaped back parts (A, B, C, D) a corner of the seat (E).

fit around the legs. Give the plywood enough clearance. Most cloth can be pulled to conform partially to shape, so be careful to not cut away too much at the notches. It helps to put a strip of covering material inside a notch, then pull the covering piece into shape over it so that the strip inside disguises any gap (Fig. 13-14E). See Table 13-3 for a materials list.

DINING CHAIR

To make even a general purpose chair comfortable, there have to be departures from the right angle design appropriate to most other cabinetwork. A sitting person does not conform to a right angled seat. This chair (Fig. 13-15) has a seat that is hollowed and slopes back slightly. The front legs and the back both slope. The seat is upholstered on a frame and lifts out. Overall sizes (Fig. 13-16) are suitable for sitting at a table.

When viewed from the front, the upright parts are parallel and the other members are at right angles to them. Assembly that way can be by normal squaring methods. In the other direction, there are no right angles. It is advisable to set out a side view full size and work to that for the sizes and positions of the joining parts. The seat is ½-inch higher at the front than the back. The bottom rails also slope up from back to front. Also, draw a plan view of half the seat to get the angles of the side seat rails. Shoulders of the side rails are slightly angled in both directions.

The back legs are curved (Fig. 13-17A). Cut the front curves, but leave the back until after cutting the joints. The front legs (Fig. 13-17B) can be square pieces (Fig. 13-16), but the example has a ball turning larger than the square ends. The wood for this can be prepared by using the size for the ends and gluing on enough to turn the ball. This might show a glue line

Table 13-3. Materials List for Side Arm Chair.

2 back legs	3½ × 37 × 1¾
2 front legs	1¾ × 25 × 1¾
3 seat rails	2½ × 18 × 1¼
1 front rail	3½ × 18 × 1¼
2 lower rails	1¼ × 18 × 1½
2 arms	1 × 20 × 3
3 back slats from	3½ × 18 × 1¾
1 seat	17 × 20 × ½ plywood

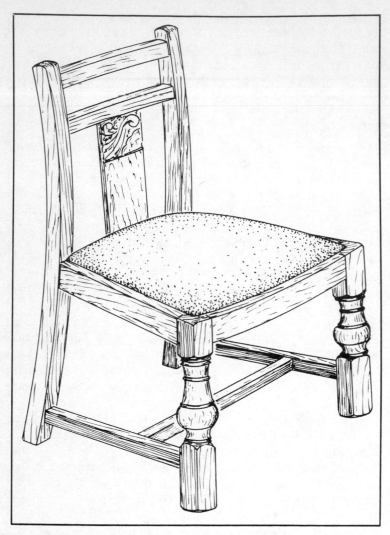

Fig. 13-15. The dining chair incorporates many features that add to comfort and appearance.

and different grain, but if the finished chair is to be stained dark it would probably not be obvious. The alternative is to start with the wood large enough to turn the ball and reduce the ends to square. In both cases, careful centering in the lathe is important to get the square section concentric with the round section.

The two side seat rails are given rabbets to support the seat (Fig. 13-18A). Front and back rails are without rabbets, but

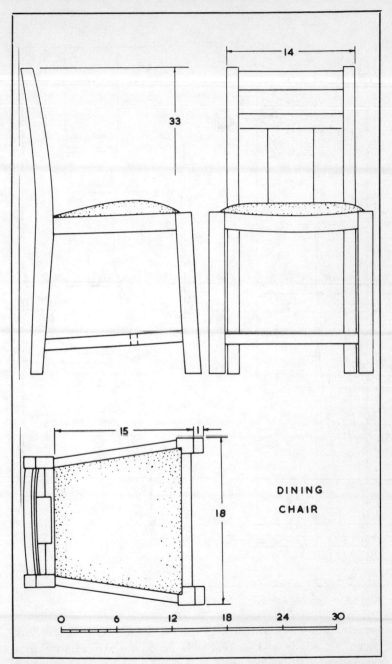

Fig. 13-16. These proportions suit a chair to be used at a normal dining table.

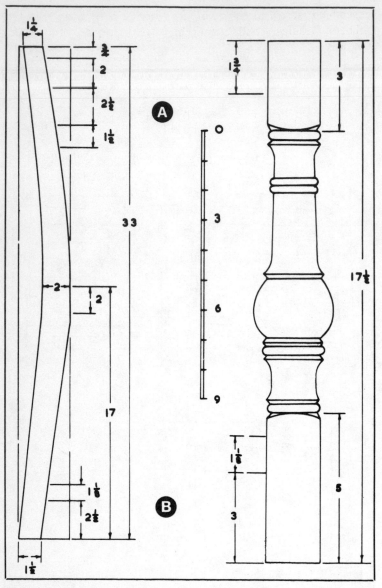

Fig. 13-17. Details of rear (A) and front legs (B)

are hollowed (Fig. 13-18B). Shape the front rail, then use this curve to mark the shorter rear rail. Tenon the back seat rail into the legs so that its front edge is level (Fig. 13-18C). At the front legs, allow for cutting in (Fig. 13-18D). When the chair is assembled, screw in corner blocks (Fig. 13-18E) level with the rabbets. Besides strengthening the corners they help to support the seat.

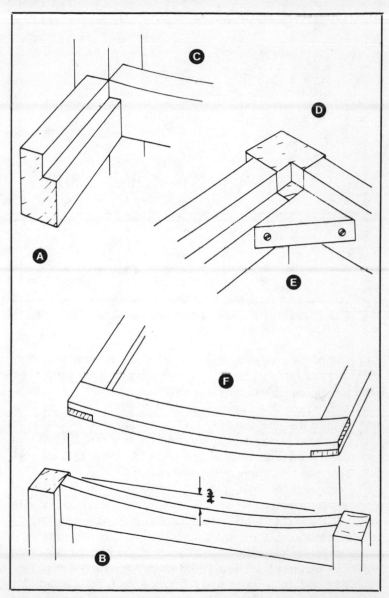

Fig. 13-18, The seat has curved front and back (A,B,C) with rabbets in the side rails (D,E,F).

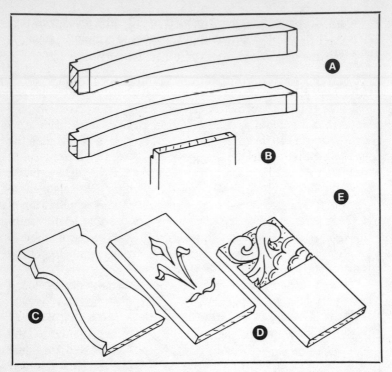

Fig. 13-19. Back rails are curved (A,B,C). Several methods of decorating the central part can be used (C,D,E).

The bottom rails have simple tenons, but their shoulders are angled and it is advisable to get the length of the center one after a trial assembly of the other parts.

At the back, the two rails are cut to curves (Fig. 13-19A) and tenoned into the uprights. The central splat tenons into the lower of these two rails and into the rear seat rail. If barefaced tenons are used (Fig. 13-19B), only only the shoulder at the rear has to be cut to the curve of the seat rail.

Because of the form of the back, it is advisable to assemble back and front as the first step. Check for squareness and lack of twist. If the corner blocks are cut to their angles from the full size seat drawing, they will help to pull the chair symmetrical when the other parts are added. Bring in the bottom crosswise rail as its partners are assembled. Otherwise it cannot be put in.

The seat frame parts have finished sections that are 1½ inches by ⅝ of an inch. Back and front are curved to match the curves of the seat rails (Fig. 13-18F). Corner joints can be halved or bridles. Upholster over webbing in the same way as described for earlier stools. Three pieces of webbing each way will give a good support. See Table 13-4 for a materials list.

CARVER CHAIR

The greatest comfort in an arm chair comes from shaping the back in its width as well as letting it slope back. The arms have to be curved and they should be wider at the front than the seat below them. This means that the rear legs have to be cut to curves in both directions. The supports have to be flared outwards. For the sake of appearance they may also curve forward. These compound curves, coupled with the hollowing of the back parts and a possible hollowing of the seat in its width, mean that the structure is an assembly of curved parts and it is not always easy to see what to use as reference points to get the chair properly trued to a symmetrical shape.

If most chairs are examined, there will usually be found some straight parts at right angles to each other. In other views, there are assemblies that can be trued by comparing diagonal measurements. In this chair (Fig. 13-20), the outsides of the front legs are at right angles to the seat sides and to a line across the seat front. If diagonals are used on the back framing, the chair should finish symmetrical. Because sizes of some parts will have to be found by reference to others during temporary assemblies, these checks should be kept in mind when trying parts in position.

Table 13-4. Material List for Dining Chair.

2 back legs	3½ × 33 × 1¼
2 front legs	1¾ × 18 × 1¾
or	3 × 18 × 3
2 seat rails	1¼ × 16 × 1¾
1 front rail	3 × 18 × 1
1 back seat rail	2½ × 14 × 1
1 back top rail	2 × 14 × 1½
1 back lower rail	1½ × 14 × 1½
1 back splat	5 × 12 × 1½
2 seat sides	1½ × 15 × ⅝
1 seat back	1½ × 13 × 1¼
1 seat front	1½ × 18 × 1½
4 corner blocks	2 × 6 × ⅞
3 bottom rails	1⅛ × 18 × ⅝

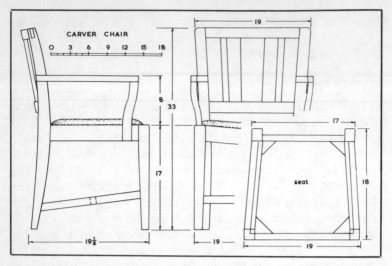

Fig. 13-20. This carver chair has more shaping than the side armchair.

There is a beauty in a nicely made joint and this chair leaves some joints exposed. The method is better for close-grained hardwoods than for open-grained woods such as oak. End grain can be finished smoothly alongside the side grain of the joints. In open joints, cut the parts too long and trim them carefully after the glue has set. Dowels made from the same wood can be put through joints and their end grain will provide decoration.

Draw a side view full size and use this as a reference for the sizes of most parts. Draw the whole, or half, of the seat plan and use this as a guide to angles when viewed from above. After the legs and seat have been made, draw over the seat plan the intended shape of an arm. Use this as a guide to the shape of the arm and the amount its support has to be curved outwards (Fig. 13-21D).

The front legs taper on the inner surfaces only from below the seat rail level (Fig. 13-21A). Leave the outsides square. Make the seat side rails, with rabbets for the seat, similar to the previous chair. Cut their joints at the front legs, but leave the other ends until the back legs are ready. Mark out the legs in side view (Fig. 13-21B). Include the positions of other parts. Cut them to shape. Then mark the other way (Fig. 13-21C) so as to make a pair. The taper of the legs below the seat is slight, but it looks better curved than straight slopes.

Make the front seat rail with a hollow in a similar way to that of the previous chair. Mark the back seat rail to the same curve. The joints for the seat rails into the legs are the same as the previous chair and the joints will be strengthened by corner

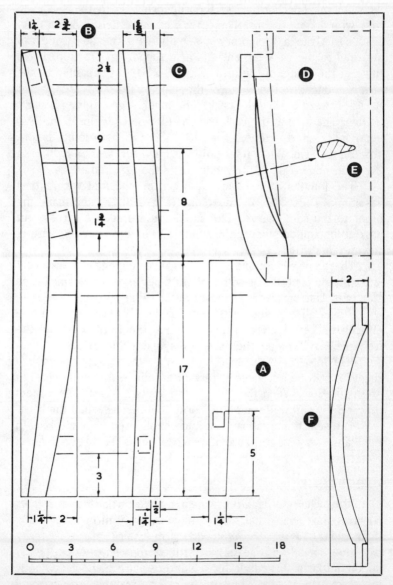

Fig. 13-21. Details of the shaped parts: (A) seat rail level; (B) side view; (C) mark a pair; (D) shape of the arm; (E) inner edge; (F) back rail.

blocks. The bottom rails are similarly made with mortise and tenon joints.

The arm supports bend forward and outward 1 inch (Fig. 13-22A). Keep the ends straight but shape to fair curves between them. The bottoms of the supports join to the seat side rails with double tenons. The outer part goes the full depth (Fig. 13-22B). Make a temporary assembly with the seat side rail attached to the back leg and the arm support in position. From this get the shape of the arm (Fig. 13-21D). At the support the arm is reduced to the width of the support (Fig. 13-22C), but it flares outward toward the back. The inner edge is given a slight hollow. The joint at the back has an outer piece going to the rear edge and a shorter tenon (Fig. 13-22D). Cut both joints before shaping the arm. When its profile has been cut, work a hollow on the inner edge (Fig. 13-21E) and round the exposed edges.

The lengths of the back rails can be checked with a trial assembly. Then cut the longer one (Fig. 13-21F) and make the other to the same curve. The shoulders are square across, but have to be angled slightly the other way to allow for the flare of the uprights (Fig. 13-22E).

There are several possible ways of arranging the back. That shown has a central slat with a slight taper and narrow ones each side of it. Use barefaced tenons into the rails.

Round all exposed parts and particularly those that will be difficult to get at after assembly. Glue the front legs and the front seat rail. Glue the back rails and slats. Glue the arm supports into the side seat rails. With these sub assemblies ready, it will be advisable to further assemble the whole chair in one operation. When the glue in the joints has set, clean them off carefully and well round the corners of the arms and the back.

The seat frame is made up and upholstered over webbing in the same way as the previous chair. See Table 13-5 for a materials list.

TURNED CHAIR

Many chairs of traditional design have turned parts in their construction. Some chairs are almost entirely turned (including their seats). *Windsor chairs* are arm chairs made in many patterns, but all with seats having their tops shaped and nearly all other parts turned. If the chair does not have arms, it is incorrect to call it a Windsor chair. The making of successful ones with arms calls for considerable experience. Much of the

Table 13-5. Materials List for Carver Chair.

2 front legs	1⅝ × 18 × 1⅝
2 back legs	4 × 34 × 2
2 side seat rails	2½ × 18 × 1
1 back seat rail	3 × 17 × 1
1 front seat rail	3½ × 19 × 1
2 arms	3 × 19 × 1
2 arm supports	2½ × 11 × 2
1 top back rail	2½ × 19 × 2
1 bottom back rail	2 × 19 × 1¾
1 back slat	4 × 12 × ⅝
2 back slats	1 × 12 × ⅝
3 bottom rails	1¼ × 19 × 1
4 corner blocks	2 × 6 × ⅞
1 seat front	1½ × 18 × 1½
1 seat back	1½ × 16 × 1¼
1 seat front	1½ × 17 × ⅝

work, such as the drilling of holes at the correct angles, has to be done by eye and the first-time chair maker might make mistakes. If a chair is made without arms, the amount of work that depends on estimation is reduced and a successful result should be obtained first time if the work is done in the correct sequence.

This chair (Fig. 13-23) has a seat that could be left flat, although it is shown shaped in Windsor style. All of the turned parts are shown plain, but they could be turned with beads and other patterns. Whatever design is used in the length of the turned parts, the ends should be parallel for a short distance from each end. This allows for adjustment during assembly. The shape of the chair can be corrected if necessary by moving an end in or out a little in its hole, or even by cutting some off, but that would not be possible if the end tapered or there was a shoulder to come against the mouth of the hole. Of course, the ends must be good fits in their holes. Have the holes drilled in scrap wood with the bits that will be used for testing when the parts are turned. It would be possible to foxwedge rails into blind holes, but it is usual to rely on a good fit. The legs and back posts can go right through the seat and their exposed ends can be wedged.

The lengths of parts required are better visualized from a drawing showing just the centerlines of the turned parts (Fig. 13-24). Construction is best approached in two stages: First the seat and legs and then the back. Cut the seat to its outline (Fig.

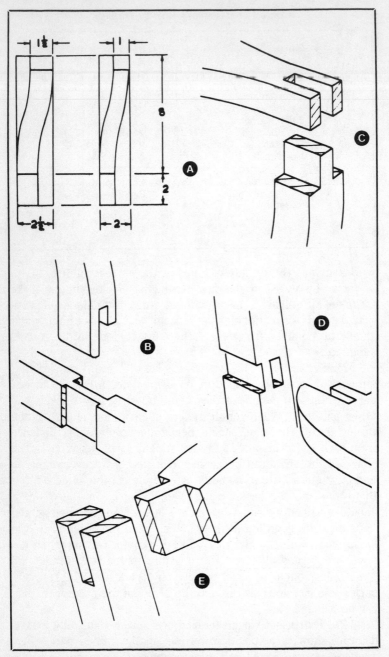

Fig. 13-22. Arm details: (A) arm supports; (B) outer portion (C) flare; (D) short tenon; (E) flared uprights.

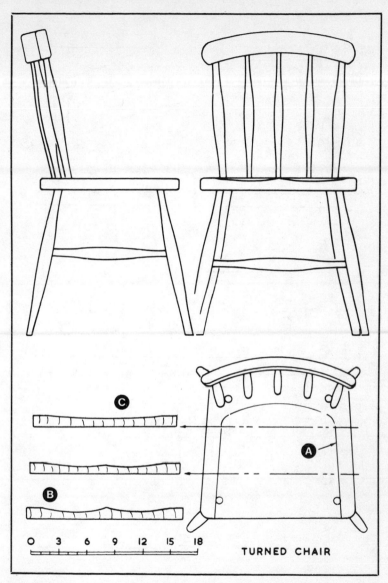

O 3 6 9 12 15 18

TURNED CHAIR

Fig. 13-23. The turned chair is lathe work except for the seat (A) and back (B,C)

13-24A). There is no need for any rounding or shaping at this stage. Mark on it the positions for the holes for the legs 2 inches from each edge (Fig. 13-24B). The legs will splay out to points 1 inch outside the line of the seat (in each direction they go 3

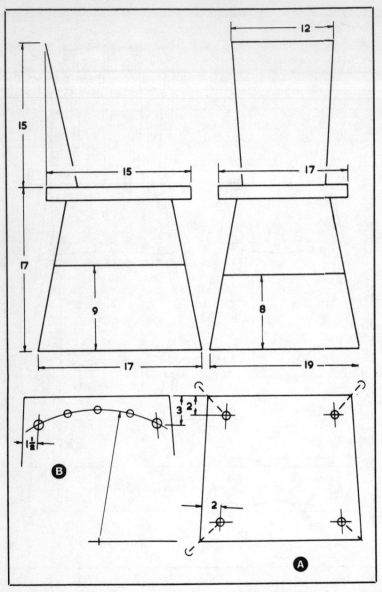

Fig. 13-24. How to set out the turned chair: (A) outline; (B) holes.

inches). If a 3-inch square is drawn, its diagonal is the total amount of splay. If a line is drawn to the seat height on the diagonal, a slope from this is the angle the legs will be (Fig. 13-25A). Set an adjustable bevel to this angle and use it on a diagonal at the corner as a guide when drilling (Fig. 13-25B). Drill from the top downward so there is little risk of grain breaking out where it will show. Drill back from below or clamp on scrap wood to prevent roughness there.

Use ¾-inch holes for the ends of legs and the ends of the outer back posts. All others can be ⅝ of an inch. The turned

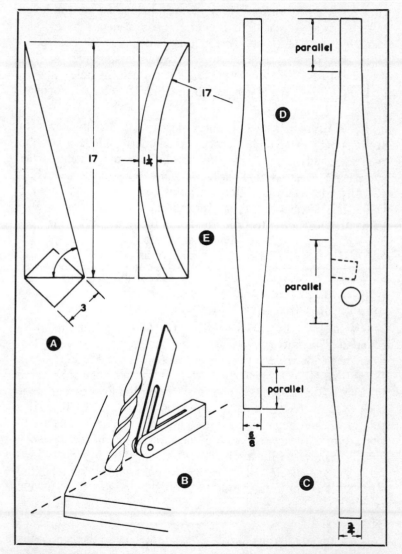

Fig. 13-25. Getting the leg angles and drilling for them (A,B). Shapes of legs and rails (C,D,E).

parts with ¾-inch ends can be 1⅜ inches at their greater diameters and the others can be 1¼ inches. It is more important to get parts matching. Slightly smaller or larger diameters do not matter so long as parts that should be similar really are similar. Use calipers when repeating after the first of a type.

The chair legs (Fig. 13-25C) are made parallel for a sufficient length to allow for drilling the rail holes. To get the holes at right angles to each other, wrap a strip of paper around and mark the circumference. Divide this into four. The hole positions around the curve come on two adjoining marks. The drawing (Fig. 13-24) shows the angles at which the holes have to be drilled. Make the lower rails (Fig. 13-25D). Pair the opposite ones.

For strength, the two outer back posts are thicker with ¾-inch ends. The other three can be more slender, but the shapes should match. Make sure the bulbous parts come at the same level all around the back. Mark the holes in the seat (Fig. 13-24B). Make sure that the side holes come far enough forward of the leg holes to not break into them. Use the drawing as a guide to the angles to drill the holes for back posts. Besides sloping back, the outer holes allow for the posts splaying outward and the next two splay a smaller amount.

Cut the back from solid wood (Fig. 13-25E). Smooth all surfaces. Then well round the ends and the front so that it is comfortable to lean against. Mark and drill the post holes.

If the seat is to remain flat, its outer corners should be rounded. Then the edges are rounded and the front edge is given a considerable curve in section. If the seat is to be shaped, mark the outline of the shaping (Fig. 13-23A). At the front edge, mark the shape (Fig. 13-23B). The raised center diminishes as it goes back until it blends into a complete hollow (Fig. 13-23C). How this is worked depends on the equipment available. The traditional craftsman used a curved adze. Some of the waste wood can be removed with a power router and then broad shallow-curved gouges used. Curved scrapers could follow to smooth the surface. It is not always easy to see that opposite sides match, so use card templates to check that the hollow is symmetrical at various points.

Assemble the rails to the legs and the legs to the seat at the same time. Because of the compound angles, each joint has to be entered a little at a time. It would not do to fully assemble a side before joining in the other parts. Have saw cuts already made in the tops of the legs at an angle that will bring them across the grain of the seat ready for wedging. Do not use a quick-setting glue. It might be necessary to take the assembly apart to trim ends. A dry test assembly is not advised, as that tends to wear and loosen joints.

The back is easier. Glue the posts into the curved back and then press them into the seat holes. If force is needed, put a piece of wood over the back to spread the effect of a blow. At all stages of assembly, stand back and view the chair from several angles. This will show if the slopes of legs match or the back assembly is going on without twist. Adjustment can be made before the glue has set. Also check that the seat is parallel with the floor. Slight trimming of the bottoms of the legs might be necessary. If the legs start the same length and there is much error, the amount of splay will be found to differ. See Table 13-6 for a materials list.

ROCKER

One method of upholstering a chair is to use loose cushions supported by webbing or coil springs. Ordinary webbing can give sufficient support, but rubber webbing, with its slight elasticity, gives a little more comfort, Coil springs have a similar effect to rubber webbing, but frames have to suit their stock lengths. Webbing can be cut to any length.

This chair uses cushions for the seat, the back (Fig. 13-26) and the method of support that must be chosen before starting on the woodwork. For rubber webbing, there are metal fittings to squeeze on to cut ends (Fig. 13-27A). A nail or screw can go through the fitting or a common way of attachment is to use an angled plowed groove (Fig. 13-27B). A coil spring will hook on to a nail or screw in a rabbet (Fig. 13-27C) or a groove (Fig.

Table 13-6. Materials List for Turned Chair.

1 seat	15 × 17 × 1¼
4 legs	1½ × 19 × 1½
2 rails	1⅜ × 15 × 1⅜
2 rails	1⅜ × 18 × 1⅜
1 back from	3½ × 18 × 2½
2 back posts	1½ × 18 × 1½
2 back posts	1½ × 18 × 1½

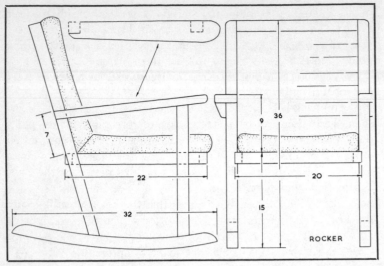

Fig. 13-26. A rocker chair of simple proportions (with loose cushions).

13-27D). It is also possible to get metal strips to screw to the wood and take the springs at intervals (Fig. 13-27E).

Start by making the seat frame. The webbing or springs will fit crosswise. Prepare the side pieces to suit the chosen type.

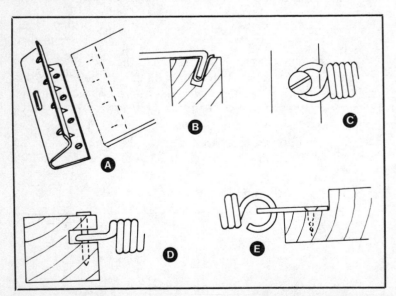

Fig. 13-27. Methods of attaching rubber webbing (A,B) or coil springs (C,D,E).

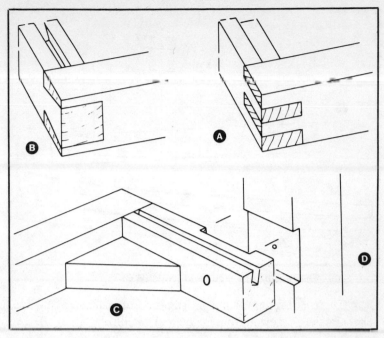

Fig. 13-28. Seat joints: (A) dovetails; (B) bridles; (C) triangular blocks; (D) glued joints are fastened with screws.

Corner joints can be dovetails (Fig. 13-28A) or bridles (Fig. 13-28B). See that the assembly is square. If there are doubts about its rigidity, put triangular blocks low down in the corners (Fig. 13-28C). When springs or webbing are fitted, space them at about 5-inch centers.

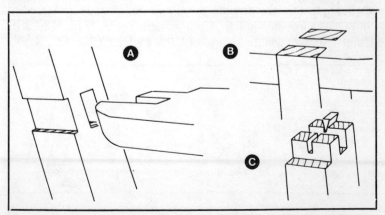

Fig. 13-29. Arm joints: (A) tenon; (B) exposed joint; (C) fox wedging.

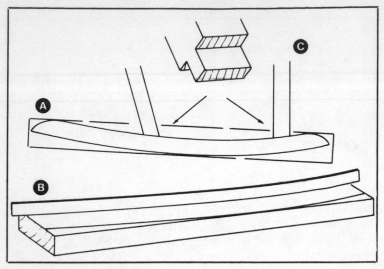

Fig. 13-30. The rocker (A) shapes and joints (B,C).

The front legs cross at right angles. Both parts are notched. The joints are screwed from inside and glued (Fig. 13-28D). The rear legs are notched to the same depth so front and back legs are in line.

Mark out the back legs with some extra left at the bottoms. Prepare the parts that come behind the cushion to take webbing or springs. Joints to the crossbar forming the top can be the same as in the corners of the seat. The back is drawn at 15 degrees to vertical. Mark the joint to the seat at this angle.

The arms tenon into the back leg (Fig. 13-29A) with a shallow notch at the outside. If an exposed joint is preferred at the front, use a similar arrangement there (Fig. 13-29B). Otherwise, use double tenons with fox wedging (Fig. 13-29C).

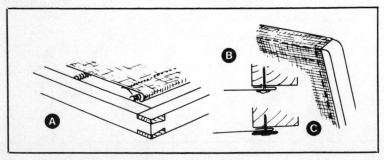

Fig. 13-31.Covering springs (A) and back (B,C).

Table 13-7. Materials List for Rocker.

2 front legs	1¼ × 25 × 1¾
2 back legs	1¾ × 38 × 1¾
2 seat frames	1¾ × 23 × 1¼
2 seat frames	1¾ × 21 × 1¼
1 top	1¾ × 24 × 1¾
2 arms	3½ × 25 × 1¼
2 rockers	5 × 33 × 1¾

The rockers are cut from solid wood (Fig. 13-30A). A curve can be drawn using a long piece of wood and an awl as a compass. The best rocker curve is not quite part of the circumference of a circle. It is better if the curve flattens toward the extended rear end. It can be drawn around a sprung lath that is manipulated in the hands to get the required shape (Fig. 13-30B). When the chair is at rest, it should be resting on the part of the curve just behind the halfway mark between the legs. The seat should then be slightly lower at the back than the front.

With a temporary assembly of one side, position a rocker over its legs and mark both legs and rocker with each other's positions. Use these marks as guides for marking and cutting the mortise and tenon joints (Fig. 13-30C). Do not weaken the rockers by cutting deep mortises.

Take off all sharp edges and round the outer corners. In particular, thoroughly round the parts of the arms that project forward. Check for squareness. Otherwise cushions will not fit evenly.

The cushions are rectangular pieces of 3-inch thick foam covered in suitable material. There can be suitable stock cushions or they can be made by sewing the covering inside out for all but the last seam at a narrow end. With the cover turned the right way and the foam pad pushed in, the last edge has to be sewn from outside. It is best to arrange for this to come where the cushions meet and it will not show.

Cushions can rest directly against webbing, but with springs it is better to put light, flexible cloth between them and the cushions. This can be tacked to the frame or it can be sewn around the end springs (Fig. 13-31A). The underside of the seat will not be seen, but the reverse side of the back will be covered with a piece of cloth. Use either a plain piece or one that matches the cushions. It would then be wrapped over the top and tacked to the frame (Fig. 13-31B). Use ornamental nails or thin nails through gimp (Fig. 13-31C).

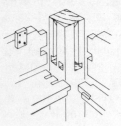

Chapter 14
Chests, Cabinets and Other Furniture

Much cabinetwork involves making items for storage. The name of the craft comes from the making of cabinets. Other furniture is associated with increasing comfort and convenience in modern homes. Modern materials are finding their way into furniture construction largely because of their suitability for quantity production. Some furniture that is made of manufactured boards is satisfactory and is aesthetically pleasing. Other furniture of this type might have to be accepted for economic reasons even though it is not otherwise attractive.

Furniture made of these modern materials has not yet settled down as a style in the same way as earlier styles were typically Queen Anne or Chippendale. Undoubtedly, future generations will speak of a 20th century style. Meanwhile, good cabinetwork is regarded as furniture made mostly of solid wood. Plywood panelling is used where appropriate, but not with particleboard or other manufactured boards as main constructional material. Joints mostly follow traditional methods. These considerations are more applicable to cabinets and chests where many parts are wide boards.

Items in this chapter are examples of the application of good techniques to furniture of sound construction. Chests and cabinets can have a much more elaborate appearance, but underneath the construction will follow the standard techniques. Inlaying and veneering can give a different appearance. Carving can be quite extensive. Curved spaces can take the place of flat ones with bow fronts to cabinets or drawers. These things add complications and give a craftsman an opportunity to express himself, but the joints and other constructional considerations should be similar to those of a plainer piece of work. If the object is to produce a reproduction of some earlier piece of fine craftsmanship, the work will be justified. Remember that the current preference is for a much plainer style of furniture. Another craftsman might appreciate your elaboration, but the ordinary user of the furniture might regard something that accounted for many hours work as a nuisance they would rather not have. An enthusiastic craftsman, wanting to show his skill, should strike a balance between the elaboration of earlier years and the starkness of some modern furniture—particularly in chests and cabinets.

CLASSIC CHEST OF DRAWERS

This is a three-drawer chest (Figs. 14-1 and 14-2) made by traditional cabinetmaking methods. It is comparatively plain and gets its beauty from its proportions and the use of attractive wood. Other chests of drawers are mostly made in the same basic way, but they can be complicated by veneering, molding, carving or the use of bowed fronts. Drawers have to be parallel sided and given a smooth action whatever the overall design of the chest. This example is a good piece of furniture in its own right, but it also serves as an introduction to anyone still learning how to make furniture with drawers.

In this sort of furniture, there have to be some parts fitted together with the grain crossing. Therefore, wide boards might not have much allowance for expansion and contraction. This means that the wood used should be properly seasoned. It would be advisable to keep the wider boards in the same atmosphere as the chest will eventually be used in, for a few weeks before completion of assembly, so that the wood moisture content can stabilize. This is particularly important if the normal wood storage and the shop are comparatively cold and the furniture is expected to be used in a centrally heated room. The regular heat can cause a loss of moisture that will make the wood shrink slightly. If a wide board has cross members firmly attached and the assembly is made when the moisture content is high, drying out will probably cause cracking.

Fig. 14-1. This chest of drawers has classic proportions.

The top and two ends will almost certainly have to be made up by joining two or more boards. It is these parts, preferably slightly oversize, that particularly ought to be prepared in advance of further work and stored in the final atmospheric conditions for a few weeks.

It is the pair of ends which are the controlling parts for arriving at dimensions of all parts of the chest. Mark out the sides (Fig. 14-3A). Use the actual pieces of wood to get the widths of the parts marked across. Rabbet the rear edges to take the plywood back (Fig. 14-3B).

Top and bottom lengthwise parts are best dovetailed into the ends (Fig. 14-3C). The top will be covering to within ⅛-inch of the edges (Fig. 14-3D). Keep the joints far enough back to be hidden by this. The runners that go back to front across the ends must not move in relation to the lengthwise parts so that their ends have short tenons to lock them (Fig. 14-3E). Prepare top and bottom parts in this way. Rabbet the long top piece for the back, but at the bottom the plywood can go over that part.

The two intermediate assemblies between the drawers are very similar, but their ends join to the chest ends with tenons (Fig. 14-3F). Of course, it is important that all long parts across the chest should be exactly the same length between shoulders. Mark these distances all together, but then tenons and dovetails will have to be dealt with separately.

Assemble with glue. This might be sufficient everywhere except where the runners go across. It might be worthwhile to use some screws as a guard against any tendency to warp in the chest ends. Obviously, screws from outside would spoil appearances, so drive the screws from inside. Counterbore so that there is no need to obtain long screws (Fig. 14-3G). Be careful of squaring the assembly and leaving it for the glue to set while standing on a truly flat surface. Any twist will make the action of drawers difficult. It helps to have one corner of the plywood back already truly square. Use this in a top corner and trim the other edge to fit into the rabbet and to hold the assembly square. The bottom edge can overlap to be trimmed later. Use fine nails or screws as well as glue through the plywood into the rabbets and to the lengthwise parts

The top can be molded around the edge in several ways. The example here cuts down ⅛ of an inch and allows for the wood to be set back ⅛ of an inch from the front and sides (Fig. 14-4A). There is no need to mold the back edge if the chest goes

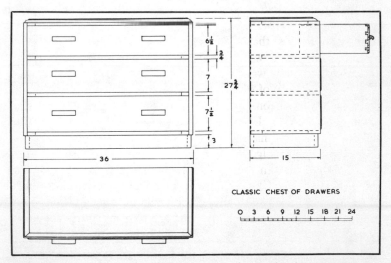

Fig. 14-2. Graduating the depths of drawers gives a pleasing appearance.

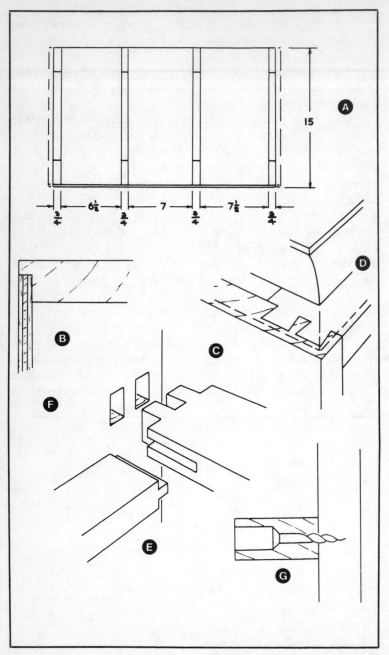

Fig. 14-3. Constructional details of the chest of drawers: (A) sides; (B) rear edges; (C) dovetail; (D) top; (E,F) tenons; ((G) counterbore.

into the usual position against a wall. The top will be glued and screwed from below through the framing, but the fitting of the drawers is more easily dealt with if the top is left off until you are satisfied with the drawer action.

The plinth is made like a box. The front corners should be mitered and reinforced with a block inside (Fig. 14-4B). The rear corners can be dealt with in the same way. However, for a position against a wall, they can be simple butt joints or the back can be rabbeted into the sides (Fig. 14-4C). Allow for the plinth coming level with the chest at the back, but set it in about ¼ of an inch at front and sides (Fig. 14-4D). Mark where it comes on the underside of the chest and drill for screws at about 6-inch spacing through the chest framing.

Have the chest itself completed except for attaching the top. Check that there are no blobs of glue anywhere inside that might interfere with the smooth sliding of the drawers. Each drawer has to slide on its runners and the one above acts as a kicker to prevent the drawer from tilting as it is pulled out. The chest ends act as side guides. Be sure that they are smooth.

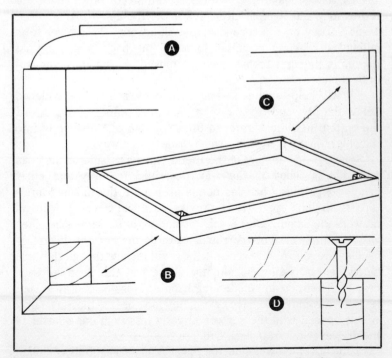

Fig. 14-4. The top and plinth (A,B,C,D) are set back on the chest.

The drawers are made with dovetails on the back and front and the bottom is let into plowed grooves (Fig. 14-5A). Although the drawer fronts must be made of the same wood as the rest of the chest, the sides and back can be inexpensive wood. Softwood is not recommended because it will wear quickly against the hardwood.

Make the front of a drawer first and planing it to be a close fit in the front of its space in the chest. The completed drawer will have to be eased by planing later, but start with the front fitting with only slight gaps around its edges. The front surfaces can be made flush with the front of the chest. In many chests, that is the way a traditional cabinetmaker made the drawers. Letting the fronts project ⅛ of an inch with rounded edges does something to disguise the gaps inevitable around a drawer and is more tolerant of slight inaccuracies.

Drawers can be made so that they close tightly against the plywood back, but pushing in a loaded drawer can put a considerable shock against the plywood. It is better to use stops at the front so that the drawer does not quite reach the back (Fig. 14-5B). The stops are two widely spaced pieces of wood about 4 inches long and ¼ of an inch thick under the upper divider (Fig. 14-5C). They have a secondary use in keeping the drawer from falling out when it is pulled forward (the back comes against them). If the drawer has to be removed, lifting its front will draw it clear.

It will help to spread wear if the drawer sides are widened below the plywood (Fig. 14-5D). A similar effect is obtained if the bottom fits into a grooved fillet (Fig. 14-5E) instead of into the side. Many old drawers were made in this way.

Handles can be any of the metal types available or they can be made of wood in the way described for tray and other handles. Spacing of handles needs planning if the finished furniture is to look right. It is unwise to make a chest with all drawers the same depth. If they actually are the same size, they will look progressively narrower towards the bottom. If drawer handles are put exactly central, they will look as though they are below center. Get them slightly above half the depth of each drawer. There could be one long handle across each drawer, but it is more common to have two. They look best if they are fairly widely spaced with the centers slightly less than one-quarter of the drawer width from each end.

Chests of drawers do not usually have any finish applied inside. If you feel that something should be done to prevent

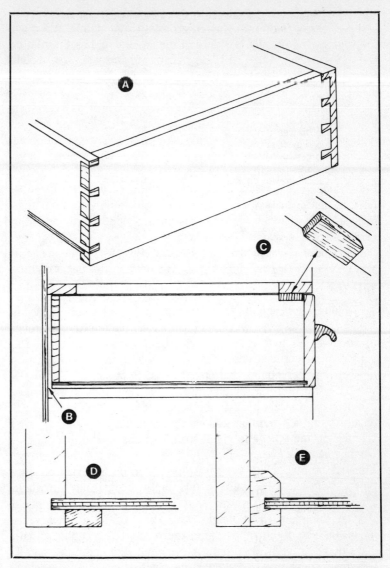

Fig. 14-5. Drawers are of standard construction (A,B). They have a stop at each front rail and the bottoms are strengthened for heavy wear (C,D,E).

absorption of moisture inside, you could allow a coat of varnish to soak in. Drawer sides will need some planing and sanding to get them to slide easily, but be careful of overdoing it. Candle wax, or something similar (not oil) will ease sticking drawers. See Table 14-1 for a materials list.

Table 14-1. Materials List for Classic Chest of Drawers.

1 top	14¾ × 36 × ¾
2 ends	15 × 25 × ¾
8 dividers	2½ × 36 × ¾
8 runners	1½ × 12 × ¾
1 back	25 × 36 × ¼ plywood
2 plinths	3 × 36 × ¾
2 plinths	3 × 15 × ¾
1 top drawer front	6½ × 36 × ¾
1 top drawer back	6 × 36 × ⅝
2 top drawer sides	6½ × 15 × ⅝
1 middle drawer front	7 × 36 × ¾
1 middle drawer back	6½ × 36 × ⅝
2 middle drawer ends	7 × 15 × ⅝
1 bottom drawer front	7½ × 36 × ¾
1 bottom drawer back	7 × 36 × ⅝
2 bottom drawer ends	7½ × 15 × ⅝
3 drawer bottoms	15 × 36 × ¼ plywood
handles (if wood) from	1¼ × 36 × 1¼

TALLBOY

Chests and cabinets of substantial size can be very heavy as well as bulky. It has always been common practice to make them in sections so that each part can be moved separately. The ability to reduce sizes is even more important for getting into modern smaller homes and apartments. Sections also allows a variety of furniture arrangements. In addition, the cabinetmaker can produce a part which can be regarded as a complete piece of furniture in itself and than add another part later.

The name *tallboy* is given to a high chest of drawers. The obvious name of *lowboy* for a low chest is not so commonly used. This can be made with a separate pedestal, on high or low legs, then a main chest on which stands another chest and the whole can be topped by a crown molding (Fig. 14-6A). The piece could stop at the main chest height with the surface given a table finish. Instead of the upper chest, there could be a cupboard with glass doors (Fig. 14-6B). If an in between size chest is wanted, the main chest can be taken higher with more drawers (Fig. 14-6C) and the upper chest omitted. The crown molding goes with a fairly ornate treatment and patterned brass drawer pulls. With a more severe modern theme, a much simpler top would be appropriate.

The example described here has all four parts and a treatment reminiscent of the 18th century (Fig. 14-6D). It can easily be adapted to a reduced form or simplified in many details.

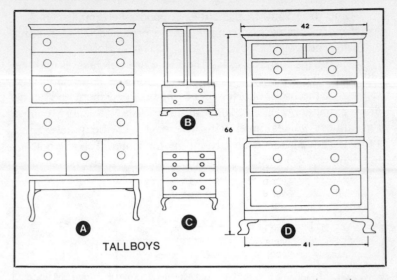

Fig. 14-6. Tallboys may take several forms and are usually in sections.

The pedestal could be on cabriole legs (Fig. 14-7A) as already described, but shorter legs give greater storage space (Fig. 14-7B). However, leave enough clearance for cleaning the floor. The legs are like dumpy cabriole legs with square sections cut from solid blocks and with ears attached (Fig. 14-7C). The frame is made up like that of a table and preferably with a bead along the lower edge and with a rabbet at the top to locate the main chest (Fig. 14-7D). The assembly will probably be strong enough as it is, but if necessary glue blocks in the corners.

The main chest is flat-fronted. Some chests have the drawer fronts curved, but that means cutting thicker wood to waste. If there is much bowing, the surfaces should be veneered. There are two deep drawers. Decoration is provided by having the drawer fronts overlapping and molded and there are molded pillar effects at the side (Fig. 14-8A). Hidden parts need not be of such good quality wood as the face wood.

The ends of the chest can be made by gluing boards to make up a sufficient width or plywood faced with matching veneer could be framed (Fig. 14-8B). Rabbet the rear edges for the plywood back. At the front, the two pillar pieces (Fig. 14-8C) could be plain. However, they look better if worked to a bead similar to that on the plinth, but carried around and the edges of the end bevelled.

Glue the pillars to the ends. A good glued joint should be satisfactory, but extra strength can be provided by secret-slot screwing the joints as well.

The strips that go across the chest are notched around the pillars at the front and come level with the bottoms of the rabbets at the back. Shorter pieces fit between them and act as drawer runners (Fig. 14-8D). Join these parts with short tenons. Put drawer guides level with the edges of the pillars (Fig. 14-8E). They also provide strength in the joints. Top and bottom assemblies are the same as those between the drawers.

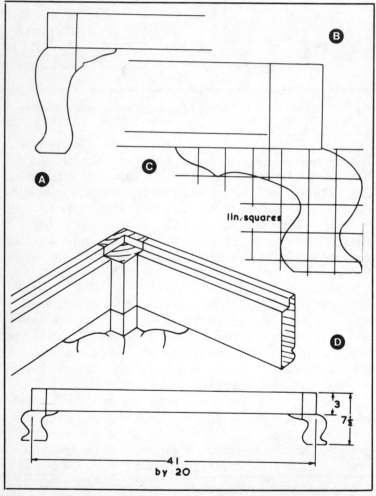

Fig. 14-7. The bottom of a tallboy (A,B,C) is built up like a table frame (D).

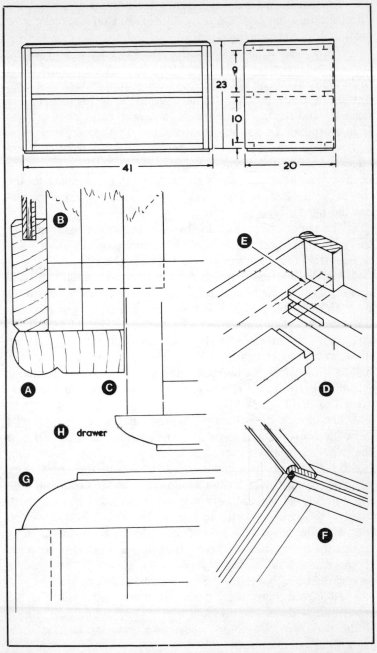

Fig. 14-8. The main part of the tallboy has pillars at the sides (A,B,C) and the drawer fronts overlap (D,E,F,G).

Underneath the bottom, arrange locating strips so that the chest fits into the pedestal (Fig. 14-8F). But do not make it so tight that it cannot be lifted out.

If the chest is to be finished without the upper part and its top will be exposed, the top can be made from solid wood like a table top or it can be of framed plywood with a veneered surface forming a central panel. If there is to be a top chest or a glass-fronted cupboard, the top of the lower chest need only be framed around. To seal it, there could be a plywood panel set in a plowed groove. Miter the corners. Mold the front and end edges. A simple pattern is shown in Fig. 14-8G, but other sections are possible. Screw these parts to the framing on the top of the chest. If it is set back, see that the margin is parallel and the same all round.

The upper chest (Fig. 14-9A) is made in the same way as the main chest, but its sizes allow for it being set in an equal amount from the sides and front of the main chest.

For the division between the top drawers, tenon in a wide runner in the frame below and another in the frame above to act as a kicker (Fig. 14-9B). At the front and back, put uprights between the frames and tenoned into them (Fig. 14-9C). Then put guides between them. It would be sufficient to put thin plywood on top of this part of the chest to keep out dust, but nailing it on might not be considered good cabinetmaking and it would be better to let it into grooves when the top frame parts are assembled (Fig. 14-9D).

The type of crown molding depends on what molding can be cut with available equipment or bought already shaped. To give the tallboy a balanced appearance, it should broaden at the top. Make a frame of the same size as the top of the chest (Fig. 14-10A). Around this, form a shallow box on to which can go a top frame (Fig. 14-10B). Arrange the lower edge of the box to overlap the chest slightly to locate the parts. Both of these pieces can be shaped on their edges to form part of the molding so that they blend in with the molding proper which fits between them (Fig. 14-10C). There is no need to carry the molding around the back, but miter the front corners neatly.

To prevent movement, the upper chest can be joined to the lower part with four screws and the crown molding can be held in the same way. Do not use glue. The parts can be disassembled whenever necessary.

The drawers are made in the usual way, with dovetails and plywood bottoms, but there are overlapping fronts. Make the

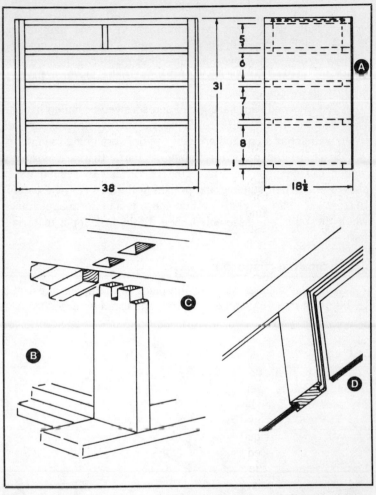

Fig. 14-9. The upper part has tapered drawer widths (A,B,C) and a division between top drawers (D).

drawers with the main fronts level with the fronts of the chest parts, but make false fronts to overlap at sides and tops by ¼ of an inch (Fig. 14-8H). Mold the false fronts to match the molding used on the top of the main chest or that of the crown. Attach the false fronts with screws from inside. See that the edges of the drawers finish level with each other when all drawers are pushed home and there are no parts out of parallel. It is advisable to fit the false fronts and do whatever trimming is necessary before molding their edges.

This type of furniture looks best with decorative brass drawer pulls rather than wooden ones. It is the pair of top drawers which govern the handle spacing. The handles must be central across each drawer and the other drawer pulls should be vertically below them. On each drawer, locate the handles slightly above center.

The plywood backs are glued and screwed or nailed in. The drawers should not quite reach them, but overlapping drawer fronts will act as stops and prevent the drawers going too far.

Separate the parts for finishing. Parts that are normally hidden can be given a single coat of varnish to reduce water absorption. When staining and polishing the exterior, be careful to treat each part similarly so that there is a uniform appearance when the tallboy is assembled. See Table 14-2 for a materials list.

GLASS-FRONTED CUPBOARD

A display cabinet can take the place of the upper chest of a tallboy. The large number of drawers can be of value in a

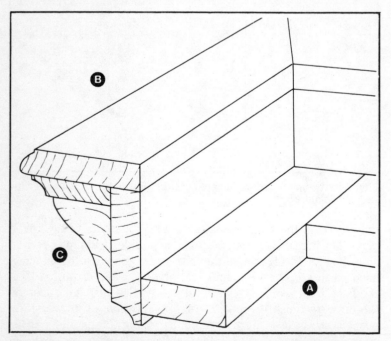

Fig. 14-10. The molded top (A) is built up to rest on the top section (B) of drawers (C).

Table 14-2. Materials List for Tallboy.

Pedestal

2 frames	3 × 42 × 1
2 frames	3 × 20 × 1
4 legs	2½ × 8 × 8½
8 leg ears	1 × 3½ × 1

Main chest

2 ends or	20 × 23 × ⅝
¼-inch plywood framed with	2 × ⅝
6 strips	2 × 41 × 1
6 strips	2¼ × 18 × 1
4 drawer guides	¾ × 20 × ¾
2 locating strips	½ × 41 × ½
2 locating strips	½ × 20 × ½
1 back	20 × 41 × ¼ plywood
1 top	20 × 41 × 1
or	
¼ plywood framed with	2 × 1
2 pillar pieces	2 × 23 × 1

Upper chest

2 ends	18½ × 32 × ⅝
or	
¼ plywood framed with	2 × ⅝
10 strips	2 × 38 × 1
10 strips	2¼ × 18 × 1
12 drawer guides	¾ × 19 × ¾
1 back	31 × 38 × ¼ plywood
1 top	18 × 30 × ½ plywood
2 pillar pieces	2 × 31 × 1
2 drawer dividers	2 × 8 × 1

Crown molding

2 frame pieces	2 × 38 × 1
2 frame pieces	2 × 19 × 1
1 top frame	3 × 43 × ⅝
2 top frames	3 × 22 × ⅝
molding from	2½ × 80 × 1½

Drawers

2 first fronts	5 × 19 × ⅝
2 first fronts	5½ × 19 × ⅝
2 backs	4½ × 19 × ⅝
4 sides	5 × 19 × ⅝
2 bottoms	19 × 19 × ¼ plywood
1 second front	6 × 36 × ⅝
1 second front	6½ × 36 × ⅝
1 back	6 × 36 × ⅝
2 sides	6 × 19 × ⅝
1 third front	7 × 36 × ⅝
1 third front	7½ × 36 × ⅝
1 back	7 × 36 × ⅝
2 sides	7 × 19 × ⅝
1 fourth front	8 × 36 × ⅝
1 fourth front	8½ × 36 × ⅝
1 back	8 × 36 × ⅝
2 sides	8 × 19 × ⅝
1 fifth front	9 × 38 × ⅝
1 fifth front	9½ × 38 × ⅝
1 back	9 × 38 × ⅝
2 sides	9 × 19 × ⅝
1 sixth drawer front	10 × 38 × ⅝
1 sixth drawer front	10½ × 38 × ⅝
1 back	10 × 38 × ⅝
2 sides	10 × 19 × ⅝
5 bottoms	20 × 40 × ¼ plywood

bedroom. In a living room, the display of crockery or other valuables looks good through glass. The shelves can be arranged for books and the glass doors will provide protection. This glass-fronted cupboard (Fig. 14-11) is intended to take the place of the upper chest of the tallboy and it can be fitted with a similar crown molding. Internal arrangements can be varied. The shelves are shown permanently installed. If variable needs are expected, they can be arranged with the type of shelf brackets that can be moved up and down a column of holes.

It is possible to make the cupboard a similar depth back to front as the upper chest of drawers if maximum storage space is wanted. For most purposes, it is better shallower and the top of the main chest must be given a front projecting part of its top that will match the rest of the assembly.

Make the sides of solid wood or with plywood panels to match the sides of the main chest. The front pillar pieces are the same as for the chest. Because the back of the cupboard will be visible through the glass doors, it should be plywood faced with

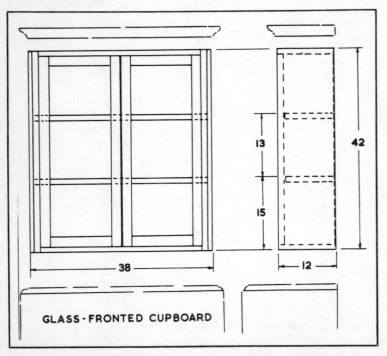

GLASS-FRONTED CUPBOARD

Fig. 14-11. A glass-fronted cupboard can take the place of the top block of drawers on a tallboy.

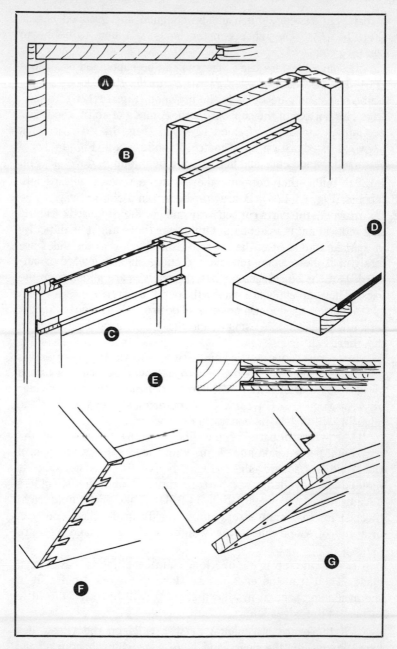

Fig. 14-12. Constructional details of the glass-fronted cupboard; (A) tongued and grooved; (B) dadoes; (C) strips; (D) framed plywood; (E) lip; (F) dovetail; (G) rabbet.

a matching veneer or it could be tongued and grooved boards (Fig. 14-12A). The rabbets in the sides will have to be cut to suit.

If solid sides are used, shelves can be supported by dadoes (Fig. 14-12B). If framed plywood is used, cut dadoes in the frame parts and glue strips to the plywood (Fig. 14-12C).

The bottom of the cupboard is best made of solid wood. For economy, it could be framed plywood (Fig. 14-12D) or thick plywood faced with a lip of matching solid wood (Fig. 14-12E). With solid wood ends and bottom, the best joint is dovetail (Fig. 4-12F). With other bottoms, there can be screws upward into rabbets (Fig. 14-12G). Deal with the top in a similar way.

Have all the parts cut squarely and get the cupboard carefully squared when it is assembled. Otherwise there might be difficulty in making a good fit of the doors. Also, check that the sides are straight. If there is any tendency to curve slightly inward or outward, that can be corrected when the shelves are slid in from the back. Then the cupboard back will lock the parts.

Wood for the door frames should be properly seasoned (keep it for a few weeks before using it) and reasonably straight-grained so that there is little risk of warping. The glass fits into rabbets and is held by narrow strips and fine pins (Fig. 14-13A). At the center it is better for the doors to overlap than to just meet. So that they have a similar visible width all round the front, one meeting part is a wider piece of wood (Fig. 14-13B). If the outer piece has a bead on the edge, it will match the decoration elsewhere.

The vertical parts of the doors follow through and the horizontal parts tenon into them, with the shoulders stepped, if the wood has square edges (Fig. 14-13C). If the inner edge is molded or bevelled, that part is mitered and the shoulders become the same length (Fig. 14-13D). Take the tenons right through for maximum strength. A weakly made glass door can drop out of shape due to the weight of the glass and insecure joints.

Leave the uprights overlong until the joints have been made. Then trim the ends level. Make the doors a close fit in the available space at first so that there will have to be a little planing of the edges later.

If there are ornamental drawer pulls on the chest, use brass hinges for the doors and have a matching handle on the door that overlaps. A handle on the other door is not essential, but it might be fitted for the sake of appearance. In a traditional

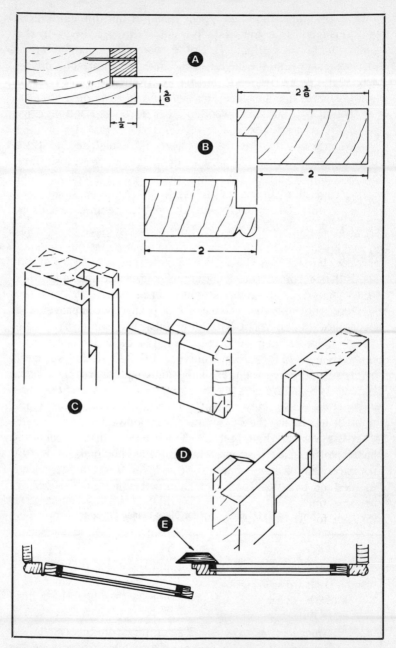

Fig. 14-13. Door details of the glass-fronted cupboard: (A) rabbets, strips and pins; (B) wider wood; (C) square edges; (D) shoulder; (E) wooden stops.

piece of furniture, the inner door is held at the top and bottom with small bolts on the first door going through holes in the cupboard top and bottom. The other door has a handle which turns an arm behind the center of the inner door surface. Similar fastenings can be used on modern furniture, but magnetic or spring catches are simpler. The catch might provide a stop for the door. If not, put small wooden stops at top and bottom (Fig. 14-13E) or on a shelf edge.

When fitting the glass, do not have it cut so close that it has to be forced in. Miter the corners of the retaining strips. Have the pins lightly driven into each piece. Put a piece of stout cardboard against the glass and slide the hammer along it to drive the pins. Use a nail punch for final tightening. See Table 14-3 for a materials list.

CORNER CHEST

Fitting furniture into a corner uses up space that might not otherwise be used, gives storage space where it does not interfere with the general use of a room and improves the appearance of the room by hiding the plain angle. A simple triangle does not give much space (Fig. 14-14A). However, it is all that is needed for display shelves. If the points are squared, the area is increased and there is better scope for hanging a door (Fig. 14-14B). If drawers are to go into the corner and they are to be cut square, they cannot go far if they are wide (Fig. 14-14C). Increasing their depth means making them narrow with wider wing pieces (Fig. 14-14D). The back of a drawer could be shaped to increase its capacity, but this would be unusual. Partly shaping a pair of drawers would be simpler (Fig. 14-14E). The length along each wall does not have to be the same (although

Table 14-3. Materials List for Glass-fronted Cupboard.

2 sides or	12 × 43 × ⅝
plywood framed with	2 × 1
2 tops and bottoms	12 × 39 × 1
or framed as in text	
2 shelves	11 × 39 × 1
1 back	38 × 42 × ¼ plywood
3 door sides	2 × 41 × 1
4 door ends	2 × 17 × 1
4 glass strips	½ × 40 × ½
4 glass strips	½ × 16 × ½
2 pillars	2 × 43 × 1

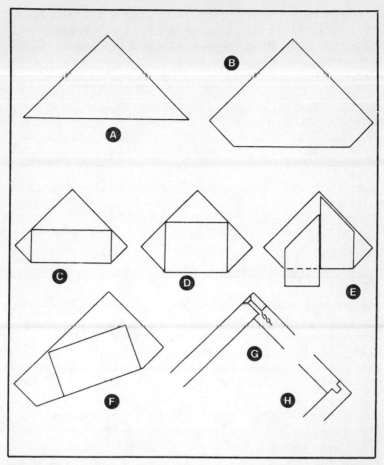

Fig.14-14. Design considerations in a corner cupboard: (A) triangle; (A,B,C,D) squared points; (E) partial shap; (F) corner fitting; (G) upright parts.

that is common). If the room is much longer one way than the other, the corner fitting can match. This gives an individual look to the piece (Fig. 14-14F).

Corners of a room are not always as square as they appear and sometimes they are not upright. If a piece of furniture is intended for a particular place, it can be made to match. Otherwise it will have to be right-angled and an adjustment will have to be made to edges or trimming pieces will have to be added. Upright parts meeting in the corner can be glued and screwed (Fig. 14-14G) or they and the front corner joints can be tongued and grooved (Fig. 14-14H).

This chest has two drawers and a top at low table height (Fig. 14-15 and 14-19). However, it could be made higher with an extra drawer. It can be used alone or it will take the display cabinet or mirror (as described next).

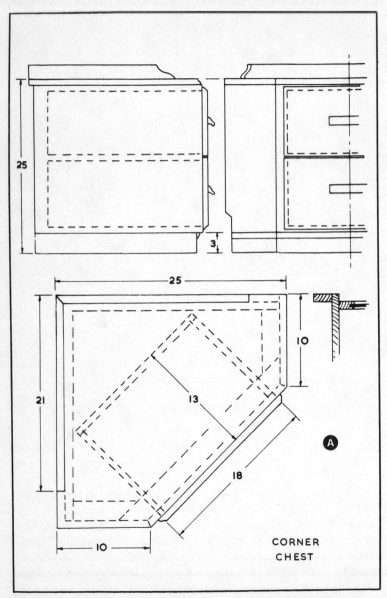

CORNER
CHEST

Fig. 14-15. The corner chest makes the most of available space.

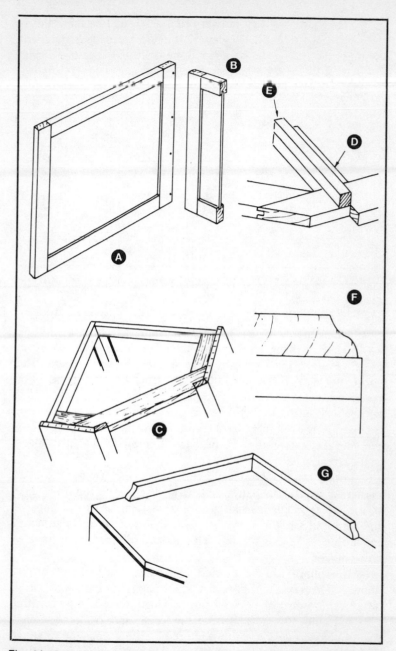

Fig. 14-16. Framing (A) of a corner chest: (B) corner joint; (C) top and bottom frame; (D) runners and kickers; (E) strips; (F) molded front edge; (G) miter, round and shape the outer ends.

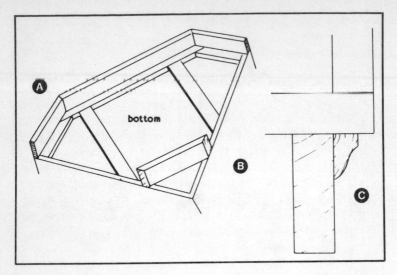

Fig. 14-17. Plinth details of the corner chest: (A) front; (B) bottom; (C) molded to match.

Tenon pieces to act as drawer runners and kickers (Fig. 14-16D). Put strips on them to keep the drawers in line (Fig. 14-16E). Make the top with its grain the long way across. The corners of a room are generally not sharply angular, so bevel or round the point at the back slightly. The front edge can be left square and set back slightly or it can be molded (Fig. 14-16F). Screw through the front frame from below, but use buttons into the side frame tops toward the back to allow for slight changes in the wood width.

There can be border pieces. Miter and round the rear corners and shape the outer ends (Fig. 14-16G). If the front edge of the top is molded, make a similar molding along the tops of the borders. Screw the borders from below. Use oversize holes for the necks of the screws. This should allow enough for any wood movement.

The plinth can be carried all round, but only the front shows. That is the only part that need be complete (Fig. 14-17A). Toward the back, put a small crossbar below the bottom frame (Fig. 14-17B). Set the front plinth back far enough for it to be screwed down through the bottom frame and to allow for molding to be taken around. It could be a plain piece, if other parts are plain, or molded to match molding elsewhere (Fig. 14-17C).

The drawers are the standard construction. The fronts could finish flush and with stops at the back. A traditional finish that looks good in a contrasting wood is a narrow beaded piece taken around the front (Fig. 14-18A). Top and bottom edges of the front can be kept narrow during construction, but rabbets over the joints are better made after the drawer has been glued

Start by making a full size drawing on scrap plywood or hardboard. If the wood for the top is available, it could be drawn on the underside of that. If the room has a baseboard, keep the sides inside that. The top and the face pieces will reach the wall (Fig. 14-15A). The sides can be solid wood, but it would be more economical to frame plywood (Fig. 14-16A). One frame is longer than the other along the walls to allow for the corner joint (Fig. 14-16B). These frames and other hidden parts need not be of the same wood as the face parts.

Make the wing pieces and prepare the joints to the sides. Either shape the boards over the wall baseboard or allow for a filler piece to be put in later. The uprights at the sides of the drawers can be glued only or there could be secret slot screws. Top and bottom frame parts are the same (Fig. 14-16C). The front crossbars that show should be the same wood as the other face parts. There is no need for a full frame between the drawers, but put a similar crossbar there. Allow for the internal parts to be glued and screwed to the other parts, but do not fit them until after the joints for the drawer guides have been made.

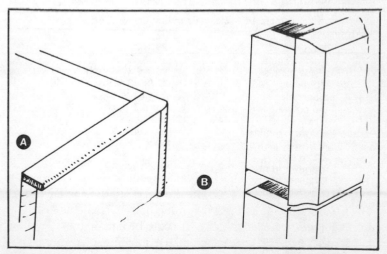

Fig. 14-18. The drawer fronts can have beads (A) or be molded (B).

and otherwise finished. The drawers shown have false fronts, brought close together over the central divider and with molded edges carried around (Fig. 14-18B). Wooden drawer pulls can have matching molding.

There is no need to fasten the chest into the corner. To pull it away, partly withdraw the top drawer and grip the underside of the top frame. In use, there are spaces empty on each side of the drawers. They can be regarded as secret compartments. The design can be adapted as a cupboard or closet by fitting a door instead of drawers. The bottom would then have to be given a flat surface with plywood behind the front piece of framing. See Table 14-4 for a materials list.

CORNER MIRROR

A mirror above the corner chest would convert it into a dresser. It would be particularly useful in a bedroom where space is restricted. Because it cannot be tilted, it should be tall enough to give a good view for users of different heights. See the example shown in Fig. 14-19. The mirror shown is of ample size, but if the available mirror is a different width it can be positioned at a different distance from the corner to suit.

If the mirror has polished edges, it can be mounted frameless with clips on plywood (Fig. 14-20A). A mirror of this size is quite heavy, so use enough clips. About 12-inch spacing should be satisfactory. At the bottom, the weight can be taken on a border piece.

Table 14-4. Materials List for Corner Chest.

1 top	25 × 36 × ¾
8 side frames	1½ × 25 × ¾
2 side panels	23 × 23 × ¼ plywood
2 uprights	10 × 23 × ¾
2 uprights	2 × 23 × ¾
3 dront frames	3 × 27 × ¾
6 side parts	2 × 9 × ¾
6 drawer runners	2 × 14 × ¾
4 drawer guides	¾ × 14 × ¾
2 borders	2 × 22 × ¾
1 drawer front	9 × 19 × ⅝
2 drawer fronts	10 × 20 × ⅝
1 drawer front	11 × 20 × ⅝
2 drawer sides	9 × 14 × ½
2 drawer sides	10 × 14 × ½
1 drawer back	9 × 19 × ½
1 drawer back	10 × 19 × ½
2 drawer bottoms	13 × 18 × ¼ plywood

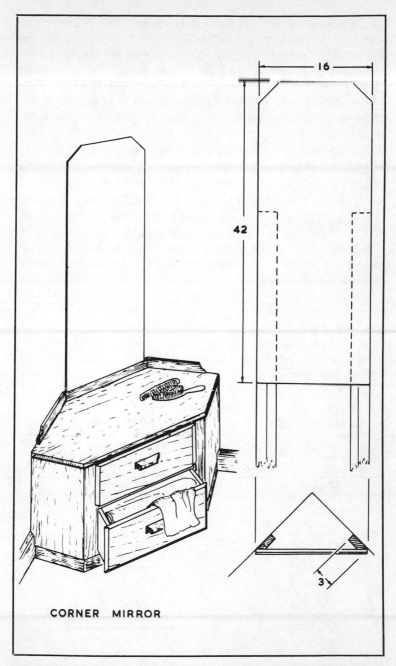

16

42

3

CORNER MIRROR

Fig. 14-19. A corner mirror on a chest provide dresser faciilities where space is limited.

If the mirror is to be framed, the front of the frame can be rounded, bevelled or molded to match other molding on the chest (Fig. 14-20B). Because the back will not show, let the glass into a rabbet and allow for a plywood back to be screwed on (Fig. 14-20C). Do not force the back too tight, but allow for a pad of cloth behind the glass. Miter the corners of the frame, but strengthen them with veneers across (Fig. 14-20D) or small dowels.

The mirror supports are strips going through the chest top to the sides (Fig. 14-21A). Their position is found by placing the mirror across the chest top. Leave a small clearance at the walls. Bevel the edges of the supports (Fig. 14-21B). With the overhang at the top, there might not be much need for cutting in. Notch the framing to take each support and there may have to be a packing against a side plywood panel (Fig. 14-21C). Screw the supports in place so that they can be removed for transport if that is ever necessary.

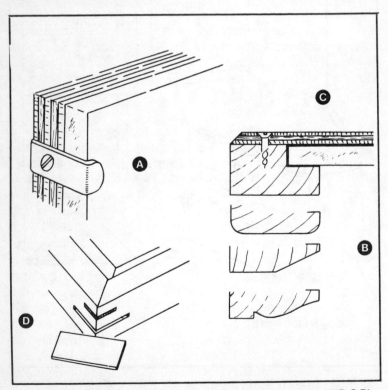

Fig. 14-20. The mirror can be clipped (A) to a backboard or framed (B,C,D).

1 mirror back or	16 × 42 × ½ plywood
1 mirror back	16 × 42 × ¼ plywood
and 2	1½ × 44 × ¾
and 2	1½ × 18 × ¾
2 posts	3 × 52 × 1

The border pieces do not go behind the mirror, but are in three pieces in front of it (Fig. 14-21D). The mirror rests on the central one. The plywood back of a frameless mirror can be screwed into the supports before the mirror is clipped on. For a framed mirror, cut down the tops of the supports to allow screwing into the frame (Fig. 14-21E). At the bottom, use a strip behind the border (Fig. 14-21F).

In a first assembly, check to be sure that the mirror stands upright and square to the surface of the chest. If the room walls are upright, this will fit into the corner with the mirror edges parallel with the walls. If positioning it shows that there is a difference, the bottom screws in the supports can be moved sideways to bring the mirror to a matching position. See Table 14-5 for a materials list.

CORNER DISPLAY CABINET

A corner is a particularly good place for displaying valuables and items of interest. A corner display cabinet has to be a compromise between the need for wide glass doors and the width of shelf space that necessarily gets less as doors are made wider. This corner display cabinet (Fig. 14-22 and 14-23) is designed to stand on the corner chest. However, it could be put on another corner fitment or provided with legs. Most of the constructional details are similar to those of the chest. Doors are made in a similar way to those of the glass-fronted cupboard.

For display purposes, it is better for the inner surfaces of the sides to be flush than to have plywood panels in a grooved frame. The plywood could have a light-colored veneer or the inside of the cabinet might be lined with cloth to show off the contents. If the sides are not made of solid wood, let the plywood into rabbets and support the shelves with strips instead of dadoes (Fig. 14-24A). Shelves are shown level with the internal corners, but they could be brought forward a little if maximum width is needed.

351

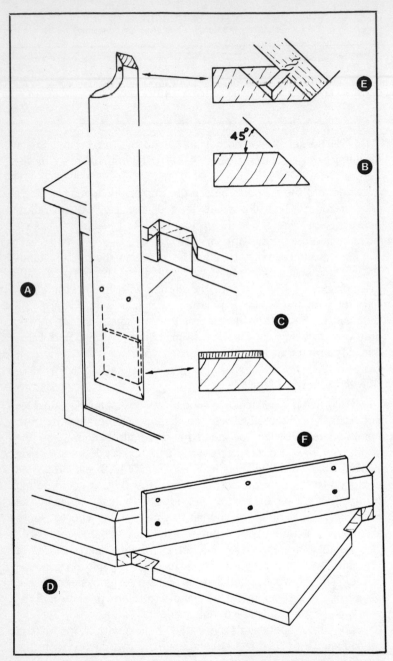

Fig. 14-21. Mirror supports extend below the chest top (A): (B) bevel; (C) notch; (D) border pieces; (E) screw into the frame; (F) use a strip.

352

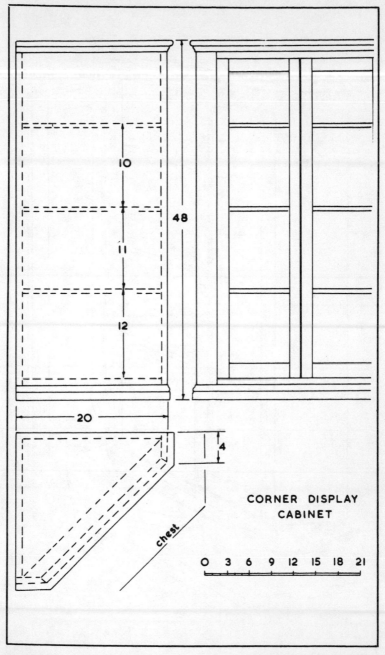

Fig. 14-22. A corner display cabinet has broad glass doors in front of triangular shelves.

Fig. 14-23. The corner display cabinet will stand on the corner chest.

At the top, a piece fits between the uprights. Then there is a molding put around and the covering piece goes over the lot (Fig. 14-24B). The top is sealed by plywood let into rabbets in the visible front. It could be nailed or rabbeted to the tops of the sides.

At the bottom, there is a solid base or one made by framing around plywood in a rabbet, enclosed by the front uprights and sides, than a rabbeted plinth encloses these parts (Fig. 14-24C). A fillet glued around inside provides strength at the plinth miters as well as the horizontal joints.

The inner edges of the uprights should provide sufficient bearing for hinges. The extra width is due to planing at 45 degrees. The doors have similar sections to those of the glass-fronted cupboard, but their bottom pieces are wider than the others. This improves the appearance of the tall narrow shapes. Use catches at the top and bottom and handles on both doors just above their centers.

There should be sufficient weight in the cabinet to stand firm on a level surface. If there is any doubt, screw through to the wall inside near the top or put blocks above the top and screw through them. See Table 14-6 for a materials list.

FULL-LENGTH MIRROR

A mirror that shows the full length of the viewer does not have to be very big, providing it can be tilted, but it has to be a reasonable size and mirror glass can be quite heavy. The mirror supports have to be stout enough to remain rigid. Better mirrors, particularly if one is obtained from an old piece of furni-

Table 14-6. Materials List for Corner Display Cabinet.

4 side frames	1½ × 50 × ¾
4 side frames	1½ × 20 × ¾
top and bottom framing from	150 × 2 × ¾
2 side panels	18 × 46 × ¼ plywood
2 top and bottom panels	16 × 26 × ¼ plywood
2 uprights	4 × 50 × ¾
top molding from	36 × ¾ × ½
plinth from	36 × 2 × 1
1 top of door opening	1½ × 24 × ¾
4 door sides	1½ × 50 × 1
2 door tops	1½ × 12 × 1
2 door bottoms	2½ × 12 × 1
3 shelves	13 × 27 × ½ edged plywood
6 shelf supports	¾ × 20 × ½

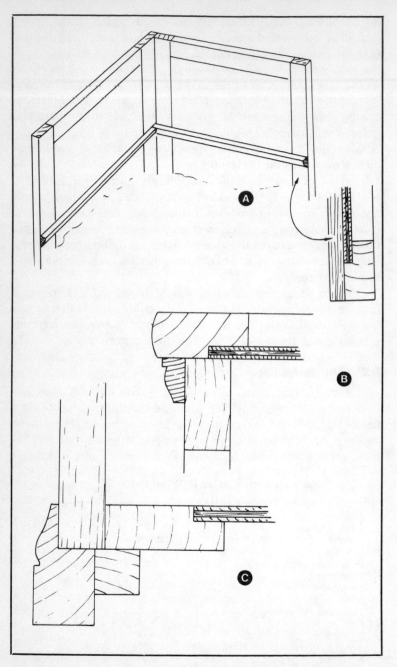

Fig. 14-24 The carcase (A) of the cabinet is framed plywood (B,C).

ture, will be found to be thick glass. Obviously, it is the condition of the "silvering" on the back which is important. Handle a mirror carefully and avoid putting it down where there could be a risk of damaging the back.

Because the size of the stand depends on the mirror size, get that first and plan the other sizes to suit it. The frame has to be supported between the posts with fittings that allow the mirror to tilt while providing enough friction to keep it at any angle. There are several types. A simple one has a deep V-shaped socket to fit to the post and a part with a domed extension to drop into the socket. That way it is possible to lift the mirror frame off. Because the clearance for a fitting at each side governs the spacing of the posts, these fittings should also be obtained before starting on the woodwork. The design shown in Fig. 14-25 suits a mirror about 18 inches by 42 inches and the sections of wood specified will serve as a guide if dimensions have to be modified.

The parts can be made with straight lines and square edges, but the necessarily fairly stout sections can be lightened in appearance by using curves and rounding the corners of sections.

The frame around the glass has a deep section for stiffness and the back is stiff enough to relieve the glass of strain (Fig. 14-26A). The sections of the rabbets should suit the glass and plywood, but allow for a piece of cloth, thin plastic foam or even paper, between the plywood and the back of the mirror.

The visible part of the frame can be molded in several ways, depending on the equipment available, but the curved section shown here can be worked with ordinary planes followed by sanding. The plywood back should be made a good fit in the frame, but there can be a little clearance around the glass so that it is the plywood and not the glass that keeps the frame in shape. Whatever finish is used for the rest of the woodwork, paint the inside of the glass rabbet black to avoid an unattractive reflection around the edges.

The plywood back screwed in place provides stiffness and strength, but the corners of the frame should have joints stronger than would be acceptable for a picture frame. A mitered bridle joint is suitable (Fig. 14-26B). For clarity, this is shown on wood of square section, but it can be used with the rounded section and any other except a deep molding. Alternatively, cut simple miters. Then drill across them at different levels for thin dowels, glued in and planed level (Fig. 14-26C).

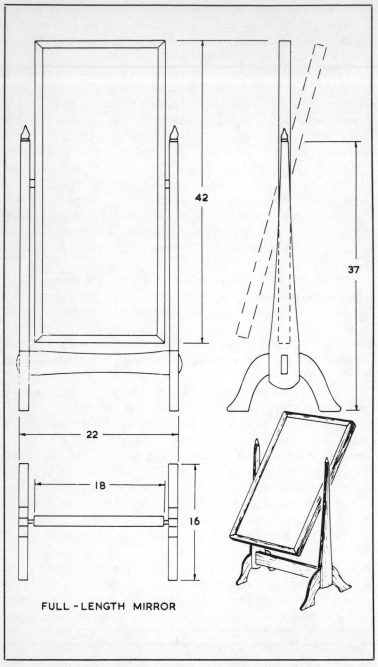

FULL-LENGTH MIRROR

Fig. 14-25. A large tilting mirror shows a person full-length.

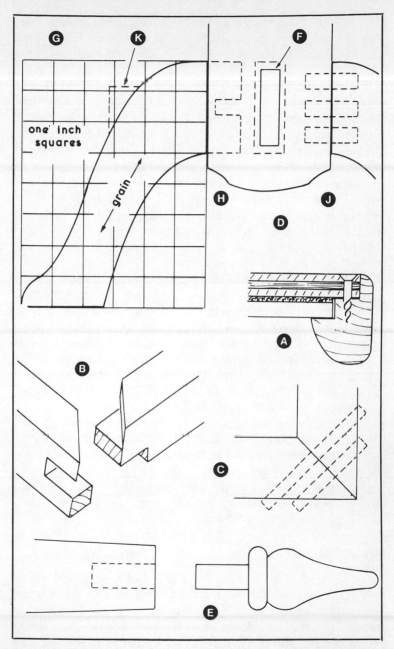

Fig. 14-26. Details of the full-length mirror: (A) frame; (B) mitered bridle joint; (C) planed level; (D,E,F) parallel post; (G) leg; (H) mortise and tenon; (J) dowel; (K) projection.

Arrange the pivot point slightly above halfway up each side. About 1 inch above the middle should suit a 42-inch depth. If the pivot is exactly on the point of balance, the mirror will swing too easily.

Each post has a parallel lower part (Fig. 14-26D). Then it tapers to a square end above the pivot. Instead of a straight taper, appearance is improved if each is slightly hollow. A ¼-inch greatest depth in the length is enough. The top can be rounded or a turned finial can be added. These can be bought, but a suitable design to turn is shown in Fig. 14-26E.

The rail provides stiffness in a crosswise direction and should be securely joined to the posts. Dowel joints might not be strong enough. It would be better to shoulder the rail ends and have a tenon through each post and then round its exposed end (Fig. 14-26F). If the posts are hollowed along their tapers, give the edges of the rail matching hollowing.

Draw a leg full size (Fig. 14-26G). Make a template or use one leg as a pattern for the others. Arrange the grain the long way. The joints to the posts can be mortise and tenon (Fig. 14-26H) or dowels (Fig. 14-26J). In both cases, there will be difficulty in pulling the joints tight if the legs are fully finished before assembly. It is better to leave on a small projection for clamping (Fig. 14-26K) while the rest of the outline is finished to size and rounded. Leave just the small area to deal with after the projections have been cut off.

Assemble the pair of posts with their feet and see that they match and will stand level. Then join them with the rail. Check squareness carefully and leave the assembly for glue to set while it is standing on a level surface.

Finishing is most easily done before the mirror goes into the frame, but a trial assembly with a few screws in the back is advisable. See Table 14-7 for a materials list.

BEDSIDE CABINET

A bedside cabinet needs to be at a useful height and with a top of a good area so things are unlikely to get knocked over the edge. An open shelf provides storage for things not immediately needed. What goes below that depends on needs. There could be more open shelves, but it is usually better to enclose that part. There could be drawers or a door enclosing storage space (Figs. 14-27 and 14-28).

Table 14-7. Materials List for Full-Length Mirror.

2 frame sides	1½ × 45 × 1
2 frame ends	1½ × 20 × 1
1 frame back	20 × 45 × ⅜ plywood
2 posts	4 × 36 × 1¼
4 legs	3½ × 11 × 1¼
1 rail	3 × 24 × 1¼
2 finals	1¼ × 4 × 1¼

Externally the cabinet should be of solid wood of good quality, but the rear parts of some shelves and other parts can be plywood or particleboard. The front edges can be made of wood to match the rest of the cabinet. The external wide boards will almost certainly have to be made by gluing pieces to make up the width. The depth of the cabinet back to front is not critical and this measurement can be adjusted to suit available boards.

Construction and appearance is very similar to the classic chest of drawers. If the two pieces are to be used in the same bedroom, handles and the molding of the top edges can be the same.

Prepare the boards for the sides with carefully squared ends. Mark out the positions of the other parts (including the depths of drawers and shelf positions). A rod made from this

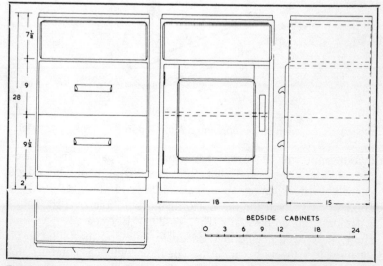

Fig. 14-27. A bedside cabinet may have drawers or a door.

Fig. 14-28. An open shelf supplements the top in this bedside cabinet.

marking out will be useful in marking other parts. The bottom can be the same wood, but for economy it could be edged particleboard or an inexpensive solid wood (Fig. 14-29A). If solid wood is used for the bottom, the best joints to the sides would be stopped dovetails (Fig. 14-29B). Because they will not show, they need not be marked out evenly and the tails can be fairly wide. Dovetails cannot be cut in particleboard and are not very satisfactory in plywood. The alternative is to screw upward

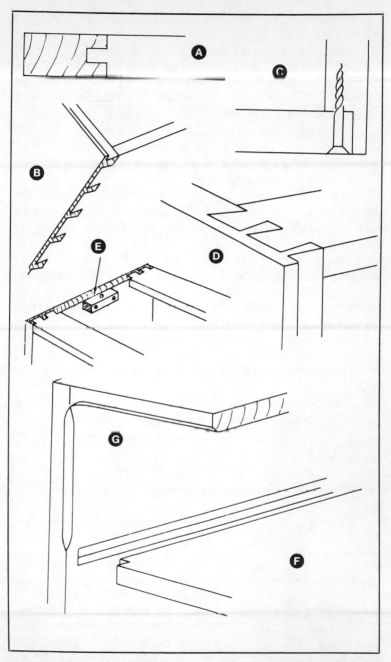

Fig. 14-29. Assembly details of the bedside cabinet carcase: (A) bottom; (B) stopped dovetails; (C) rabbet; (D) rail; (E) cleat; (F) shelf; (G) lipped edge.

into a rabbet (Fig. 14-29C). Rabbet the rear edges of the sides for the back plywood.

At the top, join in the top rails with dovetails. The plywood back can go behind the rail (Fig. 14-29D) because its edge will be covered by the top. It is inadvisable to put a strip across the top rails at each side for the full width. That would cause a side to split if it shrank. However, there has to be a fastening point. A short cleat can be used (Fig. 14-29E). Have the top ready and make sure it will finish parallel and with an equal setback at front and sides. At the back, it goes to the edge of the sides so that it covers the plywood.

Check these sizes and have the joints cut, but do not assemble yet. The shelf fits with a stopped dado joint at each side (Fig. 14-29F). It can be made up with a lipped edge like the bottom (Fig. 14-29G).

The plinth is made in a similar way to those already described on other furniture. It is set back a small amount at sides and front, but is level at the back so that it covers the edge of the plywood there. Miter the front corners, but the rear corners can overlap (Fig. 14-30A). Make up the plinth as a unit. Stiffen inside the miters with glued blocks (Fig. 14-30B). If the cabinet is to have drawers, screws can be driven downward into the plinth because the heads will be hidden. Screw holes can be drilled before assembly. If there is to be a cupboard, screw heads would show. It would be better, at least across the front, to use pocket screws driven upward (Fig. 14-30C).

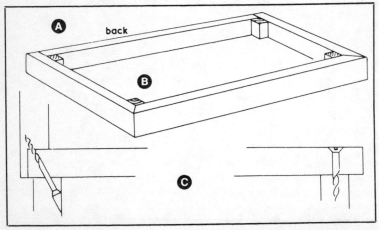

Fig. 14-30. The plinth is made up as a unit and screwed under the cabinet: (A) overlap; (B) block; (C) pocket screws.

The drawers have overlapping fronts and there is no need for a front rail between them. Fit runners for the top drawer at each side (Fig. 14-31A). The bottom drawer runs on the bottom of the cabinet. A solid bottom for the cabinet is not essential, although that is allowed for in the materials list. There could be front and back rails only, with runners between them for the botton drawer.

Assemble the cabinet. Square it carefully or you might find difficulty in getting the drawers to run smoothly. Use the plywood back and cut squarely as a guide to the accuracy of the other parts. It will probably be easier to fit drawers if the plywood is not yet screwed or nailed in permanently. If you leave the back of the cabinet accessible, it will be easier to see how the drawers fit and what adjustment, if any, is needed.

All of the internal parts of the drawers can be made of inexpensive wood. When the drawers are pushed fully in, only the overlapping fronts will show. Construction is similar to drawers for other furniture. The best joints are dovetails. Make the sides of each drawer first. Have it slightly too long. Then test to be sure that it slides easily and mark its length from the cabinet side. Cut it a little short at the back so that when the completed drawer is pushed in it is the false front that acts as a stop and not the plywood back (Fig. 14-31B).

Plow grooves for the plywood bottom. Make the main front the same depth as the sides and plow that. Then cut the dovetails to cover the groove (Fig. 14-31C)). Make the back so that it comes above the plywood bottom and check its length so that the drawer will finish the same width at back and front. The overlapping front of the bottom drawer only extends at the sides, not at the bottom edge, but its top edge goes high enough to hide the ends of the drawer runners (Fig. 14-31D). The overlapping front of the top drawer extends a matching amount at the sides and top, but its bottom edge is level. Make both fronts to the full depth at first, then try them in position. Their meeting edges will have to eased a little with a plane so that they do not foul each other.

Attach the false fronts by screwing from inside after the corner dovetails have been cleaned off level. If wooden handles are made to match other furniture, screw them from inside (Fig. 14-31E). Drawer edges are shown with a simple rounding and this can be repeated on the cabinet top (Fig. 14-31F). Both edges can be molded. Another decorative feature is to use the

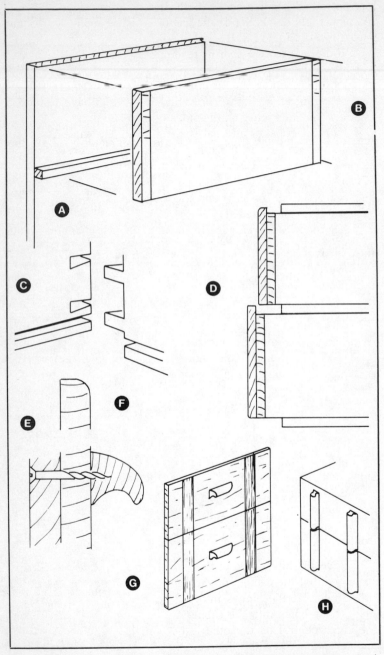

Fig. 14-31. Drawers overlap the carcase front (A,B,C,D) and can have wood handles (E,F,G,H)

upright inlaid banding across both drawer fronts (Fig. 14-31G). A comparable decoration is the use of upright handles across the two drawers (Fig. 14-31H).

If there is to be a door instead of drawers, make the cabinet carcase in the same way. Because the bottom will show then the door is open, finish its surface well and avoid driving screws downward into the plinth. The main shelf should have a stopped chamfer to match toose on the sides of the open part.

There can be an internal shelf at about the same height as the drawer runners in the other construction. However, set it back from the front. Because it will not have to carry much load, it can be made of plywood with a solid wood lip. That would hide the bearers (Fig. 14-32A) and the shelf could be left loose for removal if it is not needed.

The door is shown panelled with a stopped chamfer around the edge. The plywood panel should be veneered or faced with a surface to match the solid wood. Plough grooves in the frame material to suit the plywood. If the groove cannot be made an exact fit, it is better to have it slightly too small. Thin the plywood at the reat. A tightly fitting panel braces the door.

Make up the frame for the door with the uprights slightly over long. Use mortise and tenon joints at the corners (Fig. 14-32B). The tenons need not go through, but they should penetrate far enough to give good glue areas. After cutting the joints, note where the parts will meet and mark out the stopped chamfers so that the curved ends blend into each other there (Fig. 14-32C).

Assemble the door with the ends projecting. Trim these parts after the glue has set and trim the outline of the door to match the opening. Hang the door with 2-inch hinges. At the other side arrange stops. There can be a small strip of wood on the side (Fig. 14-32D) or two pieces at top and bottom (Fig. 14-32E). Use a ball or magnetic catch. For this sort of door, it is better to avoid any sort of catch that needs a turn or other action to release it. Fit a handle that matches those of the drawers.

Have the hinge side of the door away from the bed. If it is expected that the cabinet might have to be altered for use at the other side, let the hinges into the door only so that there are only screw holes into the cabinet side. Arrange the handle and the catch central on the other side. Fit the stops with screws and no glue. When the door is turned round, it will still look correct and there will be a minimum of adjustments and filling screw holes.

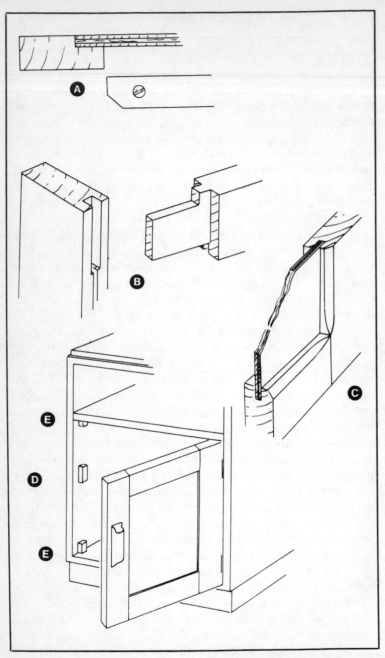

Fig. 14-32. A door has mortise and tenon joints at the corners (A,B,C) and is closed against stops (E,F).

Table 14-8. Materials List for Bedside Cabinet.

2 sides	15 × 26 × ⅝
1 top	15 × 18 × ⅝
1 shelf	15 × 18 × ⅝
1 bottom	15 × 18 × ⅝
2 top rails	3 × 18 × ⅝
1 back	18 × 28 × ¼ plywood
2 plinths	2 × 18 × ⅝
2 plinths	2 × 15 × ⅝
if drawers fitted	
2 drawer fronts	8⅝ × 18 × ⅝
4 drawer fronts	8⅞ × 18 × ⅝
2 drawer fronts	9⅛ × 18 × ⅝
2 drawer sides	8⅝ × 15 × ⅝
2 drawer sides	8⅞ × 15 × ⅝
1 drawer back	8 × 18 × ⅝
1 drawer back	8¼ × 18 × ⅝
2 drawer bottoms	15 × 18 × ¼ plywood
2 drawer runners	¾ × 15 × ⅝
if cupboard fitted	
2 door frames	2½ × 18 × ⅝
2 door frames	2½ × 15 × ⅝
1 door panel	14 × 15 × ¼ plywood
1 shelf	12 × 17 × ⅝

Another way of arranging the door is to hinge it across the bottom with a handle at the top. Opening then gives good access via the top. However, there would have to be a folding strut at one side or a cord between eyes to limit the fall of the door.

The cabinets are shown with the tops flush, but there could be a ledge across the back to prevent things from sliding off there. A low ledge can be screwed downward with counterbored and plugged holes. If the cabinet goes against a base board at the bottom of the wall, so the top is away from the wall, it would be better to arrange the ledge behind the top to fill the space. Round its ends. The same idea could be used along the sides—either one or both—if there seems a need for protection there. See Table 14-8 for a materials list.

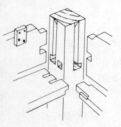

Chapter 15
Designing

A cabinetmaker can be quite skilled craftsman, yet he needs to have a design prepared by someone else. There always have been more craftsmen than designers. When Chippendale and other famous craftsmen/designers published books of designs, these books become very popular. Much furniture attributed to the designers must have been made by craftsmen who were probably just as good at handling tools, but they lacked the ability to produce their own designs.

It is still possible to enjoy a hobby or career in making furniture without ever originating a design. There are magazines and books with plenty of ideas, usually with dimensioned drawings, that can be followed. At the other extreme are those who like to call themselves artist/craftsmen who produce pieces of work that do not conform to accepted standards. Some are so way out that the desire to be different has meant that practical requirements give way to a novel appearance.

Between these extremes are capable cabinetmakers who have enough experience to be able to adapt designs to suit particular needs or who can look at someone else's design or product and know that something is wrong or could have been arranged in a better way. From there it is only a step towards producing your own designs.

Modern techniques have made possible constructions that could not have been used only a few years ago. However, that does not mean that designs have to be altered. There is no virtue in making a table that cantilevers on a single leg at one corner just because laminating might have made that feasible. A chair that only has back legs to splayed feet is a gimmick that might give some satisfaction to its designer and maker, but it is unlikely to stand up to hard use for long. It certainly will not be in use a century later as some of the famous cabinetmaker's chairs are.

If anything is to be designed with the hope that it will be acceptable to others besides the maker, and especially if it is to be offered for sale at an economic price, certain things that have proved their worth over the years must be incorporated. Most things should stand on four feet, seats should be at suitable height for use with a chair and there can be some original points about a design. The average person does not want to be always surrounded by flambuoyant or impractical extras that might overshadow the practicality of the item.

Most users of furniture are conservative in their require-ments. Centuries of furniture development have produces ac-ceptable sizes and overall designs. Anything new should not be too far off these standards. Materials will change, constructional methods will change, but people still have the same characteris-tics. We are rather bigger than our ancestors of a few centuries ago, but this does not mean much difference in our posture, the heights we can reach and the proportions furniture has to be if we are to use it comfortably and satisfactorily.

PRELIMINARIES

Before developing an original design, take a few measure-ments from something else intended for the same purpose. You might not be intending anything like what you are measuring, but it is no use producing a dining table 36 inches high when the comfortable height is nearer 30 inches. You will not be thanked for arranging drawers at a height where a user cannot look into them or so shallow that they will not hold a worthwhile amount. One of the attractions of producing your own designs is being able to adapt to needs. A bookcase can have shelf spacing to hold particular books. A cabinet can be made to stand in a particular place. Drawers and closets can have their sizes made to ac-comodate certain things.

Get together all the facts and if the furniture is for someone else, make sure that they tell you their needs explicitly. It is disappointing to be part way through a job and the customer says that he meant to ask for the whole thing to be wider. The availability of materials is imporant. Some woods are unavailable in great widths. Some are more readily available in stock sections. If stock sections can be used without spoiling your design, it obviously makes sense to use them. Check on hardware before getting far into production. Hinges, catches, knobs and drawer pulls have their peculiarities. Some are easier to fit if the wood is slightly thicker or thinner than you planned.

In general avoid near square shapes. In any direction that you look at a piece of furniture, it should be longer one way than the other. A reasonable proportion is a length between 1¼ and 1½ times the width of any panel (Fig. 15-1A). Obviously there will be some that are very different from that. The major lines of good furniture will be parallel with edges. Occasionally there can be a line running diagonally, but it is safer to keep things like door panels, drawers and anything else producing a visible line, parallel with an external edge. Veneering might include diagonals, but lines between veneer pieces will not be very prominent.

Panels made by drawer fronts or doors should be oblong rather than square (Fig. 15-1B). To avoid an appearance of top-heaviness, try to have a light look high up, while lower parts should appear more solid. This usually happens in any case, but it is possible to get a rather overpowering pair of doors above drawers. Avoid an even spacing or having greater widths at the top. Instead, have wider gaps or drawers low down (Fig. 15-1C). It is better visually to reduce the depths of drawers or shelf spaces progressively rather than to have a sudden great reduction at one level.

Think of the stability of what you are planning. Feet should usually be as far out as the edges of the top they support. However, something large and heavy will have some inherent stability that will take care of feet that are within the top outline. Avoid a great height on a small base. Three feet will always stand level even if the floor is uneven. Four feet might wobble. If possible, arrange weight low down. A bookcase is obviously better, both visually and with regards to stability, if larger books are on the bottom shelf.

Consider stiffness. A fully enclosed cabinet that reaches to the ground without legs, or with only low feet, will almost certainly have more than adequate stiffness built in due to its

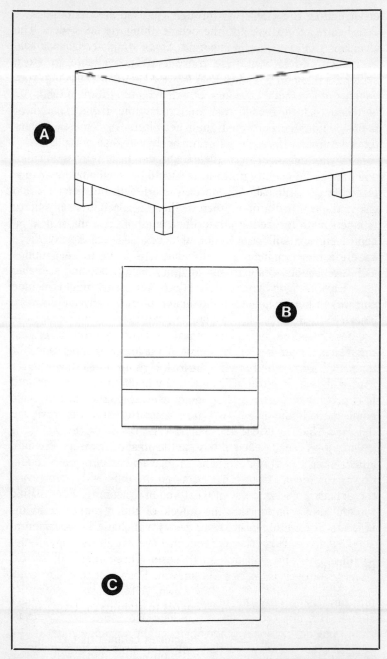

Fig. 15-1. Good design uses rectangular shapes: (A) length; (B) panels; (C) drawers.

construction. But stools, chairs and tables are subject to misuse. If any form of seat would only be sat on gently, it need not be given the stiffness that is essential to stand up to the user who tilts it on two legs or tries to slide it across the loor while sitting on it. People tend to lean against tables or they might put an unnatural strain on the legs when trying to move the table.

Legs can be braced with rails fairly low down. The lower the rail, the more it contributes to stiffness. But there are practical limits, because the rails have to be kept clear of users' legs. If the legs are to be stiff enough without lower rails, they will have to be slightly thicker and the top rails should be deeper to add to the stiffness they provide. With a table for use with a chair, there is a limit to the depth of top rail if it is not to interfere with the users' knees. The ends of the rails should be kept deep, while most of its length is at a reduced depth to give knee clearance. Examples of building stiffness into assemblies with legs can be seen in previous chapters.

Allow for good joint areas. Where two parts meet, the glue surfaces in joints should extend to as near full width as possible. There should be plenty of glue area, preferably between side grain surfaces, because glue on grain is not very strong. Imagine the wracking strains that will come on a joint during possible misuse. A good width of glued area will stand up to strain better than if it is concentrated near the center of the joined parts. If four parts join to give a rectangular assembly, they will provide some mutual support. If two parts have to depend on the joint between them without the support given by other joints, a greater joint area is needed to take the strain. So far as possible, allow for a sufficient thickness in legs and similar parts to let dowels or tenons from other parts go in sufficiently. However, the deisgn must not be such that the leg is weakened by cutting too much away in mortises or dowel holes that meet. Examples of joints in furniture previously described should be analyzed to see how strength is retained.

DRAWING

With a fairly simple project, it is possible to make a piece of furniture using only the ideas you have without even a rough sketch. But this can be dangerous because some sizes that just would not do, or some other snag, might not appear until after you have cut some wood that will then have to be scraped. It would be better to have a drawing, even if it is only a freehand rough sketch.

Rough sketches have their uses. You do not have to be an artist or a draftsman, but try to visualize what it is you want to make. It might help to attempt a pictorial view. This is particularly true if you want someone else to understand what it is you propose to make. Try to get the proportions about right so that the sketch gives an approximate picture of the final thing. Get the overall proportions right before you put in detail.

It is a help in laying out a rough sketch to put in some guide lines first. Imagine that you are looking diagonally down at the job from above one corner. Upright lines can be upright, but other lines go off at an angle in each directon. In more advanced drafting, this is called *isometric projection*. Draw a upright line freehand or with a straightedge, then two others off it at about 30 degrees to horizontal (Fig. 15-2A). These show where the main lines should be going. A surprising number of things can be enclosed in a box shape, so draw other lines to represent the box that will contain the drawing (Fig. 15-2B). The upright lines can all remain upright, but other lines as you may know, appear to go off to a vanishing point. To make your drawing a better pictorial representation, bring in the angles of the further lines rather than make them parallel with the guide lines (Fig. 15-2C).

Now put in main lines. If it is a stool, there will be the thickness of the top and rails and then the outline of the legs. Mark these things first at the outside (Fig. 15-2D), then project other visible edges, such as the leg bottoms in this case, from them (Fig. 15-2E). If the further leg will show, draw its outer lines in the same way and project in (Fig. 15-2F). With a little practice you can sketch in all of these lines lightly, then go back and darken the ones that show and even put in a few grain lines (Fig. 15-2G).

Such a sketch helps you see if what you have in mind is going to come out right and it allows you to discuss the work with another person. What it cannot do, is give you the working out sizes.

For a working drawing you need to draw views from the side and end as well as from above. For some things, you can dispense with one view. For others, you might need extra views and section drawings. Drawing can be done on almost any paper, but if you are likely to want to take measurements from the drawing later, choose a fairly stable drawing paper. Some paper will expand and contract enough to distort a curve or line. The larger the drawing, the easier it is to get information from it

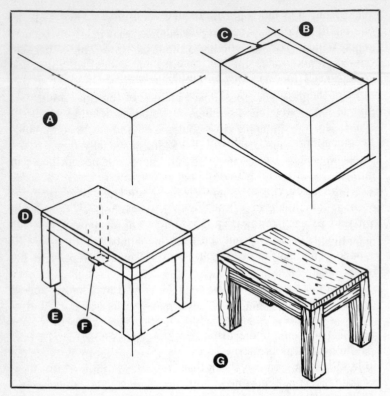

Fig. 15-2. A freehand sketch (G) is built up on a pattern (A,B,C,D,E) of lines.

accurately. For some things, a full size drawing on a piece of hardboard might be preferable to a smaller drawing on paper. Even if you use a small drawing for general information, you will have to draw some things full size if they are curved or carved.

Although a comprehensive kit of drafting instruments would have its uses, it is possible to make satisfactory working drawings using only your shop tools. At least one set square is needed for marking right angles. This can be cut from plywood. It is the right angle that matters, but if you can make one set square with 45 degree corners and another with 30 degree corners and 60 degree corners they will have additional uses.

SCALE

Most drawings will have to be made to scale. There are special scale rules, but if you keep to the proportions ½, ¼, ⅛ and so on, it is not difficult to use an ordinary shop rule. At one-eighth, 1½ inches represents 1 foot, so every ⅛-inch represents 1 inch. You are not likely to need to draw smaller than one-sixteenth scale. In that case, ⅜ of an inch on the rule represents 1 foot and 1/16 of an inch represents 1 inch. Overall sizes of the item you want to draw will have to be adapted to the size of the available paper and that will show you the choice of scale. Do not draw any smaller than necessary because detail becomes increasingly difficult and even the thickness of a pencil lines begins to have a scale size. Fasten the paper to a flat surface (usually with adhesive tape at the corners).

The three views are known as *side elevation, elevation* and *plan*. It is suitable in a first drawing to get them in a particular relation to each other (Fig. 15-3A), but it is sometimes more convenient, or it may suit the paper size better, to move them around. This can be seen from some of the illustrations in this book.

Draw a line to form the base of the elevations. Project up and down at right angles for the side elevation and plan (Fig. 15-3B). Use these lines as datum lines for measuring other lines parallel to them. If the distance of the end elevation from the side elevation is the same as the distance of the plan below the side elevation, you can check that dimensions, such as the width of the object are the same in both views, by swinging or dividers (Fig. 15-3C).

As with the sketch, for most things you can draw the outlines of the enclosing rectangle (Fig. 15-3D). In this case, you have to make sure that sizes that have to match in two views really do—either by measuring or by comparing with dividers.

If it is the stool of the rough sketch that is being drawn, draw the thickness of the top on the two elevations as well as the depth of the rails. Even if the legs are to be tapered, start by drawing their full widths (Fig. 15-3E). In the plan view, draw the squares representing the tops of the legs dotted and show the thicknesses of the rails (Fig. 15-3F).

Mark how far down the legs are to remain square, then draw in their tapers (Fig. 15-3G). You could try the effect of cutting away the lower edges of the rails or give them decorative curves. Possible carving could be drawn in.

The top should not have screw heads above and gluing only to the rails might not be enough. Draw a section full size and see

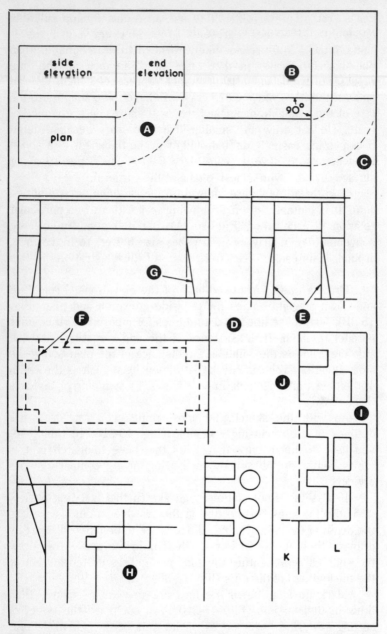

Fig. 15-3. A working drawing can usually be arranged in three views (with enlargements of details): (A) first drawing; (B) side elevation; (C) check dimensions; (D) rectangle; (E) full widths; (F) rails; (G) tapers; (H) fullsize section; (J) corner; (K) inside view; (L) barefaced tenons.

if you prefer socket screwing or buttons (Fig. 15-3H). Another problem is the arrangement of the tenons or dowels. A full size plan view of a corner will show you how far the joints can go in to meet or if there will be more strength by not going to so deep in thicker legs (Fig. 15-3J). In a side view, you can see how to arrange dowel holes at different levels (Fig. 15-3K) or how to cut the barefaced tenons (Fig. 15-3L).

With this stool, there is actually little need for the plan view except that you see the actual proportion of the top at the sizes you can intend. If you do not like that proportion, now is the time to vary it. In another project, there might be more need for the plan than one of the elevations. Most furniture you make is symmetrical, so some views need only be drawn half width (as in some drawings in this book). You can get all the constructional information from a half view. However, it does not give you much guide to proportion and it might not make sense to another person. If you want someone else to understand what the item will look like, it might be better to draw a full width even if you can get all you want from a half width.

Because your drawing will be correct to scale, you can get the sizes of parts by direct measuring. It will help if you write in at least some measurements. it will help if the final drawing is made in association with the actual wood being used. You might decide on 2-inch square legs, but when you get the wood, it might be 2-inches when sawn. After planing it might be 1⅜ of an inch so draw the legs that size. You can make your cutting list from the drawing. Again, you can relate it to the wood you have in stock or a stock length obtainable from the lumber yard. Those four legs, with a little allowed for trimming, might total 6 feet 3 inches but the yard might have the wood in 6-foot or 8-foot lengths. Would it matter if you shortened the legs slightly or will you buy the extra wood?

The use of a *rod* has been previously mentioned. For something as simple as this stool, it is unnecessary. But in as more complex item, with parts at different places that need to have matching lengths, a strip of wood marked on the edge with the necessary positions is less likely to lead to errors than if a rule or tape is used for measuring each time. If the rod is put against a piece of wood to be marked, the distance should be the same each time. If a measurement is taken, particularly if it is fractional, human error might lead to something being rather more or less than it should be. Get all the measurements you expect to need from the drawing and mark them on the edge of the rod. Using a rod in preference to measuring with a rule is always better practice.

Glossary

Adam. A period of furniture and decoration. Ascribed to Robert and James Adam.

Alburnum. The botanical name of sapwood.

annular rings. The concentric rings which form the grain of a tree. One ring is added each year.

annulet. A turned raised bead around a cylindrical part.

apron. A piece of wood below a drawer that might have its lower edge decorated by shaping or carving.

arch back. An armchair where the arms continue at the back to make an arch (as in a Windsor chair).

architrave. Outer molding around a door.

arris. The line or sharp edge between two flat or plane surfaces.

astragal. A raised molding or bead on a flat surface.

auger. A long drill, with its own handle, for deep drilling.

autumn growth. Part of an annual ring in a tree. It is formed by the descending sap.

axis. An imaginary line about which a body can be assumed to revolve. The centerline of a solid object.

backboard. The piece of wood closing the back of a cabinet.

back-flap hinge. A hinge designed to swing back further than a normal hinge. It is often used under a drop leaf on a table.

bail. A swinging loop handle.

ball-foot. A turned round or elliptical ball on the bottom of a leg.

baluster (balluster). Pillar to support a rail.

banding. A strip of inlay laid around and usually parallel with edges of panels, such as drawer fronts, table tops and cabinet parts.

barefaced tenon. A tenon shouldered on one side only.

base. The foundation of anything or the main bottom portion in an architectural or other assembly.

batten. Any narrow strip of wood. A strip fitted across boards to join them, cover a gap or prevent warping.

balk (baulk). Roughly squared lumber before cutting into boards.

bench stop. A wood or metal stop on a bench top. Wood is pressed against it when planing its surface.

bevel. An angle or chamfer planed on an edge. Also the name of an adjustable tool for testing angles.

bezel. Ring around glass over the face of a clock or other instrument.

blind. Not right through. A stopped hole for a dowel or a mortise for a short tenon.

blind nailing or screwing. Using the fastener in a rabbet or elsewhere that will be covered by another part so that the head is not visible in the finished work.

bolection. A rabbeted molding. It is particularly used around door panels.

bolster. A pad to withstand a thrust.

bonnet. Decorative shaping and molding or carving at the top of any piece of cabinetwork, but particularly on a clock.

Boston rocker. A version of the rocking Windsor chair. The rear of the seat is raised where it is bored for the spindles.

bow back. A chair back with a curved bow and spindles enclosed in it, but not necessarily an arched back.

bow saw. A small frame saw for cutting curves by hand.

bracket. An angular support used particularly to support a shelf or flap.

bullnose plane. A plane with its cutting edge very close to the front of the body. Usually the edge is the full width of the body for getting close into the end of a stopped rabbet.

bureau. A writing desk with a closing front and storage places inside.

burl (burr). An outgrowth on a tree. It can be cut across to show a very twisted grain that is valued for its decoration when cut into veneers.

cable molding. Molding with a rounded part carved diagonally to look like stranded rope or cable.

cabriole leg. Leg given a flourish so that it curves out from a corner in a stylized form of an animal's leg. Usually it finishes in a ball foot.

capping. The top molding on a pedestal or post.

carcase. The main assembly parts that make up the skeleton of a piece of furniture, such as the framework of a table, cabinet or chest of drawers.

cast. Twisting of a surface that should be flat.

chamfer. An angle or bevel planed on an edge.

check. A lengthwise separation in a piece of wood.

clamp. A device for drawing together that is used especially during gluing. A piece of wood joined across a wide board to prevent warping.

cleat. A small piece joining other parts together or an alternative name for a wood clamp.

cock head. A strip with a projecting rounded edge that fitted around a drawer front.

cocksedge hinge. A narrow hinge with a decorative outline and a slim knuckle.

coniferous. A cone-bearing tree which is the main source of softwoods.

contact adhesive. An impact adhesive which adheres as soon as parts are brought together. Movement for adjustment is impossible.

conversion. The process of cutting logs into boards.

comb. An undulating edge that is found particularly on a chair back.

core. Base wood on which veneer is laid.

cornice. A molding above eye level that projects around the top of a cabinet.

counterbore. Set the head of a screw below the surface of the wood. Then the hole is closed with a glued plug.

countersink. Bevel the top of a hole so that a screw head can be driven level with the surface.

cramp. British name for *clamp*.

cross banding. Decorative veneering that uses narrow strips cut across the grain.

cross-lap joint. Two pieces cut so as to fit into each other where they cross.

crotch (crook). Wood cut from the point where a branch leaves the tree. Cut to take advantage of the curved grain to get maximum strength in a shaped part or for decoration.

cup shake. Defect in lumber. A crack around the lines of annular rings.

curly grain. A pattern on the wood surface due to having been cut across an uneven grain.

dado. A groove in wood.

Deal. Trade name for some softwoods, such as pine or fir, but now less commonly used. May also mean a plank or board.

dead pin. A wedge.

deciduous. Leaf-shedding tree and the source of most hardwoods.

dentil. Rectangular ornaments on cornice moldings.

dessication. The artificial drying of lumber in kilns.

distressing. Intentionally damaging furniture to make it look old.

doatiness. Speckled marking in wood indicating the start of decay.

dog's tooth. A carved molding of the Early English Period.

donkey. A quick-action vise used for holding the work during the cutting of marquetry designs.

door pull. Door handle.

dowel. A cylindrical piece of wood that is particularly used as a peg in holes for making joints.

double-quirk bead. A rounded bead molding worked along an edge to disguise its joint to another board.

dovetail. The fan-shaped piece that projects between pins in the other part in a dovetail joint.

draw bore or draw pin. A peg or dowel across a mortise and tenon joint to draw the parts together.

drop leaf. A flap which swings down at the edge of a table and which can be supported when raised to enlarge the table top.

dry rot. A timber disease caused by dampness.

Dutch foot. A turned tapered leg finishing in a foot extending outwards.

ebony. Very hard almost black wood.

ellipse. The inclined transverse section of a cylinder or cone.

escutcheon. A keyhole or the plate covering and surrounding it.

face marks. Marks put on the first planed side and edge to indicate that further measuring and marking should be made from them.

facet. Narrow band between the flutes of a column.

fall front. A flap that lets down to be supported in a horizontal position. An example is the writing surface of a bureau.

fastenings (fasteners). Anything, such as nails and screws, used for joining.

fiddle back. Grain pattern when some wood is quarter-sawn, particularly mahogany used in violin backs, but also seen in sycamore, maple and other woods.

figure. Decorative grain pattern and particularly that shown when the medullary rays are prominent in quarter-sawn wood. Especially seen in oak.

fillet. A narrow strip of wood used to fill or support a part.

fillister. A rabbet plane with fences to control depth and width of cut. Sometimes confused with a plow, which can have a similar appearance, but is used for cutting grooves.

finial. A turned end to a post.

firmer chisel. A strong general purpose chisel.

flush bead molding. A bead worked into a surface, instead of standing above it, as in an astragal.

fluting. Rounded grooves that are the reverse of beads.

folding wedges. Two similar wedges used overlapping each other to provide pressure.

foxiness. Reddish color in wood indicating the onset of rot.

foxtail wedging. Using wedges in the end of a tenon so that it spreads the wood to make it grip when it is driven into a blind mortise.

framed construction. Built of strips of wood to form the carcase with the spaces filled by panels.

frame saw. A narrow saw blade tensioned in a frame.

fretwork. Pierced work done with a very fine fretsaw.

gallery. A shelf that is often bordered with turned spindles. On a table, the assembly at the top of a pedestal that allows the top to turn and pivot.

gate leg table. A table with drop leaves that can be held up by swinging legs like gates.

gauge. A marking tool or a means of testing. A definition of size. The thickness of sheet metal or the diameters of wires or screws.

glaziers' points. Small steel triangles used like headless nails to hold glass in a frame.

grain. The stripped marking seen in wood due to the annular rings.

groundwork. The base surface to which veneer is applied.

groove. Any slot in wood such as a dado. Less commonly a rabbet.

gunstock stile. The upright at the side of a panelled door. It is wider beside the lower panel than beside the upper one.

haft. The handle of a tool.

halving joint. Two crossing pieces notched to fit into each other.

hand screw. A wooden clamp.

heartwood. The mature wood nearer the center of the tree.

handed. Made in pairs.

hanging stile. The stile on which the hinges are attached.

haunch. A short part of a tenon in a corner joint.

housing joint. One part grooved to take the end of another piece such as a shelf.

impact adhesive. Alternative name for contact adhesive.

inlaying. Setting one piece of wood in another. It can be either solid pieces of wood or veneer.

jamb. Vertical side of a window or door.

jointing. The making of any joints, but particularly planing edges straight to make close-glued joints.

joist. Wood to support a floor or ceiling.

kerf. The slot made by a saw.

keying. Fitting pieces of veneer into kerfs. Used particularly to strengthen a miter joint.

knot. A flaw in wood due to where a branch left the tree.

knuckle. The pivot part of a hinge.

knuckle end. A carved end to the arm of a chair with an appearance like clenched fingers.

lacquer. A transparent varnish. Traditionally a brushed finish on gilded work, but now more often a sprayed finish.

ladder back. A chair back with several cross members between uprights.

laminate. Construct in layers with several pieces of wood. Used particularly in curved work.

lap joint. The general name for several types of joints in which one piece of wood overlaps and fits into another.

lattice work. Pierced strapwork.

laying out. Setting out the details of design and construction.

lineal. Length only. Sometimes used when pricing quantities of wood.

locking stile. The upright against which a door shuts.

lunette. Semicircular carving in a bonnet.

marking out. Marking ends and positions on wood before cutting, shaping and drilling.

marquetry. A system of inlaying that uses many woods to produce a pattern or picture using solid wood or veneers.

matched boarding. Joining boards edge to edge with matching tongues and grooves.

medullary rays. Radiating lines from the center of a log, which can be seen in some woods radially cut, but they are invisible in others.

miter (mitre). A joint where the meeting angle is divided, as in the corner of a picture frame.

miter box or board. Guide for the saw when cutting miters.

miter square. A testing tool, similar to a try square, but with its blade at 45 degrees.

molding (moulding). Decorative edge or border which may be a simple rounding or an intricate section of curves and quirks. Many are of named classical form and used in architecture and cabinetwork.

mortise (mortice). The rectangular socket cut to take a tenon.

mortise and tenon joint. A method of joining the end of one piece of wood into the side of another with the tenon projecting like a tongue on the end to fit into the mortise cut in the other piece. The most common joint in good cabinetwork.

mullet. A grooved block used for testing the thickness of the edge of a panel or drawer bottom that will have to fit in a groove.

muntin. An internal rail in a framed assembly as between the panels or panes in a window frame.

mullion. Vertical division of a window.

necking. Turned bead on the upper part of a pillar, pedestal or finial.

needle-leaf trees. Alternative name for cone-bearing trees.

nosing. Semicircular molding.

ogee molding. A molding with a convex curve above a concave one. It is named for its likeness to a combination of the letters O and G.

onion foot. A squat version of a ball foot.

oil slip. A shaped oilstone used on the inside curves of gouges.

orbital sander. A power sander in which a flat sanding pad makes small orbital movements very rapidly. Used for finish sanding.

ovolo. Classic quarter circle or ellipse molding.

parquetry. Wood block flooring laid in geometric designs. Not to be confused with marquetry.

patina. Surface texture that is particularly due to old age.

pedestal. A supporting post.

pediment. A top shaped and molded or carved. Larger than a bonnet.

pegging. Dowels or wooden pegs through joints.

pendant, pendil, pennant. A hanging turned or carved decoration. The revers of a finial.

piercing. Decoration made by cutting through the wood such as in the splat of a chair back. Similar to fretwork, but more robust.

pigeon hole. A storage compartment that is often built into a bureau.

pilaster. A decorative half column fitted on a flat surface.

pilot hole. A small hole drilled as a guide before using a larger drill.

plain sawn. Lumber cut actoss a log in slices.

pintle. A dowel or peg on which parts pivot. The name taken from the pivot of a boat's rudder.

planted. Applied instead of cut in the solid. Molding attached to a surface is planted. If it is cut in the solid wood it is stuck.

plinth. The base part around the bottom of a piece of furniture.

plow (plough). A plane for cutting grooves with guides to control depth and distance from an edge. The traditional type has a general appearance similar to a fillister with which it might be confused.

pluck up. Tear up the surface of wood by planing against the grain.

plywood. Board made with veneers glued in laminations with the grain of each layer at right-angles to the next.

punchwork. Background to carving made with punches having patterned ends.

quartered (quarter-sawn). Boards cut radially from a log to minimize warping and shrinking or to show the medullary rays as figure in oak and some other woods.

quatre-foil. A tracery detail based on four interlocking circles.

quirk. A narrow or V-shaped groove beside a bead or the whole bead when worked to form part of a cover or disguise for a joint. A raised part between patterns in turned work.

rail. A horizontal member in framing.

rake. Incline to horizontal.

rabbet (rebate). Angular cut-out in section as in the back of a picture frame.

relief. Cut back, usually to gain emphasis in appearance.

rift sawn. Alternative name for plain sawn.

ripples. A series of rays showing in the grain of some woods.

rive (riven). Split boards from a log instead of sawing them.

rod back. The type of Windsor chair with many spindles and the arms joined to back spindles.

rolled arm. The arm of a chair shaped for comfort and the front finished in a scroll.

router. Tool for leveling the bottom of a groove or recessed surface. Can be power or hand operated.

rule. Measuring rod. Do not spell it "ruler."

rule joint. Molded joint used between a table top and its drop flap used with a back-flap hinge. Named for its similarlity in section or the joint of a two-fold rule.

run. In a long length. Lumber can be quoted as so many feet run.

saddling. Scooping a chair seat to a comfortable shape.

sapwood. The wood nearer the outside of a long. Not as strong or durable as the heartwood in most trees.

sash. Molded and rabbeted edge of a window frame. A sash plane cuts the rabbet and molding at the same time.

sausage and ball molding. Long and short curved shapes in a molding.

saw buck. Crossed sawing trestle. The name can be applied to table legs arranged in a similar way.

scratch molding. Small molding cut with a *scratch stock* which has a cutter sharpened like a scraper.

scroll. Carved shape like end view of loosely rolled paper.

seasoning. Drying wood to an acceptable moisture content.

secret dovetail joint. Joint in which the dovetails are hidden by mitered parts outside them.

segments. Curved pieces of wood used to build up table rails and similar things of curved form.

set. To punch a nail below the surface. The tool for doing that. The bending of saw teeth in alternate directions to produce a kerf wider than the thickness of the saw metal.

setting out. Laying out details of the whole furniture or a particular part of it.

shooting board (shuting board). A holding device for wood while having its edges planed or molded.

shot joint. Planed edges glued together.

shoulder piece. An extra bracket at the top of a leg extending under the rail or framing.

shake. A defect or crack that occurs in the growing tree, but might not be found until after conversion.

skirt. Wood to form a border.

slat. Narrow thin wood, usually horizontal, as across the back of a ladderback chair.

soffit. The underside of a window or door opening.

spandrail, (spandrel). A shaped rail between the upright parts of a piece of furniture.

spindle. Rounded slender part, usually vertical, as in a chair back.

splat. Central upright member in a chair back. Usually decorated by shaping, piercing or carving.

splay. To spread out.

spline. A narrow strip of wood fitting into grooves. Strengthening two meeting faces that are glued.

split turning. A piece with semicircular section made by turning two pieces of wood glued together and separating them so that the half turning can be glued to a flat surface.

square turning. Wood of square section, but with lengthwise shaping similar to a turned outline.

star shake. A defect in a tree shown as star lines radiating from the center of a log.

stile. The vertical part at edge of furniture framing to which rails are attached.

stopped. Not carried through as in a stopped chamfer or rabbet.

strap hinge. Hinge with long narrow arms.

strap work. Carving that looks like interwoven crossing straps.

stretcher. A lengthwise rail between the lower parts of a chair or table.

surbase molding. A molding placed between the cornice and plinth such as on the table part of a bureau bookcase.

swag. Carved ornamental detail in the form of flowers or material suspended.

tang. The tapered end of a tool to fit in a handle.

template (templet). Shaped pattern to be drawn aroung when marking out.

Tenon. The projecting tongue on the end of one piece of wood to fit into a mortise in another piece.

tester. The roof over a four-poster bed.

thread escutcheon. A metal liner for a keyhole.

thumb molding. Curved edge below a small rabbetted step.

thumb plane. Any very small plane.

tote. A handle (particularly on a plane).

trunnel (treenail). Peg or down driven through a joint.

tusk tenon. A tenon projecting through a mortise and held with a cross wedge.

undercutting. In carving, cutting under the design to give it emphasis due to be better shadow.

veneer. A thin piece of wood that is usually of a decorative type and intended to be glued to a backing. If very thin and cut from a rotating log, it is cut with a knife. If it is not so thin it is cut with a saw.

veneer pin. Very fine nail with a small head.

volute. A spiral scroll in carving.

wainscot. This term means the panelling around a room, but it is also applied to quartersawn wood, such as oak, that shows figuring.

wany edge. The edge of a board that still has bark on it or is still in the pattern of the outside of the log.

warping. Distortion of a board by twisting or curving because of unequal shrinkage as moisture dries out.

wavy grain. Alternative name for fiddleback.

winding. A board or assembled frame is said to be in winding when it is nt flat and a twist can be seen when sighting from one end.

working drawing. The drawing showing elevation, plan, sections and details from which measurements can be taken to make the furniture.

Index

Index

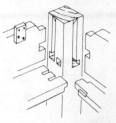

Edited by Steven Bolt